YOUNG STUDENTS

Learning Library®

VOLUME 21

United States Government—
World War I

WEEKLY READER BOOKS
MIDDLETOWN · CONNECTICUT

PHOTO CREDITS

Young Students Learning Library is a federally registered trademark of Field Publications.

ISBN 0-8374-6051-4

CONTENTS

UNITED STATES GOVERN-MENT The national government of the United States is described as a *constitutional federal republic*. It is *constitutional* because the powers and operations of the government are designated by long-established written law (the U.S. Constitution) and not by any person or group, as is often the case with monarchies, oligarchies, and dictatorships. The U.S. government is *federal* because it represents the union, or federation, of all the states. It shares authority with state governments and cannot take over the powers of the states in matters under their rule. The U.S. government is *republican* in form because the citizens directly elect the people who represent them.

Four basic features make the government of the United States different from the governments of other nations—the relationship of the states to the Federal Government; the U.S. Constitution; the separation of powers among three branches of government; and the broad powers of the U.S. President.

Federal and State Governments
The representative democracy of the United States did not just "happen." The U.S. governmental system developed gradually through the trials and errors of a new nation learning how to govern itself. The U.S. government today operates within a system that allows the state governments and the Federal Government to work together.

When the colonies won their war for independence against Britain in 1783, they knew they would have to join together in order to survive as a

◀ *Is this how planets like our Earth were formed? Great changes took place, including molten rock seething all over the planet. Volcanoes give us clues about the origins of our planet and of the universe. (See* UNIVERSE.)

nation. But the colonies wanted to retain their newly won independence and did not like the idea of too much control from a central government. In 1781, the original 13 states adopted a constitution, called the Articles of Confederation. Under this constitution, each state had almost as much power as an independent nation.

The states soon realized that the Articles of Confederation were not building a strong nation. Because each state was acting as if it were a separate nation, the union of states was in danger of collapse. State leaders had to come up with a better system if the United States were to survive as a single, whole nation.

In 1787, representatives from every state met in Philadelphia. They planned to revise the Articles of Confederation, but instead they wrote the present U.S. Constitution, in which the states agreed to give up some of their powers in order to form a more perfect union.

The Constitution specifically defines the powers of the Federal Government. All powers not specifically given to federal authority belong to the states. The Federal Government handles services that cross state boundaries and that affect the nation as a whole. Transportation, communications, military and defense needs, road-building, electric and gas power,

▲ *Federal Hall in New York City was the first capitol of the U.S. government. This is how it looked in 1797.*

The United States was the first nation in the world to plan a capital city—Washington, D.C.—specially for its seat of government.

2487

▲ *The United States Supreme Court building in Washington, D.C. Here great legal decisions are made about how the country should be governed and about rights of the individual. The Supreme Court is one of the three "checks and balances" of United States government.*

out these great upheavals and changes, the Constitution has remained a basic source of law, with which the actions and decisions of the United States can be guided. Very few new words have been added to its original language.

Much credit for the Constitution must go to persons like Alexander Hamilton, Thomas Jefferson, and James Madison, who had to devise general principles of government for specific situations they could not possibly foresee. At the Constitutional Convention in 1787, they composed a document that they knew must serve the nation for many years to come.

and natural resources lie within the federal authority. The states are free to govern themselves in more local matters, such as schools and education, state road-building, state taxes, civil and criminal laws, state parks, and natural resources within a state.

In modern times, there has been a shift of power and control away from the individual states and toward the Federal Government, in order to solve the increasingly complicated problems confronting people living in a large modern nation. Increased transportation and communication, as well as greater U.S. involvement in foreign affairs, have produced more situations in which the Federal Government must act for the nation as a whole.

The U.S. Constitution The U.S. Constitution differs from the constitutions of many other nations in its brevity, simplicity, and flexibility. The Constitution has survived with only 26 changes for 200 years. (Some nations change their constitutions quite often.) The U.S. Constitution has seen the United States through the early frontier years, Indian wars, the Industrial Revolution, the Civil War, two World Wars, the Great Depression of the 1930's, and the troubled "Cold War" period culminating in the Vietnam War. Through-

Separation of Powers The people who designed the U.S. Constitution did not want a system of government that in any way resembled a monarchy. The colonists had fought long and hard to free themselves from the rule of a hostile king and parliament. They were determined that the power of the Federal Government would never be allowed to come under the control of an all-powerful king or group of rulers. They outlined a system whereby power is divided among three branches of government—the Presidency, called the *executive branch*; the Congress, called the *legislative branch*; and the courts, called the *judicial branch*.

In their operations, these three branches of government check and balance each other so that no one person or group can gain complete control of the government at any time. The Congress, for example, can pass a law, and the President can sign it, but, if the law runs contrary to the Constitution, the Supreme Court can void (refuse to accept) it. The President commands the army, but only Congress can declare war and supply funds for the military services. A President who has acted corruptly may be impeached, convicted by Congress, and removed from office.

The Federal Government, according to the Constitution, can coin money, borrow money, set up federal courts, and in other ways run the nation. The Congress, as the lawmaking body, enacts new laws, levies taxes, and spends the tax money. The Supreme Court, as the highest court in the nation, interprets the laws of the nation. Decisions of the Supreme Court become law, and its decisions can change laws that are deemed unconstitutional. By declaring a law unconstitutional, the Supreme Court has power over both the Congress and the executive branch, and therefore has a great role in shaping the nation. Where constitutional language is vague, the Supreme Court can interpret it according to the just needs of the nation.

The Party System The system of political parties in the United States has a great effect on the President and on Congress. The two major parties, Democratic and Republican, as well as independent parties, perform special duties in the political system. U.S. political parties select candidates for elective office, provide the means for a candidate to make his or her views known to the public, and allow for individuals to participate in the selection process through nominating conventions and primary elections on the local, state, and national levels.

The Democratic, Republican, and other parties serve as checks on each other. Within each party are members with widely differing political views. The candidates of a party must usually be able to bring the various views of party members together on most issues. They must try to represent the political views of the people who nominate them. If candidates do not represent the views of the majority of their party, many party members may vote for the opposing party.

For further information on:
Agencies within U.S. Government, *see* FEDERAL BUREAU OF INVESTIGATION, FOREIGN SERVICE, LIBRARY OF CONGRESS, PEACE CORPS, POSTAL SERVICE, SOCIAL SECURITY, UNITED STATES GOVERNMENT AGENCIES.
Branches of U.S. Government, *see* CABINET, UNITED STATES; CONGRESS, UNITED STATES; COURT SYSTEM; PRESIDENCY; SUPREME COURT; VICE-PRESIDENT.
Formation of U.S. Government, *see* AMERICAN COLONIES; AMERICAN HISTORY; AMERICAN REVOLUTION; ARTICLES OF CONFEDERATON; BILL OF RIGHTS; CONSTITUTION, UNITED STATES; CONTINENTAL CONGRESS; DECLARATION OF INDEPENDENCE; ELECTION; MAYFLOWER COMPACT; POLITICAL PARTY.
Powers of U.S. Government, *see* CITIZENSHIP, CIVIL RIGHTS, IMPEACHMENT, INTERNATIONAL RELATIONS, INTERNATIONAL TRADE, LAW, MONEY, PASSPORTS AND VISAS, PATENTS AND COPYRIGHTS, TAX, TREATY, WAR.

UNITED STATES GOVERNMENT AGENCIES Besides the three branches of the U.S. government—the President, the Congress, and the federal court system—the United States has many administrative agencies to handle special problems in the course of governing a large nation. These agencies vary in size

▼ *Inside the Senate Chamber of the nation's capitol in Washington, D.C. Here senators ratify treaties and approve laws.*

Members of the U.S. Congress are the highest paid legislators in the world. Over and above salary they are allowed just over $1,000,000 every year for office help—staff, travel, communications, and so on.

SOME IMPORTANT INDEPENDENT FEDERAL AGENCIES

ACTION—controls programs for aid to needy areas at home and abroad. It administers Vista and Peace Corps organizations.

Central Intelligence Agency—is responsible for the intelligence operations of the United States government.

Consumer Product Safety Commission—establishes safety standards for consumer products and bans dangerous products.

Environmental Protection Agency—leads the government's fight against pollution.

Equal Employment Opportunity Commission—is responsible for the prevention of discrimination in employment.

Export-Import Bank of the United States—provides aid in financing exports and imports of commodities.

Federal Communications Commission—licenses broadcast stations and regulates some aspects of the programming of broadcast stations as a whole.

Federal Deposit Insurance Corporation—insures the deposits of most banks in the United States.

Federal Election Commission—controls distribution of public funds for federal elections and checks compliance with Federal Election Campaign Act.

Federal Maritime Commission—administers federal laws relating to U.S. shipping operations.

Federal Reserve System—influences the flow of credit and money in the United States.

Federal Trade Commission—attempts to keep business fair and competitive.

General Accounting Office—examines the accounts of most federal agencies and provides Congress with reports.

General Services Administration—manages federal property.

Government Printing Office—is responsible for government publications.

International Communications Agency—provides information to foreign countries about the United States and conducts cultural exchange programs.

Interstate Commerce Commission—enforces federal laws concerning transportation of people or property across state lines.

Library of Congress—provides research and other materials to Congress and members of the public.

National Aeronautics and Space Administration—develops, constructs, tests, and operates manned and unmanned vehicles used in the exploration of space.

National Foundation on the Arts and the Humanities—provides financial and other assistance to the arts and humanities.

National Labor Relations Board—prevents unfair labor practices by either unions or employers.

National Science Foundation—supports research in science by awarding grants to qualified individuals and institutions.

Nuclear Regulatory Commission—licenses and regulates the uses of nuclear energy.

Office of Personnel Management—checks competency of applicants for jobs in competitive service and classifies jobs.

Securities and Exchange Commission—enforces federal laws concerning the purchase and sale of securities.

Selective Service System—is responsible for providing enough personnel for the Armed Forces.

Small Business Administration—tries to help small businesses by use of loans and government contracts.

Tennessee Valley Authority—is responsible for the development of resources in the Tennessee Valley.

Veterans Administration—administers laws concerning benefits for men who served in the Armed Forces.

and importance. Many were created during President Franklin Delano Roosevelt's New Deal administration to cope with bank failures, widespread unemployment, and other problems during the Great Depression of the 1930's. Other agencies, such as the Lend-Lease Administration and National War Labor Board, were formed as temporary war measures during and after World War II. These agencies were then shut down.

The President appoints, and the Senate confirms, the heads of government agencies and commissions. A commissioner's term usually runs several years. Directors of agencies, such as the Environmental Protection Agency, are appointed every four years, at the beginning of each new presidential term. Commissions grew out of a definite need for small independent bodies, apart from the regular government structure, to investigate unfair practices and to settle disputes in areas affecting

▲ *The Nuclear Regulatory Commission, once called the Atomic Energy Commission, has used devices like this to try to develop controlled nuclear fusion— cheap energy without the risks of today's nuclear power stations. So far, no one has succeeded.*

the public, such as transportation, business, international trade, and foreign loans.

Once the work of a commission is completed, it is usually disbanded. After World War II, for example, the U.S. Foreign Claims Settlement Commission was set up. This agency was empowered to check into damage claims against the United States made by citizens of countries where U.S. troops had fought. The commission then recommended payment if the United States was at fault. By the early 1960's, no more war claims were being made against the United States, and the commission was dissolved.

Commissions are created by acts of Congress. The five-member Federal Trade Commission (FTC), which checks into unfair trade and business practices, and the Federal Communications Commission (FCC), which regulates communications by wire and airwaves, are examples of commissions set up by congressional acts. One of the oldest commissions is the Interstate Commerce Commission (ICC). It was established in 1887 during a public furor over railroad abuses. The ICC continues to investigate poor management of interstate commerce, overly high rates for interstate hauling of passengers and freight, and unsafe transportation.

The Reconstruction Finance Corporation (RFC) was started by an act of Congress in 1932. Its purpose was to make emergency loans to banks and trust companies during the Great Depression. Another government corporation, the Export-Import Bank, makes loans to U.S. companies that export products abroad. It also supervises various types of trade relations between the United States and foreign nations. The bank is run by a full-time five-member board.

Government agencies that are not corporations or commissions are established by acts of Congress and are each run by a director. The directors are appointed by the President with the approval of the Senate. The U.S. Arms Control and Disarmament Agency was established in 1961. It is empowered to negotiate disarmament treaties for the United States and to research and develop arms-control measures for negotiation with foreign governments. The International Communications Agency (formerly the U.S. Information Agency) spreads information about the United States abroad. The Central Intelligence Agency (CIA) is the office of government engaged in espionage work overseas. There are many more agencies and commissions within the U.S. government. The independent agencies (those not connected with any larger governmental department) are listed in the table on the opposite page.

ALSO READ: CONGRESS, UNITED STATES; PEACE CORPS; PRESIDENCY; ROOSEVELT, FRANKLIN D.; UNITED STATES GOVERNMENT.

▲ *The Voice of America is the international radio broadcasting service for the United States government. The VOA broadcasts in 42 languages and has many bureaus and relay stations around the world.*

UNITED STATES OF AMERICA

The United States of America is a large country centered on the North American continent. It was founded in 1776, when 13 colonies along the Atlantic coast broke away from Britain to form an independent nation.

Today, the United States consists of 50 states and several outlying dependencies, including partially independent Puerto Rico, the Virgin Islands in the West Indies, and Guam in the Mariana Islands. The United States is the fourth largest country in the world in both area and population. Only China, India, and the Soviet Union have more people, and only the Soviet Union, Canada, and China are bigger in size.

The Land and Climate The United States covers many different geographical regions. The Appalachian Mountains run southwestward along the Atlantic Coast from New England to Alabama. But from New York

A hundred years ago nearly three-fourths of the American people lived on farms. Today, only about one person in twenty does. But American farms have grown in size, and farmland now covers more than twice the area it did in the 1880's. Today, there are more than two million farms in the U.S., covering about a billion acres (about 400 million hectares).

UNITED STATES OF AMERICA

Capital City: Washington, D.C. (626,000 people).

Area: 3,618,772 square miles (9,372,614 sq. km).

Population: 247,100,000.

Government: Federal republic.

Natural Resources: Coal, copper, lead, natural gas, molybdenum, oil, iron ore, gold, silver.

Export Products: Machinery, transportation, chemicals, food, coal, electronics, weapons.

Unit of Money: U.S. dollar.

Official Language: English.

The most densely populated state is New Jersey, with about 1,000 people per square mile (about 390 per sq. km). The least densely populated state is Alaska, with less than one person per square mile. The average density for the whole United States is about 65 people per square mile (about 25 per sq. km). This can be compared to over 800 people per square mile (about 300 per sq. km) in Japan.

The average baby born in the United States today can expect to live to an age of about 75. In 1900, the age was less than 50.

south, a coastal plain widens to include most of Georgia and all of Florida. Vast plains cover the huge central area of the United States. West of the central plains rise the Rocky Mountains. Between them and the Pacific is an uneven, high tableland, ending with coastal ranges along the Pacific Ocean. The coastal ranges include the Sierra Nevada, a mountain chain that extends for about 400 miles (640 km) through eastern California. The highest peak in the 48 contiguous (adjacent) states, Mount Whitney, is in the Sierra Nevada; it is 14,945 feet (4,555 m) high. The Cascade Range runs north from the Sierra Nevada through Oregon and Washington.

In the state of Alaska are the highest mountains in North America. The country's tallest mountain, Mount McKinley—20,320 feet (6,194 m)—is located there. The mountains in Alaska gradually taper off to an Arctic coastal plain.

The islands of Hawaii are located about 2,000 miles (3,200 km) off the Pacific coast of the continental United States. They were formed by volcanoes that built up from the ocean floor. The islands have many volcanoes that are still active.

Most of the United States is drained by six great rivers—the Mississippi and its branches (which include the Missouri) in the center, the Columbia in the northwest, the Colorado and the Rio Grande in the southwest, the St. Lawrence–Great Lakes system in

the northeast, and the Yukon in central Alaska.

Because the United States is so large, it has many different types of climate. The southern part of the West Coast has what is called a Mediterranean climate. It is warm and sunny most of the year, with some rain in winter. North of California, the coast has a marine climate. The winds come mostly from the sea. Rain is common and forests are dense.

The sea winds are forced upward by the coastal mountains and lose their moisture. This creates a long band of dry country just east of the coast. In the south, this arid belt produces deserts as dry as Death Valley in California. Farther north, the land is often dry and barren, but it usually has some sparse growth.

The land near the Rockies has a highland climate. It is cooler, because of its high altitude, and has more rain and snow. The central plains have what is called a continental climate. Summers are hot and winters are very cold.

When the winds come from the sea, as they do on the West Coast of

▼ *A riverboat passes by tall Spanish moss in Florida's Everglades, one of the most beautiful parts of the United States.*

▲ *The world's hottest place—Death Valley in California, near the border with Nevada—seen here from an elevation of over 5,000 feet (1,500 m). Summer temperatures reach 135°F (57°C), and each year only 2 inches (5 cm) of rain falls.*

Reserves of coal in the United States are estimated to be more than 1,000 billion tons (907 billion metric tonnes). This is enough to last for 1,500 years at the present rate of consumption.

North America, they keep winters mild. Even a coastal city as far north as Juneau, Alaska, is usually warmer in January than inland Milwaukee, Wisconsin, or Buffalo, New York. On the East Coast, however, the wind brings weather mostly from the west, so the climate is generally (not always) continental. Southern Florida and Hawaii are warm and humid all year round. Most of Alaska, by contrast, has the nation's coldest temperatures. Alaska's long, southeastern arm, called the Panhandle, has a cool marine climate, but the state's central portion has a cold climate.

People U.S. citizens, usually called Americans, are descended from people from almost every country in the world. Only about 1,418,000 U.S. citizens are of North American Indian descent. Some of the earliest immigrants were from Africa. These were black slaves, brought by force to the colonies in the early 1600's. More than 26 million of their descendants live in the United States today. Roughly one out of every ten U.S. citizens is black. Most non-slave immigrants to the United States came from Europe. Of those from Europe, the greatest numbers came from Germany, Italy, Great Britain, Ireland, Austria, and Hungary. Many came

from the Scandinavian countries and settled in middle and northwestern areas of the United States.

The United States is also a land of many religions. Most U.S. citizens who belong to a religious group are Christians. Of these, about two-thirds are Protestants, while about one-fourth are Roman Catholic. About four of every 100 U.S. citizens are Jewish.

There are more women than men in the United States, by the ratio of about 52 to 48. The largest number of men are "blue-collar" workers; they work at jobs requiring physical effort or skill, such as most factory jobs. Most women and the next largest

▼ *Two examples of the great natural beauty to be found in the United States: Cape Hatteras, off the coast of North Carolina (below), and Scott Lake, in Oregon (bottom).*

group of men work at "white-collar" jobs, which include working in offices, teaching, and selling.

About two-thirds of all U.S. citizens live in urbanized areas (areas with a combined population of at least 50,000 people). The inner cities show the least growth, and the suburbs continue to increase in size.

U.S. citizens spend much leisure time watching television, listening to music on records and tapes, and reading newspapers, magazines, and books. They also enjoy going to plays, concerts, and movies as well as attending various amateur and professional sports events. Some U.S. citizens try their skill at home decorating and repairing, arts and crafts, and gardening. Others like to take study courses to enrich their education. Traveling and camping are popular with many people.

The United States has one of the world's highest standards of living. There are other developed nations that have higher incomes per person than the United States does, but the United States is the leader in the total amount of money earned by any nation.

Land and Resources The United States leads the world in developed natural resources. It produces more coal, copper, lead, natural gas, and molybdenum than any other country. Many other minerals of commercial use are found in the United States. The country still has vast forests, particularly in the West. But careless use of the country's resources in the past has made many modern U.S. citizens aware of the need to preserve their natural resources.

About one-half of the country's land area is used for farming or ranching. There are more than 2 million farms in the United States, but the number is declining steadily. Small farms cannot compete with the bigger farms, where food for people and livestock can be produced more economically.

U.S. farmers produce about one-half of the world's corn. They also grow large crops of wheat, oats, cotton, and tobacco. Very few other countries can compete with the United States in the production of cattle, sheep, hogs, poultry, fruits, vegetables, and many other farm crops.

To a large extent, the climate determines the type of farming found in the different areas of the United States. On the Arctic slopes of Alaska, for example, only a few days each year are without frost, and only mosses and lichens can survive. But central Alaska has two or three months without frost, and fast-growing crops, such as vegetables, thrive during the long summer hours of sunlight.

The midwestern states have four to six months without any freezing. This growing season is long enough to allow the huge grain crops of the prairies—wheat, oats, rye, barley, and corn. Around the cities, fruit and vegetable farming flourish.

The seven frost-free months of the Southern states permit the growing of such crops as cotton, peanuts, and tobacco. The subtropical climates of Florida and Hawaii, where it rarely freezes, are good for growing delicate

▲ *Harvesting pumpkins on a farm in New England. The United States is one of the world's leading agricultural producers.*

▼ *A rodeo in the cattle country west of the Mississippi River. Originally rodeos were staged by the cowboys for their own fun. Today, they are sporting events where the competitors can earn big money.*

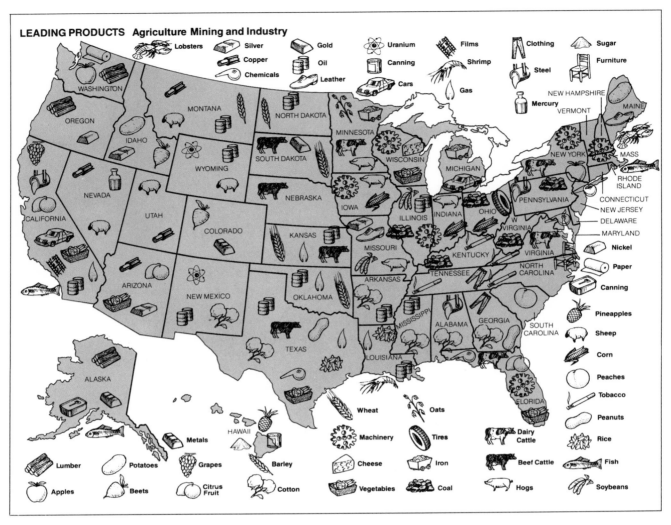

LEADING PRODUCTS Agriculture Mining and Industry

citrus fruits such as oranges and grapefruit. Citrus fruits, as well as grapes, figs, olives, and almonds, are grown in the Mediterranean climate of southern California.

Industry The United States is one of the world's industrial leaders. The manufactured goods produced by U.S. factories account for about a third of the world's total industrial output. The production of transportation equipment, steel, chemicals, and machinery are some of the most important industries. Food processing and the production of textiles, paper, and clothing are also major industries. Many of the country's

▼ *The great width of the United States means it has several time zones. When it is 7 a.m. in New York City, it is 6 a.m. in St. Louis, 5 a.m. in Denver, and 4 a.m. in San Francisco. In the far west of Alaska it is only 1 a.m.!*

▲ *A railway brings iron ore and coal to this giant U.S. steelworks.*

▲ *The world's biggest indoor theater, the famous Radio City Music Hall on Broadway, in New York City. It can seat 5,882 people.*

manufacturing states, such as New York, Ohio, Illinois, Pennsylvania, and Michigan, are located east of the Mississippi River. California, a leading industrial state, is one very important exception.

Capital and Principal Cities The capital of the United States, Washington, is located in the District of Columbia, which is not part of any state. The largest cities in the United States, in order of size, are New York City; Los Angeles, California; Chicago, Illinois; Houston, Texas; Philadelphia, Pennsylvania; San Diego, California; Detroit, Michigan; Dallas, Texas. Some older cities, such as Baltimore, Maryland, and Boston, Massachusetts, are losing population. Many people are moving to the suburbs or to other states in search of jobs. Among the busiest seaports of the United States are New York City; New Orleans, Louisiana; and Los Angeles and San Francisco, California.

For further information on:
Cities, *see* BOSTON, CHICAGO, DALLAS, DETROIT, LOS ANGELES, NEW YORK CITY, PHILADELPHIA, SAN FRANCISCO.
Geography, *see* AMERICA, APPALACHIAN MOUNTAINS, BADLANDS, CHESAPEAKE BAY, EVERGLADES, GRAND CANYON, GREAT LAKES, GREAT PLAINS, GREAT SALT LAKE, GULF OF MEXICO, MISSISSIPPI RIVER, NIAGARA FALLS, NORTH AMERICA, PAINTED DESERT, PUERTO RICO, RIO GRANDE, ROCKY MOUNTAINS, ST. LAWRENCE SEAWAY, SIERRA NEVADA, YELLOWSTONE PARK, YOSEMITE VALLEY.
Industry and Products, *see* AUTOMATION, CATTLE, CLOTHING, CORN, COTTON, DAIRY FARMING, FOOD PROCESSING, FRUIT, GRAIN, IRON AND STEEL, LUMBER AND LUMBERING, MANUFACTURING, MEAT, MINES AND MINING, PAPER, PETROLEUM, TEXTILE, TOBACCO, WHEAT.
People, *see* BLACK AMERICANS; IMMIGRATION; INDIANS, AMERICAN; SLAVERY.
For individual states, see Index at name.

UNITED STATES SERVICE ACADEMIES The armed forces of the United States have five separate branches—the Army, the Navy, the Air Force, the Marine Corps, and the Coast Guard. Each branch is composed of enlisted men and women and of officers who lead them. Many young people become officers in the armed forces without graduating from a military service academy, but the United States does provide schools for educating and training potential officers for each of these branches. The U.S. Military Academy, founded in

Two-thirds of the men who became Presidents of the United States were lawyers.

The murder rate in the United States is about 200 times greater than that of Japan. The Japanese cannot buy handguns legally. In the United States more than four handguns are sold legally every minute, and the country has the world's highest death rate from firearms.

▲ *Cadets at the U.S. Naval Academy at Annapolis, Maryland, turn out in gleaming outfits for their Dress Parade.*

▼ *Graduates at the most famous military service academy in the United States, West Point, throw their hats in the air at the graduation ceremony.*

1802, trains future Army officers at West Point, New York. Future officers of the Navy are trained at the U.S. Naval Academy at Annapolis, Maryland. It was established in 1845. The Air Force Academy, founded in 1954, is at Colorado Springs, Colorado, and the Coast Guard Academy, founded in 1915, is at New London, Connecticut. Marine Corps officers are trained at West Point or Annapolis.

Qualifications and requirements for appointment vary somewhat among the service academies, but generally candidates must be physically, mentally, and morally qualified citizens, aged 17 to 22, and unmarried. Nominations for appointment to all but the Coast Guard Academy are made by the President, Vice-President, members of Congress, or other high government officials. Other appointments are reserved for members of the regular or reserve armed forces, qualified sons and daughters of deceased veterans and Medal of Honor winners, and other special groups. Coast Guard cadets are selected by means of a competitive examination.

Each academy provides a four-year program of study, equal to a regular college course of study, plus an athletic and physical education program. This is in addition to military and professional training. Every student receives free room and board. He or she also receives a salary each month from the Federal Government to pay for uniforms, books, and some personal expenses. At graduation, the student receives a bachelor of science degree and a commission (a government certificate stating military rank and authority).

Newly graduated officers in the Army, Air Force, or Marine Corps are commissioned as second lieutenants. Newly graduated officers in the Navy and Coast Guard are commissioned as ensigns. In exchange for their education, these new officers agree to stay in military service for a certain number of years.

The U.S. Merchant Marine also operates a service academy at Kings Point, New York. Cadets there study navigation, seamanship, oceanography, and other technical subjects. These cadets are appointed by members of Congress. Graduates of the Merchant Marine Academy receive commissions as ensigns in the U.S. Naval Reserve.

ALSO READ: AIR FORCE, ARMY, COAST GUARD, MARINE CORPS, MERCHANT MARINE, NAVY.

UNIVERSAL LANGUAGE It would be wonderful if there were one universal language that people from all over the world could learn to use! No interpreters would be needed at international conferences. Nobody would feel like a stranger when traveling, because everyone could communicate in this common language.

The universal language that has met with most success is *Esperanto*. It was invented by Lazarus Ludwig Zamenhof, a Polish physician and linguist, who presented his new language in 1887. Esperanto is based on words from several European languages, making it easy for people who speak one or two of these languages to understand Esperanto. It is pronounced phonetically, exactly as it is written, and uses a 28-letter alphabet. The following paragraph is in Esperanto. Can you read it?

"Elefanto estas tre granda besto, kiu vivas en Afriko kaj Azio. La homo rigardas la elefanto kiel amiko, kaj ili ofte kunlaboras. Oni diras, ke elefantoj nemian forgesas."

Here are some hints for translating Esperanto. (1) All nouns end in "o," and plurals are made by adding a "j." (2) *Estas* means "is," *kaj* means "and," *kiu* means "who," *kiel* means "as," *oni diras* means "they say."

Another universal language that has become very useful in recent years is *Interlingua*. It was developed by the Italian mathematician and linguist, Giuseppe Peano, and presented in 1903. It has been modified since then. The words are based on scientific and technological terms that are the same in almost all languages. Many international scientific publications are now printed in Interlingua.

Other universal languages and their dates of presentation are *Volapük* (1880), *Idiom Neutral* (1898), *Ro* (1906), *Ido* (a simplified Esperanto, 1907), *Novial* (1928), and *Basic English* (during the 1920's). Basic English is interesting because it uses only 850 English words. This small vocabulary is very powerful because the words can be combined to do the work of thousands of other words. For example, the word "go" in Basic English can combine with prepositions to make hundreds of other verbs. Here are a few of them:

enter—go into   exit—go out of
break—go against   leave—go away
fetch—go for   fall—go down
return—go back   rise—go up
turn—go right (left) pass—go by
encircle—go around avoid—go past

ALSO READ: LANGUAGES.

UNIVERSE The universe includes the stars, planets, comets, galaxies, meteors, dust, and everything else in space, including space itself. In short, the universe is everything—not only those things that we know, but also those things that exist but are unknown to us. The universe is not just what people know, the universe is that which *is*. Some scientists believe that really we should say the universe is also everything that *has been* and *will be*.

Until the 1500's, people thought that the Earth was the center of the universe. This idea was so pleasing that they held to it even when astronomical observations showed that it was unlikely.

In 1543, Nicolaus Copernicus published a book suggesting the Earth moved around the sun. In the 1600's, the telescope drastically changed people's notions of the size of the universe. It was much larger than they had imagined. The nearest stars were so far away that their distances had to be measured in *light-years*—the distance light, moving at about 186,000 miles (about 300,000 km) a second, travels in a year. Nowadays, astronomers usually use an even bigger distance unit, the *parsec* (pc), which is about 3.26 light years.

The Earth is merely one planet moving around one star—the sun. The sun is one of about 100 billion stars in our *galaxy* (group of stars), the Milky Way. The Milky Way is about 80,000 light-years (24,550 pc)

▲ *The British astronomer William Herschel (1738–1822) concentrated his efforts on observing faint and distant objects in the universe. In 1781 he discovered a hitherto-unknown planet, Uranus.*

▼ *The ancient Egyptians had a strange idea of what the universe was like. They thought the heavens were spanned by the sky goddess, Nut, her body being covered with stars. Inside the "bridge" made by her body were Shu, god of air, and Geb, god of Earth, whose body was covered with leaves. Outside the "bridge" was a boat that carried the sun god, Ra, across the sky each day.*

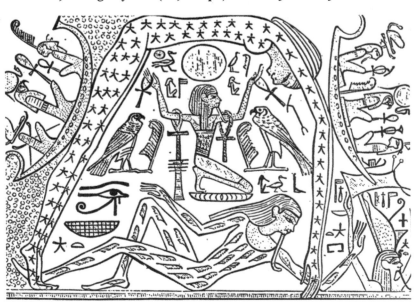

across and 13,000 light-years (4,000 pc) thick. It is one of many million galaxies. The nearest large galaxy to the Milky Way is the Andromeda Galaxy, over 2 million light-years (0.6 million pc) away.

You might well wonder how astronomers can measure distances in the universe. They can observe the stars with optical telescopes, radio telescopes, and now, because of satellites, X-ray telescopes, infrared telescopes, and so on. But how can they tell whether a star or a galaxy is one or a million light-years away?

It might seem even more difficult to tell where a star is going and how fast it is moving than to tell how far away it is. But it is often much easier. When a light source, such as a star or galaxy, is moving away from an observer, its light appears redder than it would otherwise. If the light source is moving toward the observer, its light appears bluer. These "red shifts" and "blue shifts" help astronomers to calculate the speed and direction in which stars and galaxies are moving. It was discovered that almost all galaxies showed red shifts. This meant that almost all of the galaxies were moving away from the Earth. It was also discovered that the farther away a galaxy was, the faster it was moving away from us. The U.S. astronomer Edwin Hubble showed in 1929 that the speed at which a galaxy moved away from us could be used to calculate its distance. In fact, Hubble's figures were not right (they were revised in 1956 by Milton Humason and others), but the factor used to calculate the distance of a galaxy by its red shift is still called the *Hubble Constant*.

The discovery that all galaxies are moving apart supported the *big bang*

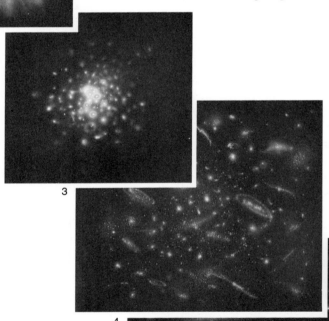

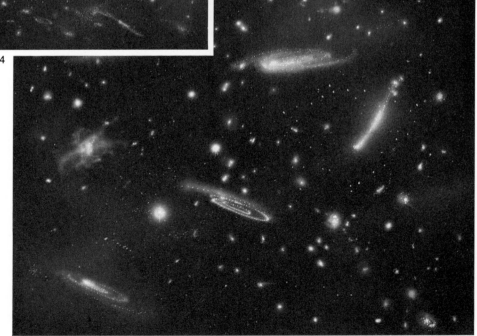

▲ *The universe probably began about 15 billion years ago in a "Big Bang," when all the energy and matter of the universe exploded into existence (1). About three minutes later, the first atomic nuclei formed (2). These were nuclei of the light element helium; hydrogen nuclei formed very soon after. After about 700,000 years, the first atoms formed; they were hydrogen atoms. Only after many million years (3) did the universe begin to look much like it does now. Now (4) the galaxies continue to fly apart.*

theory of the origin of the universe. According to the theory, the universe started with a huge explosion. At the instant of this explosion, all the matter of the universe was created. The explosion sprayed matter in all directions. The matter formed elements, and the elements eventually lumped together to form stars, planets, and galaxies. The big bang is believed to have taken place some time over 10 billion years ago. Microwave radiation detected in space in 1965 seems to be radiation left over from the huge explosion of the big bang. It seems that the universe as a whole is still expanding (getting bigger) because of that explosion.

However, cosmologists (scientists who study the origin and nature of the universe) still do not know if the universe is *open* or *closed*. If the universe is open, it will go on expanding forever. All of the matter in the universe will eventually be converted into heat energy or into black holes—there will be no matter left. This situation is described as the *heat death of the universe*.

But, if the universe is closed, it will at some time in the future stop expanding and begin to fall back in upon itself. Finally, all the matter will collapse into a single point, and there will be a "big crunch"—the converse of the big bang. Perhaps then there will be another big bang, creating a new universe.

ALSO READ: ASTRONOMY; BLACK HOLE; COMET; CONSTELLATION; COPERNICUS, NICOLAUS; GALILEO GALILEI; KEPLER, JOHANNES; MILKY WAY; OBSERVATORY; ORBIT; RADIO ASTRONOMY; RELATIVITY; SATELLITE; SOLAR SYSTEM; SPACE; STAR; SUN; TELESCOPE.

UPPER VOLTA see BURKINA FASO.

URAL MOUNTAINS The Ural Mountains are a chain of low mountains in the Soviet Union. They extend about 1,300 miles (2,100 km) from the Arctic Ocean southward to the Caspian Sea, and form the traditional boundary between Europe and Asia. They also form a natural boundary—plants and animals on each side are often different.

Most of the Ural Mountains rise only from 1,000 to 6,000 feet (305–1,830 m). The highest peak, Mount Narodnaya (6,214 feet—1,894 m), is in the northern portion of the Urals. This region has many glaciers and most of the ground is permafrost (it has a permanently frozen layer of soil). The central portion of the Urals consists of numerous high hills surrounded by deep valleys. The southern part of the Urals is made up of several parallel ridges. These mountains are covered with plant life and provide rich pastureland.

Forests cover large sections of the Ural Mountains. They yield valuable timber for the Soviet Union. Spruce, fir, pine, and larch trees grow in the north, while oak, maple, birch, and linden trees grow in the south.

Valuable deposits of oil, natural gas, coal, copper, iron ore, bauxite, gold, platinum, and other minerals are found in the Ural Mountains. The region is well known for its gems and semiprecious stones, such as emeralds, amethysts, and topazes.

ALSO READ: SOVIET UNION.

URANIUM see ELEMENT, NUCLEAR ENERGY, RADIOACTIVITY.

URUGUAY Uruguay is sometimes called the "Purple Land" because of its vast pasturelands of blue-purple grass. It is the third smallest country in South America—it is only slightly larger than North Dakota. (See the map with the article on SOUTH AMERICA.)

Uruguay is the only South Ameri-

▲ *Many stars are single. We believe such stars almost always have planets (worlds like Earth).*

▲ *Most stars are found grouped with one or more other stars.*

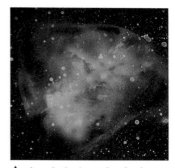

▲ *A nebula is a cloud of gas and dust in our own Milky Way galaxy.*

▲ *A globular star cluster is a group of thousands of very old stars. Our galaxy has many such clusters.*

▲ *A Spanish colonial church is almost dwarfed by this large palm tree in the town of Soriano, Uruguay.*

can country that has no large uninhabited area. People are found in almost every part, although about one half live in or near the capital city of Montevideo, in the south of the country.

Much of the country is covered with grassy plains and low hills. The climate is temperate, producing good pasture on the rich land. Only rarely are there frosts. Livestock-raising is the major agricultural activity, and wool, meat, and hides are the main exports. About three-fourths of the agricultural land is used for cattle and sheep.

Most of the population is of European background, mainly Spanish and Italian. There are almost no *mestizos* (people of mixed Spanish and Indian descent) because the native Indians have been almost entirely killed off.

International conferences, such as meetings of the Organization of American States (OAS), have been held at Punta del Este, a popular beach and resort area on Uruguay's coast.

Spanish adventurers were the first to explore Uruguay, but the Portuguese founded the first town there. Spain and Portugal vied for control of Uruguay, and later Brazil and Argentina fought to possess it. José Gervasio Artigas led the people in a fight against the Spanish government in the early 1800's, but in 1820 he was defeated and driven into exile. Then Portuguese Brazil annexed Uruguay,

in 1821. A group called the "Thirty-three Immortals," led by Juan Antonio Lavalleja, declared independence in 1825 and temporarily united the country with Argentina. Independence was finally won in 1828. Civil wars plagued Uruguay until José Batlle y Ordóñez became president in 1903. Terrorism by the Tupamaros (leftist rebels) brought a military takeover of the government in 1973. Since then, the country has been noted for its abuses of human rights—in the late 1970's, Uruguay had a higher proportion of political prisoners than any other country in the world. In 1984, military rule ended, and Julio Sanguinetti was elected president. Although the military still threatened to retake control, democracy had strengthened in Uruguay by the mid 1980's, and the economy improved.

ALSO READ: SOUTH AMERICA.

UTAH The Great Salt Lake of Utah is a small remaining part of an ancient inland sea, Lake Bonneville. The billions of tons of salt in the lake provide such buoyancy that it is almost impossible to sink while floating in it. The Jordan River flows from Utah Lake to the Great Salt Lake, which is fed also by rainfall and mountain streams.

West of the lake is the Great Salt Lake Desert. Racing cars have set speed records while racing on the desert's Bonneville Flats.

URUGUAY

Capital City: Montevideo (1,250,000 people).
Area: 68,037 square miles (176,216 sq. km).
Population: 3,000,000.
Government: Republic.
Natural Resources: Oil.
Export Products: Wool, meat, hides and skins.
Unit of Money: New peso.
Official Language: Spanish.

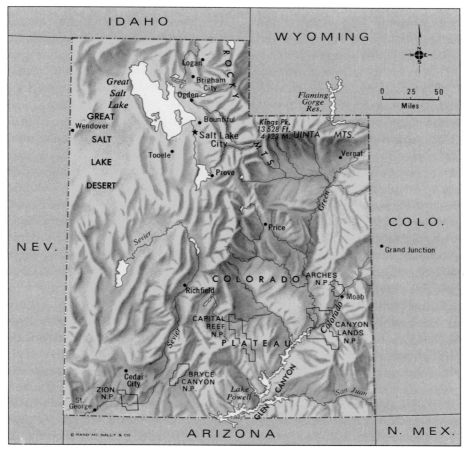

▲ *This is Temple Square in Salt Lake City where the Mormon Temple with its six granite spires stands.*

STATE EMBLEMS

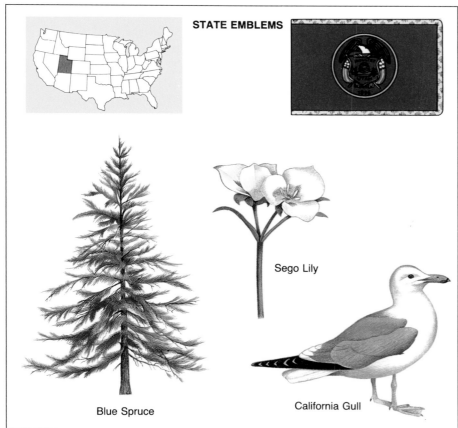

Sego Lily

Blue Spruce

California Gull

UTAH

Capital and largest city
Salt Lake City (163,000 people)

Area
84,916 square miles (219,931 sq. km)
Rank: 11th

Population
1,690,000
Rank: 36th

Statehood
January 4, 1896
(45th state admitted)

Principal rivers
Colorado River
Green River

Highest point
King's Peak;
13,528 feet (4,123 m)

Motto
"Industry"

Song
"Utah, We Love Thee"

Famous people
Maude Adams, John Moses Browning, Philo Farnsworth, the Osmond family, Brigham Young

The Land and Climate Utah lies on the western side of the Rocky Mountains. Idaho and Wyoming are north of Utah. Nevada is on its western side. Utah's southeastern corner is the only point in the United States where four states meet.

Utah is divided into two almost equal parts. Its western part is in the Great Basin. Its eastern part belongs to the big Colorado Plateau. The dividing line follows the highest ridge of a north-south highland. This highland is made up of mountains and narrow plateaus. The Wasatch Mountains, a branch of the Rockies, are at its northern end.

The highland is the state's most important part. It has most of the farmland and many of the mines. The factory centers are here, too. Most of Utah's people live in the highland. At its southern end, the highland curves westward. Here is beautiful canyon country.

The Great Basin Region, west of the dividing line, is gray and barren. It is sagebrush land. White salt flats show where lakes have dried up and left salt behind.

In the Colorado Plateau, the Uinta Mountains rise in the north near the Wyoming border. They have high, wooded peaks and deep canyons. Southward lies dry, yellow country.

The soil changes to red farther south. Rivers and the weather have carved gorges of colored rock.

Most of Utah has little rain. Only the mountains in the north receive much precipitation. A large part of this precipitation takes the form of snow. As the snow melts in spring, it feeds mountain streams.

The little rainfall that Utah receives falls mainly on the western side of the mountains. Therefore, the first settlers started farms in a strip along the western slopes of the Wasatch Range. They widened the strip of cropland by irrigation, using the water from the mountain streams.

History Dry, barren country has one advantage for the people who live there: outsiders are not likely to try to take their land from them!

For over 300 years, white people left Utah to the Paiute, Shoshone, and Ute Indians. But a change came in 1847. It came because a group of people wanted land where they could live as they pleased and be left alone by other people. They were a religious group, the Church of Jesus Christ of Latter-Day Saints. Most people call its members *Mormons*.

Mormon customs were different from those of their neighbors. The differences made their neighbors un-

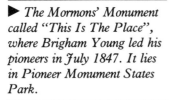

▶ *The Mormons' Monument called "This Is The Place", where Brigham Young led his pioneers in July 1847. It lies in Pioneer Monument States Park.*

friendly. Mobs often attacked the Mormons. In 1844, the founder of the group, Joseph Smith, and his brother were killed by an angry mob in Illinois. In search of peace, the Mormons moved westward. They eventually reached the Great Salt Lake in 1847.

"This is the place," said their leader, Brigham Young. They had left their former neighbors almost 1,000 miles (1,600 km) behind them—east of the Rockies. Other people of different beliefs were about 600 miles (960 km) away on the Pacific Coast. And the mountains and deserts of the Great Basin were in between.

The first settlement in Utah was named Great Salt Lake City. (Later, the "Great" in the city's name was dropped.) Nearly all the people were farmers in the beginning. They gained a reputation for their agricultural skill. Mormons were the first white North Americans to irrigate large areas.

As their population grew, the Mormons started other settlements. Their land was made a United States territory in 1850. Congress named it *Utah*. The word is a form of the Indian name *Ute*. Brigham Young, who led the Mormons into the area, was the territory's first governor.

People other than the Mormons settled in Utah. There was trouble between them and the Mormon majority. In time, though, the different groups of people learned to live peaceably together. The territory became a state in 1896. It would have become a state much earlier, but Congress disapproved of the Mormon practice of polygamy, whereby each man had several wives.

The People at Work Brigham Young liked farming, manufacturing, and trade. But he did not approve of mining. He felt it would give people get-rich-quick ideas. They might stop their useful labors and wander off to

▲ *Mesas and pinnacles worn down by centuries of wind erosion dominate the otherwise flat desert features of Monument Valley, Utah.*

hunt gold and silver. And if these minerals were found, Young believed, Utah might be overrun by hordes of rough fellows.

Mining did, however, start in Utah, and it is now the state's second largest industry. Much copper is extracted from the huge open-pit mine at Bingham Canyon. Utah is also a major producer of lead, oil, natural gas, uranium, silver, and gold.

The state's most important industry is manufacturing. Transportation equipment, primary metals, and food items are the chief manufactured products. The aerospace industry is rapidly growing.

Agriculture is a large business in Utah. Cattle, sheep, and turkeys are raised in large numbers, and large crops of hay, wheat, sugar beets, apricots, and cherries are grown. Because of limited rainfall, farmlands require much irrigation.

Utah is visited by millions of tourists every year. A popular attraction is the Mormon Tabernacle in Salt Lake City. This hall holds up to 10,000 people. It was built in the 1860's, and no nails at all were used in its construction. Wooden pins and rawhide thongs were used to hold it together.

ALSO READ: GREAT SALT LAKE; SMITH, JOSEPH; YOUNG, BRIGHAM.

Although Utah is far from the sea, a monument honoring sea gulls stands in Salt Lake City. In 1848, flocks of sea gulls came to Utah, probably from the Pacific Ocean. The birds saved the crops of the pioneer Mormons by eating a plague of locusts attacking the growing plants.

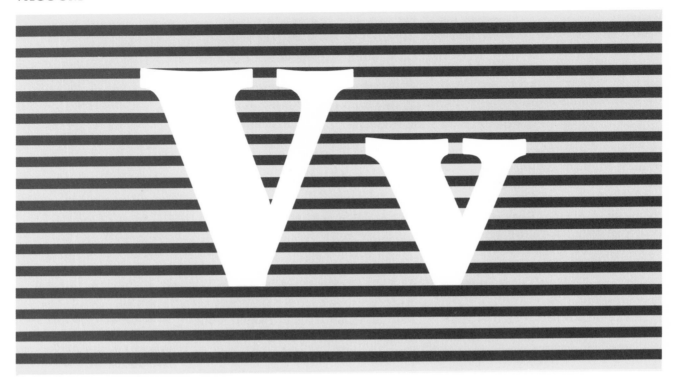

▼ *The vacuum pump, first developed in the 17th century, was used by scientists like Otto von Guericke and Robert Boyle in their experiments with air. The pump can suck almost all of the air out of a container.*

VACUUM A perfect (total) vacuum would be a space that had absolutely nothing in it—not even a single atom. A perfect vacuum of this kind is hard to find. Even in outer space, there are molecules or very fine dust particles. Even inside a glass or steel container, molecules would break away from the container's inner surface faster than they could be removed from the container. Thus, the word "vacuum" usually refers to a partial vacuum—a space from which *almost* everything has been removed.

Vacuum pumps have been invented that can suck the air out of containers. Vacuum pumps work much like ordinary pumps, except that they pump the air from inside a container until only a partial vacuum is left. A vacuum cleaner, for example, has a pump inside it that sucks air through a long hose. If a container were attached to the front end of the hose, the vacuum cleaner would create a partial vacuum within the container. Without a container, the vacuum cleaner continuously sucks dirt and dust into the hose.

Many food products are "vacuum-packed." This means that a partial vacuum has been created in the container. With almost no air inside the container, the food does not spoil as easily. To "vacuum pack" the container, the container is closed tightly while the food inside it is still hot. The heat means there are far fewer air molecules in the container than if the air were cool. When the container is shut tightly, more air cannot get inside the container. When you open a "vacuum-packed" container, you can hear a hissing sound as the outside air rushes in.

The vacuum tube, such as the radio tube, was one of the most important inventions in electronics. Early light bulbs also contained vacuums. Today, many "vacuum tubes" and most light bulbs use gases instead of vacuums. But vacuums are still important to scientists and engineers. Certain scientific experiments and chemical processes have to be performed in vacuums.

ALSO READ: ATOM, ELECTRONICS, GAS, MATTER, PUMP, SPACE.

VALENTINE'S DAY Valentine's Day is a romantic holiday celebrated on February 14. People send flowers, candies, or cards called "valentines" to their sweethearts, friends, or relatives. Valentine cards usually carry messages of love. Some cards are humorous. Valentines are often decorated with red hearts, ribbons, and pictures of Cupid, the Roman god of love.

Valentine's Day can be traced back to the ancient Roman festival called Lupercalia. This festival, held every February 15, was in honor of young lovers. Later, the Christian church established Saint Valentine's Day on February 14, in honor of two saints named Valentine who lived in the A.D. 200's. The old Roman custom of celebrating love and lovers is now celebrated on the saints' feast day.

VALLEY see MOUNTAIN.

VAN ALLEN, JAMES A. see RADIATION BELT.

VAN BUREN, MARTIN (1782–1862) Martin Van Buren, the eighth President, was the first President to have been born in the United States. The previous seven Presidents had been born in the British colonies before the colonies declared independence and became the United States.

Martin Van Buren lived in Kinderhook, New York. He graduated from the village school at the age of 14. He studied law in Kinderhook and in a law office in New York City and became a lawyer at the age of 21. Van Buren then returned to his native town to practice law. In 1807, Van Buren married one of his cousins, Hannah Hoes. The couple had four sons before Hannah Van Buren died, just 12 years after their marriage.

Van Buren served in the U.S. Senate from 1821 to 1828, when he was elected governor of New York. In the same year, when Andrew Jackson was the nominee for President, some members of the Democratic-Republican Party began calling themselves Democrats. Van Buren, one of the leaders of the new party, worked hard for Jackson's election and was appointed secretary of state when Jackson took office in 1829. Only a few months after taking office, Van Buren resigned the governorship of New York to accept this new appointment. As secretary of state, Van Buren won the confidence of President Jackson, who chose him as his Vice-Presidential running mate in the election of 1832. In 1836, Jackson urged his party to nominate Van Buren for President.

Van Buren won the election, but soon after his inauguration economic

▲ *An old Valentine's Day card shows Cupid, a Roman god of love. The Romans believed that if you were wounded by one of Cupid's arrows, you would fall in love with someone.*

MARTIN VAN BUREN
EIGHTH PRESIDENT   MARCH 4, 1837—MARCH 4, 1841

Born: December 5, 1782, Kinderhook, New York
Parents: Abraham and Maria Hoes Van Buren
Education: Village schools, studied in law office
Religion: Dutch Reformed
Occupation: Lawyer, government official
Political Party: Democratic
State Represented: New York
Married: 1807 to Hannah Hoes (1783–1819)
Children: Four sons
Died: July 24, 1862, Kinderhook, New York
Buried: Kinderhook Cemetery, Kinderhook, New York

▲ *A self-portrait by Van Gogh. This artist painted many self-portraits, probably because he was trying to understand his own mind. He painted his most famous self-portrait after he had cut off part of his ear, following a quarrel with another artist, Gauguin.*

▲ The Painter on the Road to Tarascon, *a painting by Vincent Van Gogh.*

hard times hit the country. The Panic of 1837 developed when government funds that had been deposited in certain state banks were mismanaged. Some of the loans made by the banks with government funds had not been wise, and the loans were not repaid. As President, Van Buren urged that government funds be kept in a national treasury independent of state and private banks. After three years, Congress passed the Independent Treasury Bill (1840), but it was too late to help Van Buren win a second term. He was blamed for the hard times. Van Buren made himself even more unpopular with U.S. citizens by refusing to become involved in Canadian rebellions against Great Britain in 1837. In 1840, Van Buren lost the Presidential election to William Henry Harrison.

After his defeat, Van Buren returned to his hometown to practice law. He remained active in politics for many years and even ran again for President in 1848. His last years were spent at Lindenwald, an old mansion that he restored in Kinderhook.

ALSO READ: HARRISON, WILLIAM HENRY; JACKSON, ANDREW.

VAN GOGH, VINCENT (1853–1890) Vincent Willem van Gogh was a painter whose brief, bright flash of life ended in what he thought was failure. A Dutchman, he was born in Groot-Zundert, the eldest son of a Protestant minister.

The first of his many failures took place after he went to work, at age 16, for an uncle who owned an art gallery. He fell in love with a girl who did not care for him, and he suffered a nervous breakdown. He tried another gallery and then took a job teaching in Britain. But he did not do well at either job. He studied to be a minister but failed the language exams. He tried being a minister to the coal miners of Belgium. He really wanted

to work for the poor. He lived in a shack and slept on a pallet made of old coats. He even dressed like the miners, in clothes covered with coal dust. But van Gogh was not a good speaker, and he failed as a preacher.

At this time, he began to draw and paint. Van Gogh's early works are dark and somber and show the misery of coal miners and peasant farmers. His first important painting, *The Potato Eaters*, is a dark picture of work-worn peasants eating humble food after a hard day's work.

In 1886, he went to Paris and lived with his favorite brother, Theo, an art dealer. Van Gogh became friendly with many talented artists, including several of the Impressionists, who liked to paint outside in natural light. Van Gogh began to use more color in his work, and he changed his brush technique. He used many separate brush strokes, as did the Impressionists. But under van Gogh's hand, the stroke became very loose and expressive of his feelings.

Look at his painting, *The Painter on the Road to Tarascon*, shown here. The painter walking down the road could be van Gogh. The golden scene seems sun-drenched. Can't you just feel the warmth of a summer day? You do not see the sun, but you are aware of its presence everywhere. This was van Gogh in the brief happy months of his life.

Contrast this painting with *Road with Cypresses* (shown opposite) that was painted some months later. The golden colors are gone. The sun has become a yellowish green in a wild, moody, blue sky swirling with brush strokes. For no apparent reason, there is also an orange moon in the sky. The black-green cypresses reach darkly up to the sky along a hard, green, riverlike road. The figures in the foreground are dark and look helpless in front of the swirling, high cypresses. The wheat fields (so golden and straight in earlier paintings) are now dark and wild and choppy. Van

▲ One of Van Gogh's best-known paintings, Road with Cypresses.

in the chest. He died two days later through complications of the injury. Van Gogh sold almost no paintings in his lifetime, but the value of his works has soared in recent years. In 1990, his painting *Portrait of Dr. Gachet* was sold for $82.5 million—the highest amount ever paid for a work of art at auction.

ALSO READ: EXPRESSIONISM; GAUGUIN, PAUL; IMPRESSIONISM.

VANUATU see MELANESIA, PACIFIC ISLANDS.

VATICAN CITY Vatican City is an independent nation located on Vatican Hill in the city of Rome, Italy. It is ruled by the pope and is the headquarters of the Roman Catholic Church. In size, it is the world's tiniest country—108.7 acres (43.99 hectares).

The main building in Vatican City is St. Peter's Basilica, with a large *piazza* (square) in front of it. Important church functions are held in St. Peter's. In the days of ancient Rome, Vatican Hill was a burial ground. The first basilica of St. Peter was erected in the A.D. 300's over what is believed to be the grave of St. Peter, the first pope.

Near the basilica is the Vatican Palace, which contains the pope's living quarters and offices of the church government. The Vatican Museums, housing some of the greatest works of ancient art, are located in the palace,

▲ A view from the world's smallest country, Vatican City, the pope's official home. Only about the size of a large park, Vatican City has a population of about 1,000.

Gogh expressed his feelings about life in his pictures so much that he is considered the first of the *expressionists*, a school of painters who showed their personal feelings in their art.

Van Gogh's mental illness became worse. In 1888, his friend, Paul Gauguin, whom he had eagerly awaited, came to visit. But they had a violent quarrel, and van Gogh ran after Gauguin with a razor. Gauguin stood his ground, and van Gogh went to his room. He then cut off a piece of his ear and sent it to a woman he loved.

After this, van Gogh was in the care of doctors until his death. In between fits of madness, he did several paintings. His colors became wilder and wilder. In 1890, he shot himself

VATICAN CITY

Area: 108.7 acres (0.44 sq. km).

Population: 1,000.

Government: Papal commission.

Export Products: Vatican City does not engage in trade. It depends mostly on charity for income.

Unit of Money: Vatican City lira, Italian lira.

▲ *The ceremonial guard at Vatican City is made up of soldiers called Swiss Guards. Their traditional uniform, as shown here, was designed hundreds of years ago by the great artist Michelangelo (1475–1564).*

▲ *Pat Rooney, Sr., sang and danced in vaudeville for over 50 years.*

as is the Vatican Library. Also within the Vatican Palace are various chapels, including the Sistine Chapel.

The citizens of Vatican City live in apartments surrounding the church buildings. The pope has absolute executive, legislative, and judicial powers within the city. He is assisted by a commission of cardinals, a secretary, and a lay (not of the clergy) governor. The governor administers property belonging to the Vatican, the Vatican City police, and the Vatican post office (which issues its own stamps). Vatican City also has its own militia, called the Swiss Guards, whose job it is to protect the pope. The Vatican has its own telephone system, auto licenses, flag, currency, radio and television stations, and its own newspapers, the most important of which is *L'Osservatore Romano*. As an independent state, the Vatican exchanges ambassadors with other countries.

Beginning in the 1400's, the Vatican took over and ruled large areas of land in Italy called the Papal States. Italy became a united country in 1870, and the Italian government took control of the Papal States in 1871. Throughout the next 50 years, the popes refused to accept money from the Italian government in exchange for the lands taken away. The Vatican was no longer an independent state, and the popes considered themselves to be prisoners of the Italian government. In 1929, the Lateran Treaty, made between Pope Pius XI and the Italian government, established Vatican City as an independent nation.

ALSO READ: ITALIAN HISTORY, MICHELANGELO BUONARROTI, POPE, ROMAN CATHOLIC CHURCH, ROME.

VAUDEVILLE Vaudeville is an entertainment consisting of a variety of individual acts. These acts usually include singing and dancing, magic, animal acts, juggling, acrobatics, short humorous or dramatic skits, and comedy routines. The word "vaudeville" comes from the French words *vau-de-vire*, a name applied to comic drinking songs written in the valley (*vau*) of Vire, France, in the 1400's. The songs were often sung between acts of plays and later began to be called *vaudevilles*.

Vaudeville, as a program of variety acts, began in the United States in the 1800's. Up to that time, most public entertainment was considered vulgar, and only men went to see it. Vaudeville introduced family entertainment. In 1883, Benjamin F. Keith opened the first vaudeville theater in Boston. It was called the Gaiety Museum. The new amusement house proved so successful that Keith formed a partnership with Edward F. Albee. Together they built a national chain of theaters, called the Keith-Albee Circuit. The Orpheum and Pantages were other well-known Vaudeville chains.

Vaudeville's popularity grew rapidly. In the 1920's, vaudeville performances attracted audiences of over 2 million people each day in over 1,000 theaters. Most of the acts were hired by the central agencies and sent across the country to play large cities and small towns. Tony Pastor's and the Palace in New York City were two of the most famous vaudeville houses. It was the ambition of every vaudeville actor to play in them. Some of the stars of vaudeville were Frank Fay, Pat Rooney, Bill "Bo-jangles" Robinson, Ted Healy and the Three Stooges, the Marx Brothers, Sophie Tucker, and Eddie Foy and the Seven Little Foys.

In Great Britain, music halls presented shows much like vaudeville shows. Stars such as Charlie Chaplin performed there.

Many famous television and movie comedians began their careers in vaudeville—Jack Benny, Will Rogers, George Burns and Gracie Allen, and Bob Hope, among others. Milton

Berle and Sammy Davis, Jr., were child stars in vaudeville.

Vaudeville reached its height in the late 1920's. But then it began to run into trouble. There were actors' strikes and problems with theater owners. Talking motion pictures were created, and much of vaudeville's audience turned to movies and radio. Vaudeville died out.

ALSO READ: MUSICAL COMEDY; ROGERS, WILL.

VEGETABLES All plants are vegetables, but in everyday use the word "vegetables" means plants that are grown for food. (The fruits of many plants, such as oranges and apples, are not generally called vegetables.) Any part of a plant can be used as a vegetable. In some cases, such as spinach and lettuce, people eat the leaves. Celery is the leaf stalk of a plant. Beets, carrots, and turnips are the roots of plants. Green peas are a plant's seeds. Tomatoes and green and red peppers are fruits, and broccoli is a flower. Some vegetables are grown for their oils. Corn and soybeans yield oil used for cooking and seasoning. People can buy these oils either in liquid form or as solid white shortening.

A plant (or plant part) that one society considers a common vegetable may be unknown in other parts of the world. South Sea islanders eat roots we would not recognize as vegetables. Chinese cooks use vegetables unusual to us, such as water chestnuts. French people eat more kinds of salad greens than we do in the United States, although more of these greens such as kale, chicory, and even dandelion greens, are now becoming available in our stores. Some vegetables are common in some parts of the United States but are rarely eaten in other parts. Okra is a southern favorite, but northern and western shoppers are not accustomed to its heavy pod and

somewhat sticky flesh. About 30 kinds of vegetables are commonly eaten in the United States. Many more are known but seldom served.

Vegetables usually taste better when they are ripened on the vine or stalk, but many vegetables are picked while they are immature and ripen on their way to market. Some vegetables, such as potatoes, can be stored fresh for a long time, but others, such as asparagus and peas, must be preserved in some way if they are to last long. Vegetables are usually refrigerated on their way from the farm to the market or processing plant. They can be preserved for longer periods by being canned, frozen, or pickled. In recent years, quick-freezing has become increasingly popular because it does not allow the vegetables to lose vitamins and minerals, as canning does. Vegetables such as cabbage, cucumbers, and peppers are pickled by being soaked in salt or vinegar.

Many familiar vegetables have been known for centuries, but not always as food. Tomatoes were once thought to be poisonous and eggplants to be inedible. Asparagus was used as a medicine about 2,000 years ago, long before the Romans raised it for food. Cabbage leaves were used as a dressing for bruises and to prevent baldness; when vinegar was added, they were supposed to cure dog bites.

▲ *This vaudeville team was called Crane and Alexander, and the picture was taken in 1912. Loud checks and stripes were characteristic dress for such acts.*

▼ *A giant harvesting machine helps workers gather vegetable crops on this large-scale farm.*

▲ *Various different types of vegetables: (1) a lettuce, (2) peas in the pod, (3) a cauliflower, (4) a runner bean, (5) an onion, (6) a carrot, and (7) a beet.*

Onions were a household cure for colds during the Middle Ages. Carrots came from Asia to England, where women used the leaves as hat trimmings. Persian cooks served lettuce in the 500's B.C. Melons have been grown in Africa and Asia for thousands of years. Yams were eaten by primitive African tribes. Squash, potatoes, corn, and several kinds of beans are native to North and South America and were not known to Europeans until the 1500's.

Vegetables are very important in good nutrition. But they do not all offer the same food value. Avocados contain a great deal of fat. Starchy vegetables, such as beans, potatoes, and corn, contain mostly carbohydrates. Beans and peas also contain quite a lot of protein. Most vegetables provide vitamins, especially A, the B vitamins (thiamine, riboflavin, and niacin), and C. Usually, the deeper the color of the vegetable, the richer in vitamins it is. Carrots, tomatoes, and spinach are nutritous vegetables with deep coloring. Cabbage, however, has abundant vitamin C, despite its pale green color. Vegetables are also rich in minerals, such as calcium, iron, phosphorus, and potassium. Spinach and asparagus provide iron. Beans are high in calcium.

Besides vitamins and minerals, vegetables offer substances that help digestion of other foods. All vegetables contain a great deal of water. *Cellulose*, often called *fiber*, which is the fibrous material in vegetables, adds bulk to the diet, aiding digestion.

ALSO READ: AGRICULTURE, NUTRITION, PLANT, SEEDS AND FRUITS.

VEGETARIAN A vegetarian is someone who does not eat meat or fish. A *vegan* is someone who does not eat any kind of animal material—not even eggs or dairy products. Although human beings always ate mixed diets in the past, we can live perfectly well without animal food. Our digestive systems are able to deal with almost any kind of food and, as long as we choose our diets carefully, we can get everything we need from vegetable matter. We must have regular supplies of fats, proteins, and carbohydrates, together with enough minerals and vitamins. All (except vitamin B_{12}) can be obtained from plants, although we need several different kinds of plant food to supply everything and to give us enough energy. Green leaves alone, for example, cannot supply us with nearly enough energy, although they are essential for providing vitamins. Nuts, cereals, dried peas, and dried beans provide the needed proteins and fats in a vegetarian diet, while bread (made with non-animal fat) and potatoes can provide the carbohydrates.

Many people are turning to vegetarian diets today in the belief that they are actually healthier. For example, vegetable fats are thought to be less harmful than animal fats. Although we can normally live happily on plant foods, the plants in some areas cannot get enough of certain

▼ *A selection of vegetables including leeks, carrots, beans, cauliflower and artichokes, are displayed on this fresh vegetable stall in France.*

minerals (especially iodine and fluorine) from the soil. In these instances it is necessary to add the minerals to the food in the form of supplements.

ALSO READ: FOOD, NUTRITION.

VEIN see CIRCULATORY SYSTEM.

VELÁZQUEZ, DIEGO (1599–1660)

Diego Rodríguez de Silva y Velázquez was one of the greatest artists of all time. He was born in the city of Seville, Spain.

At the age of 12, Velázquez became an apprentice to Francisco Pacheco, a well-known Seville painter. Many artists from other countries visited at the Pacheco home, and Velázquez was able to learn of new developments in painting. He became a master painter at the age of 17, and a year later married Juana Pacheco, his teacher's daughter.

Velázquez soon made a reputation for himself as an excellent painter. He painted with dark brown and yellowish tones. His early paintings—both his still lifes and his religious pictures—show that he had mastery of objects and figures when he was barely 20 years old. After five years in Seville, he journeyed to Madrid, hoping to have a chance to paint a portrait of the king, Philip III. He could not arrange to do so, but a year later he went to Madrid again. By this time, the old king had died, and his son, Philip IV, had succeeded him. Velázquez became a member of the court.

King Philip IV was very fond of Velázquez, who painted many portraits of the king. In 1628, the great Flemish painter, Peter Paul Rubens, came to Madrid on a diplomatic visit. Velázquez was chosen to be his companion. It is thought that Rubens urged Velázquez to go to Italy to see the work of the great artists there. Velázquez sailed from Barcelona to Venice. He saw the work of Titian and the other great Venetian painters. Then he went on to Rome and stayed a year at the Vatican. He studied the works of Michelangelo and Raphael. He painted two pictures there. When he returned to Spain, his paintings had become more colorful. His brush strokes were freer. Philip IV, grateful to have Velázquez back, gave him his own studio and visited him as he painted.

The Prince on Horseback (shown here) is a handsome portrait of Prince Baltazar Carlos, son of King Philip IV. The little boy looks very much a prince astride a beautiful, lively-looking pony. The prince's sash flies out behind him as he rides. The young face looks at the painter with a fresh, alert expression. The prince is in command of the situation. Velázquez's background here was unusual for portraits of the day. Beautiful clouds sail through the sky, while snowcapped mountains rise in the distance.

Velázquez made another journey to Italy in 1649. At that time, he did a portrait of Pope Innocent X. It has been called one of the finest portraits ever done. Velázquez lived out his whole life at court and left a wealth of beautiful paintings. His *Maids of Honor* is especially famous for its skillful and complicated organization. Many of his paintings are in the Prado Museum in Madrid, although fine examples of his work can be seen in most of the world's leading art museums.

ALSO READ: ART HISTORY.

VENDING MACHINES

You can buy almost anything from a vending machine nowadays. Candy, snacks, and drinks; newspapers and books; tapes, toiletries, and tickets—all can be purchased instantly at the drop of a coin. Machines like automatic carpark barriers, payphones, and cash

▲ The Prince on Horseback, *by Diego Velázquez.*

In 1970, Velázquez's portrait of *Juan de Pareja* was sold to the Wildenstein Gallery, New York, for the highest price then spent on a work of art. This record for a painting lasted for over 15 years. In today's values, the amount was close to $15,000,000.

▲ *A typical vending machine for selling newspapers. You put in your coins and take the paper from the window.*

dispensers are kinds of vending machines, too.

Today's vending machines are smart machines with computers to control them. They can identify each coin fed through the slot and reject any foreign coins. They can add up the coins and give you change as they serve you. The coins pass through special sensors. These give out magnetic signals that depend on the size of each coin and how much metal it contains. Different kinds of coins give different signals. The machine's computer identifies each coin from its signal.

Many vending machines do away with coins altogether. A special card is inserted into the slot. The card contains its own magnetic signal for a certain amount of money, or a signal in another form, such as a hologram. The computer checks the card and alters its signal to subtract the cost of the item.

VENEZUELA Venezuela is one of the richest South American countries because of its oil deposits. It lies on the northern coast of South America, bordered on the north by the Caribbean Sea. Its neighbors are Brazil to the south, Colombia on the west, and Guyana on the east. Several islands off the Caribbean coast are part of Venezuela. (See the map with the article on SOUTH AMERICA.)

Venezuela is larger than Texas and Oklahoma combined. It has four main regions. In the Andes Mountains and surrounding hills, many peaks soar up over 15,000 feet (4,570 m). The capital city of Caracas lies at 3,000 feet (915 m) and has spring weather all the year round. Most of the Venezuelan people live in the cool mountain areas.

The hot and humid coastal plain includes Lake Maracaibo and the Orinoco River delta. This region is the source of Venezuela's oil wealth. Plains, or *llanos*, lie between the Andes and the Orinoco. This hot region, where cattle graze on large ranches, at times receives heavy rain and at other times is very dry. The Guiana Highlands, a vast area of high plateaus and

▲ *Electricity pylons link up along part of Lake Maracaibo, in northwestern Venezuela. The area also has many oil wells.*

Alonso de Ojeda discovered Lake Maracaibo in Venezuela in 1499. He called the land Venezuela, or Little Venice, because the natives lived in houses on stilts.

VENEZUELA

Capital City: Caracas (1,260,000 people).
Area: 352,145 square miles (912,050 sq. km).
Population: 19,250,000.
Government: Republic.
Natural Resources: Oil and natural gas, iron ore.
Export Products: Oil, iron ore, coffee, cocoa.
Unit of Money: Bolívar.
Official Language: Spanish.

plains, extends from the Orinoco River to the Brazilian border. Primitive Indian tribes live in this ruggedly beautiful country. The world's highest waterfall, Angel Falls—3,212 feet (979 m)—was discovered there in 1935 by a U.S. pilot, Jimmy Angel, after he had crash-landed near the site.

Most Venezuelans are *mestizos* (people of mixed Spanish and Indian descent). The overall standard of living is high compared to that of other Latin American countries, but many of the people are still very poor.

In 1917, oil was discovered along the shores of Lake Maracaibo, an area now one of the largest-producing oil fields in the world. Venezuela is also a major producer of iron ore. Coffee is a leading crop.

Oil revenues are now being used for public housing and other projects to benefit the people. Caracas, with its plazas and its University City, is a rich and modern city.

Venezuela was discovered by Christopher Columbus on his third voyage in 1498. It was one of the first colonies to revolt against Spain, but it did not win independence until 1821, under the leadership of Venezuela's famous hero, Simón Bolívar. General Juan Vicente Gómez ruled as a dictator from 1908 to 1935. The country was not free from dictatorial rule until 1958. It is now a republic, administered by a president. The government nationalized the iron-ore industry in 1975 and the oil industry in 1976. Venezuela is a charter member of the Organization of Petroleum Exporting Countries (OPEC).

ALSO READ: BOLÍVAR, SIMÓN; PETRO-LEUM; SOUTH AMERICA.

VENICE Venice is a beautiful Italian city built on the sea. Most Venetians travel along canals instead of streets, using boats instead of cars for transport.

When the Roman Empire collapsed in the A.D. 400's, barbarians swept across Italy. People who lived on the northern Italian mainland fled by boat to low mud islands off the coast. On these islands and in the shallow parts of the sea nearby, they began to build a city, Venice. Venice developed into a great seafaring and trading center. Its merchants controlled the growing ocean traffic to the eastern Mediterranean. From there they brought spices, silks, gems, and perfumes to Europe.

The city's 118 islands are connected by about 400 graceful bridges. Boats carry people along the 180 canals. Motorized launches are common, but some people prefer to travel on elegant Venetian boats called *gondolas*. These decorative, flat-bottomed boats have high prows and sterns and are propelled by oarsmen called *gondoliers*.

Venice is a city of striking palaces, churches, and public buildings. The Grand Canal leads to the heart of the city, Piazza San Marco (St. Mark's Square). The Cathedral of St. Mark, the Doges' Palace (a residence of early Venetian rulers), and the Campanile (bell tower) are located here. Four gilded horses, Greek in origin and brought to Venice in the 1200's, adorn the upper tier of the cathedral. Tourists like to feed the pigeons that flock to the square. The ancient Ri-

▲ *An elevated highway sweeps through the modern city of Caracas, Venezuela.*

▼ *The Grand Canal winds through the city of Venice past some of the most graceful buildings in the world. The Church of Santa Maria della Salute is in the center background. Posts for mooring gondolas and other boats are in front of the houses on the left.*

▲ *Giuseppe Verdi, the great Italian composer of operas.*

Verdi composed the opera *Aïda* in 1871 for the khedive (Turkish ruler) of Egypt. It was written to celebrate the opening of the Suez Canal.

The people of Vermont are noted for their independence. There is a saying that states: "Vermonters will do nothing you tell them to; 'most anything you ask them to."

alto Bridge, lined with shops, and the Bridge of Sighs are also favorite sights. Galleries contain masterpieces painted by such great painters as Titian, Tintoretto, and Giorgione. Many visitors like to relax on the sandy beaches at the Lido, a fashionable resort across the lagoon from the city itself.

ALSO READ: ITALIAN HISTORY, ITALY.

VENTRILOQUISM see PUPPET.

VERB see PARTS OF SPEECH.

VERDI, GIUSEPPE (1813–1901) Giuseppe Verdi was one of the world's greatest composers of grand opera. He created works filled with more exciting drama and richer melodies and harmonies than did previous opera composers.

Verdi's father was a poor innkeeper in the small town of Le Roncole, Italy. A local parish priest gave Verdi his first music lessons. Verdi later moved to Busseto, Italy, where he studied with the conductor of the local orchestra, Francesco Provesi. A merchant of Busseto, named Barezzi, helped support Verdi, even paying for his musical studies in the city of Milan, Italy. In 1833, Verdi returned to Busseto, where he became director of the orchestra after Provesi's death.

Oberto, Verdi's first opera, was produced in Milan in 1839 with some success. But his next opera was a failure. The death of his young wife (Barezzi's daughter) and children resulted in his giving up composing for more than a year. The manager of the La Scala Opera in Milan succeeded in interesting Verdi in a new opera text, and he went back to composing.

Verdi's musical gifts developed gradually, his greatest works being written in his later years. *Rigoletto,* composed in 1851, was the first of

Verdi's operas that is still regularly performed today. It was followed by *Il Trovatore, La Traviata, Don Carlos,* and *La Forza del Destino.* His greatest successes, which formed the high point of Italian opera, were *Aïda, Otello,* and *Falstaff.* He also composed a requiem mass.

ALSO READ: MUSIC, OPERA.

VERMONT Vermont is a beautiful New England state. The Vermont countryside—with its rolling hills dotted with sugar maples, peaceful villages with steepled white churches, and clear mountain lakes—gives visitors a chance to imagine what life was like in colonial days. Beneath this lovely countryside lies very hard rock. The city of Barre in central Vermont is sometimes called the "Granite Center of the World." Vermont's early settlers chiseled millstones from granite. Today, granite blocks are used for building. The state capitol building at Montpelier is built of granite.

Visitors are seldom allowed to go down into a granite quarry. If they are given permission to do so, they step into a steel box. It is open at the top and on one side. A cable lowers the box into the quarry. Along the steep rock sides are narrow ledges. Workers standing on the ledges cut the stone with power drills. The noise is deafening.

The Land and Climate A long, rocky mountain range divides Vermont into western and eastern sections. This range belongs to the Appalachian Mountains and stretches from the Canadian province of Quebec in the north to Massachusetts in the south. The Vermont part of the range is named the Green Mountains, because of the forests of trees on the mountainsides. A hiking path follows the range all the way through the state. French explorers and settlers came to this region during the 1600's

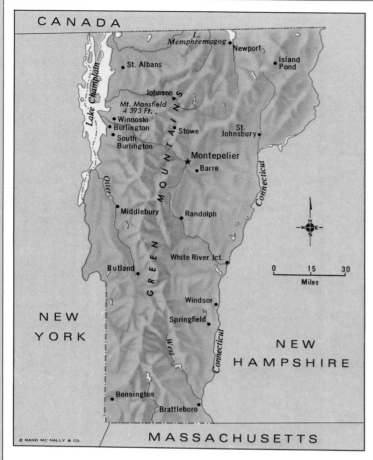

▲ *Autumn leaves line the roadside as walkers pass underneath a canopy of autumn yellows in Vermont. Many tourists visit Vermont to see its beautiful forests and mountains all year round.*

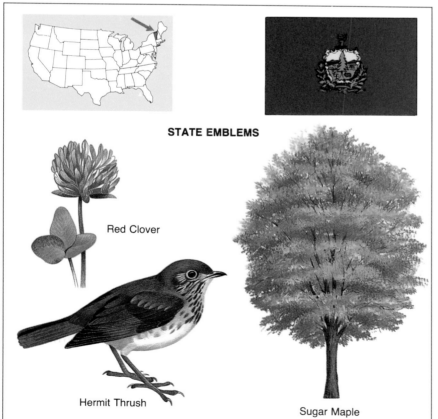

STATE EMBLEMS

Red Clover

Hermit Thrush

Sugar Maple

VERMONT

Capital
Montpelier (8,000 people)

Area
9,609 square miles
(24,887 sq. km)
Rank: 43rd

Population
557,000
Rank: 48th

Statehood
March 4, 1791
(14th state admitted)

Principal river
Connecticut River

Highest point
Mount Mansfield;
4,393 feet (1,339 m)

Largest city
Burlington (38,000 people)

Motto
"Freedom and Unity"

Song
"Hail, Vermont"

Famous people
Chester A. Arthur, Calvin Coolidge, Admiral George Dewey, John Dewey, Stephen A. Douglas

Vermont is the least populous state east of the Mississippi River having only two cities with a population exceeding 15,000.

and early 1700's; the name Vermont came from the French words *vert* and *mont* ("green mountain"). Vermont's nickname is the "Green Mountain State."

West of the Green Mountains, the land slopes toward Lake Champlain and the border of New York State. Burlington, the state's largest city and site of the University of Vermont, overlooks the lake. The Champlain Valley has much beautiful scenery. Part of the lake itself, as well as several islands and a peninsula, are in Vermont.

Addison County, near Lake Champlain, might be described in biblical terms as a "land of milk and honey." Vermont's biggest honey producers are in Addison County. Dairying is also important, as it is in more than half of the entire state. The Taconic Mountains cover a strip in the southwestern region of the state. The Valley of Vermont separates them from the Green Mountains.

East of the Green Mountains, the land slopes mostly toward the Connecticut River. However, a branch of the White Mountains rises in the northeast. Most of this range is in the state of New Hampshire, just across the Connecticut River. Eastern Vermont is horse-raising country. Miles of riding trails wind through woods,

along streams, and past waterfalls and lakes.

Vermont's summers are cool, and rain is usually plentiful. Vacationers from many states come to the cool, green hills to escape summer heat. Snow falls in Vermont in late autumn. From December until the end of March, the state is generally under a white blanket.

History In the days of the Indians, Vermont was a borderland. It lay between the territory of the New York Iroquois and that of the Algonkin tribes to the east. Other Algonkin tribes lived north of Vermont. The Algonkins of Canada and their neighbors, the Hurons, were enemies of the Iroquois.

By 1609, the French explorer, Samuel de Champlain, had made friends among the Algonkins and Hurons. They persuaded him and other French people to fight the Iroquois with them. Their war party paddled south on Lake Champlain. For the first time, Europeans saw Vermont's Green Mountains. The fight with the Iroquois took place on the New York side of the lake. French guns won the battle for the Canadian Indians. Later, the French built log forts in the Champlain Valley. The first one was built on Isle La Motte, an island in the lake.

The British entered Vermont from the southeast. In 1724, they built Fort Dummer where Brattleboro stands today. The fort was the first permanent British settlement. With the help of the vengeful Iroquois, the British began to fight the French. By 1758, the French had lost all their forts in Vermont.

Many people began to come from Massachusetts and Connecticut to settle in Vermont. But nobody was sure whether the area was part of New York or New Hampshire. In 1764, the British king, George III, declared that it belonged to New York. When New York tried to claim

▼ *Lake Champlain (in the distance) is part of Vermont's border with New York. Some of Vermont's best farmland is found around this scenic lake.*

it, Vermont settlers chose Ethan Allen to take charge of their defense. He armed a force that he called the "Green Mountain Boys." But before the matter could be settled, the American Revolution broke out. The Green Mountain Boys marched on Fort Ticonderoga, west of Lake Champlain. On May 10, 1775, they took it from the British soldiers.

Vermont declared itself an independent republic in 1777. For about 14 years, it had its own postal system and coined its own money. In 1791, Vermont joined the Union, the first state to do so after the original 13 colonies. Vermont was the first state to ban slavery and give the vote to all adult males.

As long as farming was the main business in America, Vermont was at a disadvantage. It had little good land for growing crops, although sheep raising brought prosperity for a while. Many farmers gave up their struggle against stony soil and moved west. But French Canadian settlers who were unable to obtain fertile land in Quebec began to come to Vermont in the late 1800's. They bought the farms that Vermonters had given up. Dairy farming became the main type of agriculture.

Vermonters at Work Today, manufacturing is Vermont's most important business. Machinery is the chief manufactured product.

Agriculture and tourism are also important. Dairying is still the principal kind of agriculture. The state is famous for its tasty milk and Cheddar cheese. But one of Vermont's best-known agricultural products—maple syrup—is not a dairy product. The maple sap is gathered from the state's official tree, the sugar maple. Many apples are also grown.

Vermont is a popular place to vacation. Many youngsters from eastern industrial cities go to summer camps in Vermont. The state's natural beauty draws visitors at all times of the year, but especially in autumn, when the leaves change colors. Winter brings skiers to the snowy slopes of the long chain of the Green Mountains.

ALSO READ: ALLEN, ETHAN; CHAMPLAIN, SAMUEL DE; GRANITE; QUARRYING.

VERNE, JULES (1828–1905) Jules Verne was a writer who is sometimes called the "Father of Science Fiction."

Jules Verne was born in Nantes, France. As a boy, he once tried to run away to sea. He studied law in Paris but was more interested in writing. He began to compose plays and poetry.

He was deeply interested in geography and in aeronautics, the science of flight. He wrote a scientific essay suggesting an expedition to Africa in a balloon. A publisher persuaded him to turn the essay into a novel. The novel, published in 1863, was called *Five Weeks in a Balloon*. This book was immensely successful, and Verne wrote several other novels of adventure and science fiction, including *A Journey to the Center of the Earth* (1864) and *From the Earth to the Moon* (1865).

Long before such inventions were seriously believed to be possible, Verne wrote about helicopters, airplanes, television, and space travel. His book, *Twenty Thousand Leagues Under the Sea* (1870), is about a sea captain named Nemo, who travels about in a submarine far beneath the surface of the seas. *Around the World in Eighty Days* (1873) tells the story of Phileas Fogg's exciting trip around the world, using all sorts of transportation. To make the trip in such a short time was an unheard-of feat in those days. Many of Verne's books have been made into motion pictures.

ALSO READ: SCIENCE FICTION.

▲ *A church in Vermont, typical of the kind of architecture built in New England during the early years after the American Revolution.*

▲ *Jules Verne, French writer of "scientific romances"— stories that told readers what the future might be like. His books have thrilled people to the possibilities of the future.*

▲ *The Hall of Mirrors in the Palace of Versailles, near Paris, France.*

▲ *The Palace of Versailles not only has beautiful interiors, but also has superb outdoor statues, ponds, lakes, and landscaped gardens.*

VERRAZANO, GIOVANNI DA (about 1485–about 1527)

Giovanni da Verrazano was an Italian explorer and pirate. He was one of the first Europeans to explore the coast of North America.

Little is known about Verrazano's life. He is first mentioned historically in the 1520's, as a pirate paid by the French to capture Spanish ships. In 1523, the king of France, Francis I, commissioned Verrazano to find a "northwest passage" to the Orient around the northern continent of America. The Spaniards were preventing French merchant ships from using the southern route around South America. Records of Verrazano's expedition are scanty and inaccurate. He seems to have landed on the coast of present-day North Carolina. He then sailed northward, exploring the coast as far as what is now Maine. He was the first European to enter New York and Narragansett bays. On a later expedition, Verrazano explored the West Indies, where he is believed to have been killed by Indians or Spaniards.

The entrance to New York Harbor between Brooklyn and Staten Island is known as the Narrows. The Verrazano-Narrows Bridge is one of the longest suspension bridges in the United States, with a main span of 4,260 feet (1,300 m).

ALSO READ: EXPLORATION, NORTHWEST PASSAGE.

VERSAILLES

Versailles is a city in France, about 12 miles (20 km) southwest of Paris. The magnificent Palace of Versailles, home of the French kings for about 100 years, stands at the center of the city.

About 350 years ago, Versailles was a tiny village in the middle of a forest. King Louis XIII of France liked to hunt in the forest, and in the 1620's he built a hunting lodge at Versailles.

After Louis XIII died, his son, Louis XIV, decided to build a huge palace at the same place.

This palace was finished in 1682, though large additions were made to it later. Louis XIV moved there with his court. The palace faced a vast park with many fountains and statues, and its rooms were decorated with priceless works of art. Two smaller palaces, the Grand ("large") and Petit ("small") Trianon, were built in the park away from the palace.

The Palace of Versailles and its gardens cost an enormous sum of money. The people of France resented the fact that their tax money had been spent on a lavish palace. When the French Revolution began in 1789, King Louis XVI and his family were forced to leave Versailles. The palace was never again used as a residence.

Today, the Palace of Versailles is a national museum. Visitors can walk through the gardens and the rooms of the palace. The Treaty of Versailles, which ended World War I, was signed between Germany and the Allied Powers in the great Hall of Mirrors at Versailles.

ALSO READ: FRENCH HISTORY; FRENCH REVOLUTION; LOUIS, KINGS OF FRANCE.

VERTEBRATE

Vertebrates include all the animals that have backbones, from giant whales to tiny field mice. All mammals, such as deer, cats, and human beings, are vertebrates. Reptiles, amphibians, birds, and fish are also vertebrates. Besides having backbones, all vertebrates are alike in other important ways. They have a body plan that makes them different from *invertebrates*, or animals without backbones, such as mollusks, insects, and worms. A vertebrate has a skeleton inside its body. A skeleton is a framework that supports muscle and tissue. It is made of bone

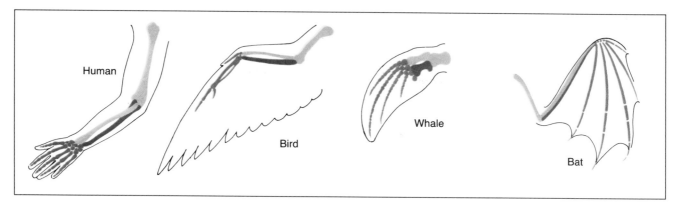

Human
Bird
Whale
Bat

and *cartilage* (a type of firm but bendable tissue). Invertebrates often have hard outside coverings (*exoskeletons*), like shells. Or they may have no supporting framework at all.

An important part of a vertebrate's skeleton is its skull. It holds and protects the animal's brain. Almost all vertebrates have jaws. One exception is the lamprey eel, which has a sucking device instead of jaws. Many vertebrates have limbs, such as arms or legs. Fish have certain fins that take the place of legs and are used for swimming. The limbs and swimming fins are always found in pairs. Vertebrates never have more than two pairs of legs. Human beings and apes, for example, have two arms and two legs. Most other mammals have two pairs of legs. Birds have two legs and two wings. Snakes once had limbs like other vertebrates but lost them in the process of evolution. The number of legs varies among invertebrates. Insects, for example, have six legs. Invertebrates such as oysters and worms have no limbs.

ALSO READ: AMPHIBIAN, ANIMAL KINGDOM, BIRD, DEEP-SEA LIFE, EVOLUTION, FISH, MAMMAL, MARSUPIAL, REPTILE, SKELETON.

VESPUCCI, AMERIGO (about 1454–1512) Amerigo Vespucci was an Italian merchant and ship's pilot, or navigator. He is mainly remembered as the person in whose honor the Americas were named.

Vespucci was born in Florence. As a young man, he worked as a merchant and also studied navigation. He traveled to South America as a ship's pilot on a Spanish expedition in 1499, and on a Portuguese expedition in 1501. During these voyages, Vespucci explored the coast of South America and discovered the mouth of the Amazon River. In a letter written in 1504, Vespucci stated that he had also made an earlier voyage to the New World in 1497. He claimed that he was the first European to set foot on the continent. Before 1498, the Italian explorer, Christopher Columbus, had landed only at the West Indies.

Scholars today doubt that Vespucci actually made the voyage in 1497. But Vespucci certainly was one of the first Europeans to realize that the new lands being discovered were not part of Asia, but a whole new continent. In 1507, a German mapmaker, Martin Waldseemüller, suggested that the new continent be named "Americus or America," "from Amerigo the discoverer" (he perhaps had not heard of Columbus).

ALSO READ: AMERICA, EXPLORATION.

VESUVIUS see VOLCANO.

VETERANS DAY Veterans Day is a national holiday in the United States. It is celebrated in most states on November 11 every year in honor of all the men and women who have

▲ When animals' bodies have things in common it usually means that, over many million years, they have evolved from the same ancestor. Humans, birds, whales, and bats look very different from each other today, but they all have five special bones in their front limbs. In humans, these bones are the fingerbones. All vertebrates (animals with spines) are related, but often the common ancestor lived a very long time ago. For example, you are more closely related to a bat than you are to a fish!

▲ *Amerigo Vespucci, a great Italian explorer. America is named for him.*

served in the U.S. armed forces during wartime. On this day, veterans parade, patriotic speeches are made, and a special ceremony takes place at Arlington National Cemetery in Virginia, at the Tomb of the Unknowns.

Veterans Day was originally called Armistice Day. It commemorated the end of fighting in World War I, which took place on November 11, 1918. President Woodrow Wilson first proclaimed November 11 as Armistice Day in 1919. In 1954, the U.S. Congress changed the holiday to Veterans Day, to honor the veterans of all wars.

ALSO READ: HOLIDAY, PARADE, TOMB OF THE UNKNOWNS.

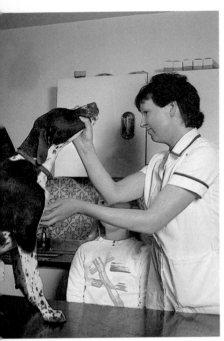

▲ *A Pointer dog is inspected by a veterinary nurse.*

VETERINARY MEDICINE Animals become sick just as human beings do. And animals can be injured. A doctor who treats sick or injured animals is a veterinarian. His or her profession is veterinary medicine.

Veterinarians working in cities usually have private practices and treat mostly pets. These doctors often have animal hospitals where pet owners can take their sick pets. Sometimes the veterinarian only has to give the pet a check-up or an injection, such as one to prevent rabies. The veterinarian who treats pets should know how to get along with people. The owners of sick animals often become more nervous than the sick animals.

Veterinarians in rural areas usually specialize in treating cattle and other livestock, including poultry, sheep, and horses. These animals are often treated on the farm, rather than being taken to clinics or hospitals.

The office of a veterinarian has modern medical equipment, including examining and operating tables and X-ray machines. The veterinarian takes X rays and runs tests to find out what is wrong with a sick animal. If necessary, he or she performs surgery or gives drugs to make the animal well again.

In government service, veterinarians protect our country's livestock from foreign diseases by inspecting animals brought into the United States from other countries. Within the borders of the United States, veterinarians safeguard public health by inspecting meat, poultry, eggs, and butter. They also inspect the farms, dairies, and packing plants where these foods are produced.

The agricultural services of the states have many veterinarians working to advise farmers on the health of their poultry and other livestock. Some veterinarians teach in schools of veterinary medicine. Many others teach in agriculture colleges. One of the most interesting jobs in veterinary medicine is being a veterinarian in a zoo. These veterinarians must treat the diseases of hundreds of kinds of animals from every part of the world.

Training If you want to become a veterinarian, you must like animals. You must be in good health, and being strong is helpful if you want to treat large animals such as horses.

Before you can study in a school of veterinary medicine, you must take a number of preveterinary courses in college. These include work in biology and chemistry. Most schools require two or three years of preveterinary study. After completing the preveterinary work, you must study for four more years at a college of veterinary medicine. This will include courses in anatomy (organs and body structure of animals), physiology (how the animals' organ systems work), and pharmacology (the science of drugs). A veterinary student must learn to observe carefully, because animals cannot talk and tell what hurts them when they are sick. When the veterinary student graduates, he or she is awarded the degree of Doctor of Veterinary Medicine.

ALSO READ: ANIMAL, MEDICINE, PUBLIC HEALTH, SURGERY.

VICE-PRESIDENT

VICE-PRESIDENT The Vice-President is second in rank to the President of the United States and is elected along with the President. According to the Constitution, the Vice-President must have the same qualifications as the President—be a native-born citizen at least 35 years old and a resident of the United States for at least 14 years.

If a President dies in office, the Vice-President automatically succeeds (follows) him or her and becomes the President of the United States. The Constitution is vague about whether the Vice-President actually becomes President or merely performs the duties. The custom for the Vice-President to assume the Presidency was established by John Tyler in 1841, when he succeeded William Henry Harrison, the first President to die while in office.

The only specific duty given to a Vice-President by the Constitution is to serve as President of the Senate. The Vice-President presides over Senate sessions, but he has no voting power unless there is a tie. When a vote is tied, the Vice-President casts the deciding vote.

Since Franklin D. Roosevelt's administration, it has been customary for the Vice-President to attend Cabinet meetings. The Vice-President is also a member of the National Security Council which advises the President on defense and foreign policy. A Vice-President may be chosen by the President to be chairman of a government committee or commission. A Vice-President may travel to other countries to "stand in" for the President at ceremonies or act as a roving ambassador for the United States.

Historically, many Vice-Presidents have disliked their job and have felt powerless to guide government affairs. John Adams, in a letter to his wife, made his feelings known about his role in the job: "My country has in its wisdom contrived for me the most insignificant office that ever the invention of man contrived or his imagination conceived. . . ." Theodore Roosevelt, as Vice-President, thought he was being "laid on the shelf," but the assassination of President McKinley in 1901 thrust him into the nation's highest office.

Since World War II, three Vice-Presidents have taken over the Presidency. Harry Truman succeeded Franklin Roosevelt, who died in 1945, and Lyndon Johnson took over as President when John Kennedy was killed in 1963. In 1974, Gerald Ford became President when Richard Nixon resigned. George Bush, who had been Vice-President under Ronald Reagan, was elected to the presidency in the 1988 election.

In 1965, Congress passed the Twenty-fifth Amendment. This change authorizes a Vice-President who has succeeded to the Presidency to appoint a new Vice-President with the approval of Congress. This amendment also defines the procedures by which a Vice-President can assume Presidential duties when a President is too ill to do the work. The Amendment was ratified by the states in 1967.

ALSO READ: CONSTITUTION, UNITED STATES; PRESIDENCY; UNITED STATES GOVERNMENT.

▲ *Walter Mondale was Vice-President under President Jimmy Carter from 1977 to 1981. He was the 42nd Vice-President.*

Gerald Ford became the first non-elected Vice-President, when he was chosen under the 25th Amendment procedure of the Constitution to fill the vacancy left by Spiro T. Agnew, who resigned in 1974.

▼ *This is the Admiral's House, official residence of the Vice-President of the United States.*

▲ *The coronation of Queen Victoria took place in Westminster Abbey, London, England, in 1838.*

▼ *In a videorecorder, the sound signal is recorded as magnetic patterns in a straight track along one edge of the tape. It is picked up by a sound pick-up head—just as in a cassette tape recorder. The pictures are recorded as magnetic patterns on the rest of the tape. Because pictures are a lot more complicated than sounds, the tape would have to move very quickly over the vision pick-up heads—they would have to be miles long! Instead, the two vision pick-up heads are mounted on a drum that spins very rapidly.*

VICTORIA (1819–1901) Victoria was Queen of the United Kingdom of Great Britain and Ireland and Empress of India. Her reign, which lasted for 63 years, was the longest in British history. While she was queen, Britain became the most powerful nation in the world.

Victoria was born in London. Her father, Edward, Duke of Kent, died when she was very young, and Victoria was brought up by her strict German mother. Victoria became queen at the age of 18, after the death of her uncle, King William IV. By this time, Britain was a *constitutional monarchy*. The monarch was expected to follow the advice of the prime minister and not attempt to influence government policies. But Victoria took a keen interest in government affairs and soon began to state strongly her approval or disapproval of her ministers' policies.

In 1840, Victoria married her cousin, a German prince, Albert of Saxe-Coburg-Gotha. Their marriage was a happy one and became an inspiration to other families throughout Britain. Victoria and Albert had nine children, most of whom married into other royal families in Europe.

In 1861, Prince Albert died suddenly of typhoid fever. Victoria was grief-stricken and went into deep mourning for several years. She later returned to public life, at the encouragement of Prime Minister Benjamin Disraeli. Victoria now ruled over a mighty empire, and, in 1876, she took the title Empress of India. The Industrial Revolution had brought immense prosperity to Britain. In 1887, the British people celebrated the 50th year of Victoria's reign with a great festival, the Golden Jubilee. A Diamond Jubilee was held ten years later, on her 60th anniversary.

Victoria was a small, plump woman with an air of immense dignity. To the British people, she became a symbol of strength, virtue, and modesty. Her reign is often simply called the "Victorian Age."

ALSO READ: ENGLISH HISTORY, KINGS AND QUEENS.

VIDEO A video is a recording of moving pictures and sound. It is usually made on a videotape, which is like the tape in a music cassette. There are also videodiscs, which are like large versions of the compact discs used for recorded music. You can get videos of films and concerts, and also educational videos that teach you and show you how to make things. You play a videotape in a videocassette recorder, and a videodisc in a videodisc player. These machines are connected to a television set, and you see the video on the screen of the set.

A videodisc gives a better picture and sound than a videotape, but you cannot use it yourself to record pictures and sound. A videocassette recorder can record television programs on videotapes, and you can erase an old program and record a new one on the same tape as often as you like.

You can also make your own videos. You need a videocamera, which is a portable television camera. You either put the videotape into the camera or connect the camera to a videorecorder. The camera also contains a microphone for the sound. You play back the tape in a videorecorder in the normal way. People make videos of their holidays, weddings, and other family occasions, sports events and so on. It is useful to be able to edit the

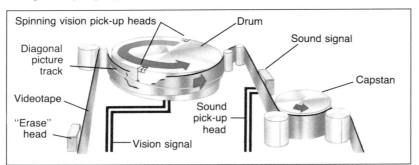

Spinning vision pick-up heads

Drum

Diagonal picture track

Sound signal

Videotape

Capstan

"Erase" head

Sound pick-up head

Vision signal

tapes you make. This involves making a copy of the parts you want in any order onto another tape. You may also include titles, by connecting a home computer to the recorder.

A videotape records the electric signals that come from the camera. It does this by magnetic recording in the same way as sound tape recording. The tape records picture signals and sound signals. The main difference from a music cassette player is that the record and replay heads in a videorecorder spin around as the tape passes. This allows the head to move over the surface of the tape very quickly, giving the high recording speed needed to record picture signals.

Many of the programs you see on television are video recordings. They are made on machines similar to home videorecorders. Rock and pop groups make videos. These are short films or video recordings that show pictures to go with a song.

ALSO READ: RECORDING, TELEVISION.

VIETNAM The Socialist Republic of Vietnam occupies the eastern and southern parts of the Indochinese peninsula in Southeast Asia. Long and narrow in shape, Vietnam is about three times the size of Tennessee. China lies to the north, Laos and Kampuchea to the west, and the South China Sea to the east and south. (See the map with the article on ASIA.)

Much of the country is mountainous and covered with forests and jungles. Most of the Vietnamese people live on the fertile coastal lowlands, near the deltas of the Mekong River in the south and the Red River in the north. Growing rice (the main crop) is a major occupation. Coffee, sugarcane, cotton, corn, cassava, and rubber are also important crops. Vietnam has a year-round tropical climate. The country's largest city is Ho Chi Minh City (formerly Saigon) in the south. Hanoi in the north is the capital.

Many Vietnamese are Buddhists. Some people worship the spirits of animals and plants or practice Taoism or Confucianism. About 10 percent of the people are Roman Catholics. Chinese, Kampucheans, and Montagnards (a mountain people) are the principal minority groups in Vietnam.

Vietnamese history is said to be 2,000 years old. The first people are believed to have come from China and parts of Southeast Asia. China controlled Vietnam for more than 1,000 years, until A.D. 939. Vietnam remained free, except for a short time in the 1400's, until the 1800's, when France conquered Laos, Vietnam, and Kampuchea (then called Cambodia), and governed these regions as *French Indochina*. The areas of Tonkin (northern Vietnam), Annam (central Vietnam), and Cochin China (southern Vietnam) made up Viet-

▲ *Rivers play a vital economic role in Vietnam, in transport as well as in irrigating the rice fields.*

VIETNAM

Capital City: Hanoi (2,000,000 people).
Area: 127,242 square miles (329,556 sq. km).
Population: 66,700,000.
Government: Communist republic.
Natural Resources: Coal, iron ore.
Export Products: Coal, farm products, fish, livestock.
Unit of Money: Dông.
Official Language: Vietnamese.

nam. During World War II, Japan occupied all of Vietnam. In 1945, after the war, fighting broke out against the French.

A Communist leader named Ho Chi Minh led a guerrilla force called the Vietminh to victory, and the French were driven out. The Battle of Dien Bien Phu, when the French forces were overrun by the Vietminh on May 7, 1954, ended French power there.

At its narrowest point, Vietnam is less than 40 miles (65 km) wide. Here a dividing line, called the 17th parallel, once separated Vietnam into two countries—North Vietnam and South Vietnam. This division was suggested as a temporary measure in 1954 at the Geneva Conference. The conference set the peace terms between France and Vietnam, called for general elections (which were never held), and allowed for resettlement of people.

In 1956, a civil war began between the northern Communist government (Democratic Republic of Vietnam) and the government of South Vietnam (Republic of Vietnam). The North Vietnamese gave aid to the Vietcong (Communist guerrilla fighters in the south). South Vietnam received help from the United States. By the late 1960's, the Vietnam War had escalated into neighboring Laos and Cambodia (now Kampuchea).

A ceasefire agreement was finally signed in Paris in 1973 by the United States, North and South Vietnam, and the Vietcong. After the withdrawal of all U.S. troops and the return of prisoners, the fighting between the South Vietnamese and Communist forces continued. In April 1975, the Communists took control. After 22 years of separation, North and South Vietnam were reunited on July 2, 1976, as one nation. Many thousands of Vietnamese fled from the country as "boat people" and settled in the U.S. and other places.

ALSO READ: ASIA, CAMBODIA, CHINA, INDOCHINA, VIETNAM WAR.

VIETNAM WAR Beginning in 1954, the Communist North Vietnamese sought to take over South Vietnam. They gave aid to the Vietcong (Communist guerrilla troops in the south). As more Communists infiltrated the south, the civil war intensified in the 1960's.

U.S. Presidents Eisenhower and Kennedy offered economic aid and advisors to train the South Vietnam army. After the Buddhists denounced the South Vietnam regime as authoritarian, a military coup in 1963 overthrew its President, Ngo Dinh Diem. A stable government did not rule the south until Nguyen Van Thieu was chosen president in 1967.

When two U.S. destroyers were attacked in 1964 by North Vietnamese torpedo boats in the Gulf of Tonkin, Congress gave power to President Johnson to repel any armed attack. Bombing raids were ordered over North Vietnam, and U.S. troops were engaged in the war.

As the fighting and U.S. casualties escalated, massive protests against the war erupted in the United States. Peace talks between the United States and North Vietnam were held in 1968 and 1969. Presidential advisor Henry Kissinger carried on secret peace negotiations in the early 1970's.

▼ Refugees are air lifted from danger by a U.S. military helicopter during the Vietnam War.

In 1973, President Nixon ordered a halt to all U.S. offensive military operations against North Vietnam. Withdrawal of U.S. troops began. A peace pact was signed in Paris by the warring parties.

When the last U.S. troops left South Vietnam on March 29, 1973, the war's dead included about 50,000 U.S. citizens, about 400,000 South Vietnamese, and about 900,000 Vietcong and North Vietnamese.

ALSO READ: INDOCHINA, VIETNAM.

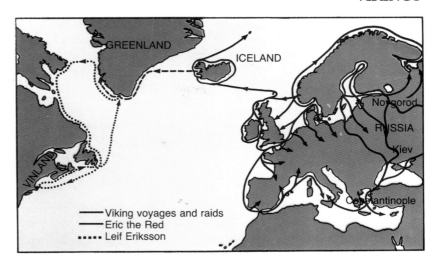

VIKINGS Also called Norsemen, Northmen, or Normans, the Vikings were a warlike, seafaring people—the ancient inhabitants of Norway, Sweden, and Denmark. In the A.D. 700's, the Vikings became known to the people of the rest of Europe when Viking pirates began to raid and terrorize settlements along the coast.

The Viking people were made up of four main tribal groups. The Norwegians lived on the west coast of what is now Norway. The Danes lived in Jutland, the area of modern Denmark and part of West Germany. The Goths and Swedes lived along the coast of the Baltic Sea in present-day Sweden and the north edge of the Soviet Union.

The Vikings were organized by tribes and lived in small villages along the lengthy Scandinavian coastlines. They took great pride in their military skills and in their ability to sail the seas. They were extremely loyal to their tribal chiefs, especially during battle. Viking men considered it the greatest honor of all to die while fighting. Viking mythology is full of tales about heroes who die valiantly in battle.

The Vikings wrote with an alphabet of 16 letters, called the *runic* alphabet. Norsemen considered runic letters to be magic, and they often tried to predict the future by "casting the runes."

As craftworkers, the Vikings were highly skilled carpenters and ironworkers. They fashioned excellent tools, weapons, and armor from iron and leather. Viking ships were probably the best fitted and most seaworthy vessels of ancient times. Both their warships and merchant vessels were swift and easy to maneuver.

In the A.D. 700's, the Viking population in Scandinavia became too large, and the poor land could not support the people. Areas of land away from the coasts were covered with dense forests that were almost impossible to get through, let alone start new settlements in. These circumstances forced the Vikings to move southward to find new places to live.

The first recorded Viking attack upon England came in A.D. 787, after which the Norsemen raided towns along the shores of present-day Belgium and France. In A.D. 878, the Saxon king, Alfred the Great, drove many of the invaders from England. But between 1017 and 1035, the Danish king, Canute, ruled a Norse empire that included Norway, Denmark, and England.

Charles III of France was unable to defeat the Vikings. Instead, Charles gave lands in northern France (modern-day Normandy) to the Viking chief, Rollo, on condition that Rollo become his subject. Rollo agreed, and in the year A.D. 911 he married King

▲ The Vikings attacked much of the known world—and some of the unknown! About A.D. 870 they discovered Iceland, and in 982 Eric the Red discovered Greenland. In about 1000, Eric's son Leif Eriksson discovered North America.

▲ The carved head of an animal from a Viking ship. Heads like this were at the fronts of ships and were made to look as menacing as possible.

VIKINGS

Without their famous longships, the Vikings could not have carried out their successful piratical raids which helped them dominate other areas. Nor could they have undertaken such voyages of discovery as Leif Eriksson's Atlantic crossing. This sail-and-oar vessel helped the Vikings dominate northern waters for over 1,500 years.

The Vikings were such a warlike race that they could not imagine a heaven without war. They buried their dead with all their weapons for use in Valhalla (their imagined great hall for dead warriors).

Charles's daughter and converted to Christianity. Rollo's descendant, William II of Normandy, invaded England in 1066 and became the English king, William I.

In other lands the Vikings were equally successful. During the A.D. 800's, they established the kingdoms of Dublin, Limerick, Waterford, and others along the Irish coast. In that same century, they discovered and colonized Iceland. From Iceland, the Norsemen sailed still farther west, settling along the coasts of Greenland.

Two important Viking seafarers and explorers were Eric the Red and his son, Leif Eriksson. Eric the Red discovered Greenland in A.D. 982 and decided to settle there. He named the country "Greenland" because he wanted to attract other people to live there; they would think, from the name, that it was a green and fertile land!

His son, Leif Eriksson, was converted to Christianity in about A.D. 1000. He set sail to Greenland to spread the faith. Either on the way there or on the way home, he got lost and accidentally discovered North America. A couple of years later, a Viking named Thorfinn Karlsefni, having heard about Leif Eriksson's discovery, tried to set up colonies in this new land. The Vikings named it "Vinland" because they said it was rich in grapes (vines).

No one knows exactly where Vinland was. Some people think it was in what we now call New England; others say that it was in Newfoundland or Nova Scotia. Certainly the Vikings did discover Newfoundland. In 1963, a team of Norwegian archeologists announced the discovery of a Viking settlement there. Scientific tests show that the buildings were probably built about the year A.D. 1000.

As early as A.D. 860, Vikings sailed into the Mediterranean Sea and founded kingdoms in southern Italy and on the island of Sicily. About the year A.D. 880, a Viking chieftain named Rurik moved southward into present-day Russia and took over the city of Novgorod. Rurik's captains went farther south, where they attacked and took the city of Kiev. Once they had Kiev, the Vikings were in control of the extensive trade route along the Dnieper River from

Scandinavia to the Black Sea. Viking conquerors mixed with the native Slavic inhabitants, and their descendants are the north Russians.

By the 1100's, Christianity had become the religion of most of Europe. Vikings converted and adapted themselves to this new religion. Their way of life had changed from that of a fierce, warring people to that of peaceful landowners and farmers. The Vikings had mixed with other Europeans and were no longer considered separate.

ALSO READ: ALFRED THE GREAT, DENMARK, MYTHOLOGY, NEWFOUNDLAND-LABRADOR, NORWAY, RUSSIAN HISTORY, SHIPS AND SHIPPING, SWEDEN.

VILLA, PANCHO (1878–1923)

The patriot guerrilla leader Pancho Villa is honored as one of the founders of modern Mexico. He was the son of a field laborer on a large estate. Orphaned as a child, Villa became a fugitive after killing one of the estate owners (who had assaulted his sister).

In 1909, he joined the revolt against the dictator Porfirio Díaz and proved himself a skillful guerrilla fighter. Northern Mexico became his personal stronghold. Díaz was overthrown in 1911, but the struggle to found a new republic continued. Villa joined forces with the revolutionary leader Emiliano Zapata.

In 1916, to prove that he was the *caudillo* (military commander) of northern Mexico, Villa attacked the United States and then eluded the force led by General John Pershing that was sent to capture him. He remained a guerrilla until 1920, when he was pardoned and retired to live on a ranch. He was murdered there in 1923.

ALSO READ: MEXICO.

The Vikings used ravens to help them find new lands. They took a number of the birds with them on their voyages and released them one by one as they sailed west. If the raven flew back along the course they had come from, the Vikings continued on a westerly course. But if the bird flew off in a different direction, the Vikings changed course to follow the raven. They knew that a new land lay in that direction.

▼ *Vikings landing on the east coast of North America. There they found grapes, wild corn, and rivers full of fish. They called the new land "Vinland the Good" because of the grapes. However, the Viking colonies here did not last long.*

▲ *In Virgil's epic poem, the Aeneid, the hero Aeneas travels across the Styx, the mythical river of the underworld.*

The book *Misty of Chincoteague* by Marguerite Henry tells the story of a wild pony brought from Assateague Island to Chincoteague Island in Virginia. A pony roundup is held each year in July at Chincoteague.

VIOLIN see MUSICAL INSTRUMENTS, STRINGED INSTRUMENTS.

VIRGIL (70 B.C.–19 B.C.) Virgil was one of the greatest poets of ancient Rome. He was born in northern Italy and grew up on his father's farm until age 12. In 37 B.C. he published the *Eclogues*, comprising ten poems about country living. A rich and powerful patron, Maecenas, encouraged further books of poems about farming.

Virgil's masterpiece, the *Aeneid*, is a long story-poem in 12 books. The *Aeneid* tells the story of Aeneas, a hero of the legendary Trojan War between the Greeks and the people of Troy, a city in Asia Minor (now Turkey). Aeneas, son of the goddess Venus, is the only Trojan hero to escape after Troy is destroyed. With a few followers, he travels westward. He visits Carthage in North Africa, where Queen Dido kills herself for love of him. He goes down into the underworld, where the ghost of his father tells him of the future greatness of Rome. Aeneas and his followers finally settle in Italy and become the ancestors of the Roman people.

Virgil died before he could finish revising the *Aeneid*. He had wanted it to be destroyed. But the Roman emperor, Augustus, had it preserved. The Romans considered the *Aeneid* to be their national poem.

ALSO READ: POETRY, ROMAN EMPIRE.

VIRGINIA The state of Virginia is one of the most historic in the United States. Part of the city of Williamsburg, Virginia, has been restored to its colonial appearance so that people may see what life was like when Virginia was a British colony. Williamsburg was made the capital of Virginia in 1699, after Jamestown

burned, and remained the capital until 1779. Today, a British flag flies from the top of the old Governor's Palace. Nearly 150 major buildings have been restored or rebuilt in Williamsburg. Craft shops practice many colonial trades of the 1700's. Inns serve meals in colonial style.

Virginia was started earlier than any of the other 13 British colonies. Permission to set up the colony was given by Britain in 1606. It was named "Virginia" in honor of Elizabeth I, known as the "Virgin Queen," who had died a little before. Settlement began in 1607, on the Atlantic Coastal Plain. By the time of the American Revolution, settlers were in the Appalachian Mountains.

Virginia is sometimes called the "Mother of Presidents," because eight of our Presidents were born there. (Ohio claims the same nickname.)

The Land and Climate Virginia's part of the Atlantic Coastal Plain is the lowest section of the state. It is called the Tidewater area. Much of the plain is almost level. In places, the low, flat land drains poorly. Such land is marsh. A good example is the Dismal Swamp, which extends into North Carolina.

Chesapeake Bay lies between the easternmost part of Virginia and the

▼ *The state capitol in Richmond, Virginia, is built in the old, classic style of architecture.*

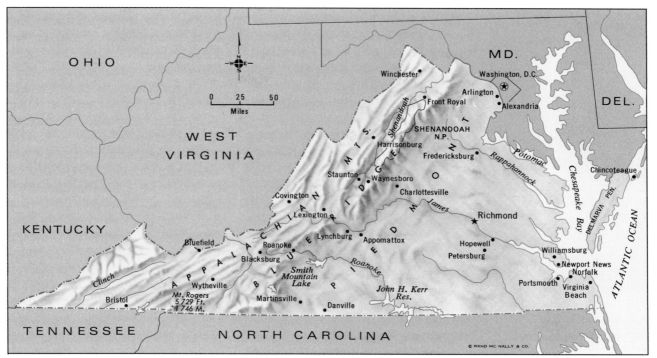

VIRGINIA

Capital
Richmond (219,000 people)

Area
40,817 square miles
(105,716 sq. km)
Rank: 36th

Population
6,015,000
Rank: 12th

Statehood
June 25, 1788
(10th of the original 13 states
to ratify the Constitution)

Principal rivers
Rappahannock River
York River
James River

Highest point
Mount Rogers; 5,729 feet
(1,746 m)

Largest city
Norfolk (267,000 people)

Motto
Sic Semper Tyrannis
("Thus Always to Tyrants")

Song
"Carry Me Back to Old
Virginia"

Famous people
William Henry Harrison, Patrick
Henry, Thomas Jefferson,
Robert E. Lee, James Madi-
son, James Monroe, Zachary
Taylor, John Tyler, Booker T.
Washington, George Washing-
ton, Woodrow Wilson

STATE EMBLEMS

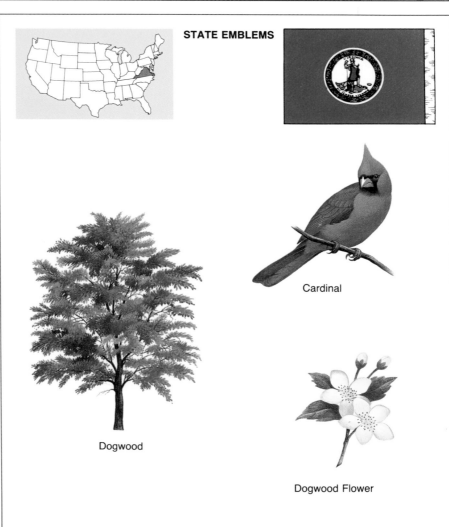

Cardinal

Dogwood

Dogwood Flower

▲ *Colonial buildings have been well restored in this settlement in Virginia.*

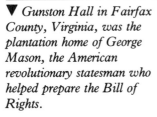

▼ *Gunston Hall in Fairfax County, Virginia, was the plantation home of George Mason, the American revolutionary statesman who helped prepare the Bill of Rights.*

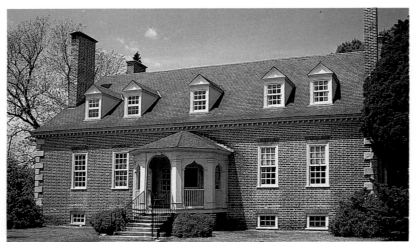

mainland. This eastern part of the state is the southern end of the Delmarva Peninsula. (The peninsula's name comes from the names of three states. What are they?) In 1964, the Chesapeake Bay Bridge-Tunnel was completed. It links the eastern shore to the mainland at a point near Norfolk. This system of two tunnels, two bridges, and a roadway is more than 17 miles (27 km) long.

The principal rivers of Virginia flow southeastward across the coastal plain to Chesapeake Bay. Virginia's middle section, the Piedmont, is higher than the coastal plain. The Piedmont is rolling, well-drained land that rises to mountains called the Blue Ridge. The fertile Shenandoah Valley lies beyond them.

To the west, Virginia's mountains are part of the Appalachians. Their forested ranges slant from southwest to northeast. Green valleys lie between the ridges. The West Virginia border is in the mountains.

History This pleasant land once had a large Indian population. When the Europeans arrived, there were about 200 Algonkin villages on Virginia's coastal plain. The 30 or more tribes here were ruled by a chief whom the British called Powhatan. Other tribes lived in the Piedmont.

The first colonists sailed up the James River in the spring of 1607. Full-sized models of their ships are tied up on the James today. They are moored not far from the place where the settlers landed. The settlers built a log fort and some huts. They named the settlement "James Towne" in honor of their king.

Hunger, disease, and Indian attacks almost wiped out the colony during its first years. The colonists had to buy tools, weapons, and clothes from Britain. They needed some way of paying for them. One of the settlers, probably John Rolfe, suggested the raising and selling of tobacco. The first shipload of tobacco went to Britain in 1614.

That same year, Rolfe aided the colony in another very different way. He married Pocahontas, the daughter of Powhatan. The marriage, which united the colonists with the Indians, brought the colony years of peace.

In 1619, the first elected lawmaking body in the New World met at Jamestown. It was called the House of Burgesses. With the governor and a council, it made the colony's laws.

Also in 1619, the first black people reached British North America. A Dutch ship landed them at Jamestown. The blacks were not slaves. Like many white newcomers, they were indentured servants. Colonists paid for their passage. Each indentured servant then worked for the colonist until the debt was paid off (about 7 to 10 years). The blacks did so well as farm workers that British colonists decided to buy slaves from Africa. The result was decades of slavery. It brought suffering to millions, white people as well as blacks.

Virginia played a big part in the American Revolution. General Washington was a Virginian. So were Thomas Jefferson, Patrick Henry, George Mason, George Wythe, and other leaders. In the 1790's, Virginia and Maryland gave land to the new Federal Government to be used as the site of the capital, later named Washington, D.C. When the land on Virginia's side of the Potomac River had not been developed by 1846, it was returned to the state.

In 1861, Virginia joined the Confederate States of America. Richmond, now the state capital, was the capital of the Confederacy during most of the Civil War. Many Civil War battles were fought in Virginia. The first Battle of Bull Run was an early battle. On April 9, 1865, Confederate General Robert E. Lee surrendered to Union General Ulysses S. Grant at Appomattox. The war left the state poor—and smaller. The northwestern part of the state had refused to leave the Union and became a separate state, West Virginia.

Virginians at Work In and near Virginian cities, you see smoking factory chimneys. Manufacturing is Virginia's biggest industry. The leading manufactures, in order of importance, are chemical products, cigarettes and other tobacco articles, foods, and textiles.

Agriculture is second to manufacturing in dollars earned. Eggs, milk, cattle, poultry, and hogs together earn more money than all crops. Winchester is a center of the apple-growing area.

The giant port area of Hampton Roads on Chesapeake Bay includes the harbors of Norfolk, Portsmouth, and Newport News. The U.S. Navy has a big base at Norfolk. Ships are built and repaired at the Portsmouth and Newport News shipyards.

ALSO READ: APPALACHIAN MOUNTAINS; CHESAPEAKE BAY; CONFEDERATE STATES OF AMERICA; HENRY, PATRICK; JAMESTOWN; JEFFERSON, THOMAS; LEE, ROBERT E.; POCAHONTAS; POWHATAN; SLAVERY; SMITH, CAPTAIN JOHN; TOBACCO; WASHINGTON, BOOKER T.; WASHINGTON, GEORGE; WEST VIRGINIA.

VIRGIN ISLANDS see WEST INDIES.

VIRUS A virus is a tiny bit of matter that is not definitely living or nonliving.

Viruses are smaller than the smallest bacteria. Viruses are too small to be seen with a light microscope, but they can be photographed with an electron microscope.

When viruses attack living cells, they seem to be alive—and they can cause disease in plants, animals and humans. Among the human diseases caused by viruses are poliomyelitis, yellow fever, chicken pox, smallpox, measles, mumps, rabies, the common cold and the deadly modern-day affliction known as acquired immune deficiency syndrome—or AIDS for short.

Before the 1900's scientists believed that bacteria diseases were caused by liquid. A Dutch scientist, Martinus Beijerinck, named this liquid *virus*, the Latin word for "poison."

Soon scientists began to believe that viruses were not liquids but things that could dissolve in liquids. In 1935, a U.S. scientist, Wendell M. Stanley, found that pure tobacco-mosaic virus, when dried, forms crystals. These crystals are in themselves harmless, but as soon as they are dissolved in liquid, they are able to cause the disease. Stanley had shown that viruses are both living and non-living, and shared the 1946 Nobel Chemistry Prize for having done so.

At the end of the 1930's, Vladimir Zworykin invented the electron microscope, and soon scientists could for the first time "see" viruses.

All viruses are made up of an outer shell of protein enclosing a core of nucleic acid (a genetic material). Proteins are the basic substances of living matter. The nucleic acids carry reproductive information.

In order to infect a living cell, a virus must first attach itself to the cell. The nucleic acid of the virus then invades the cell. It takes over the cell's

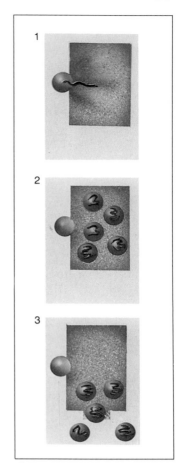

▲ *When a virus invades a cell, it injects its nucleic acids into it (1). In the cell, the nucleic acids are copied and new viruses made (2). The cell bursts open and the new viruses are released (3). In AIDS (Acquired Immune Deficiency Syndrome), the HIV-1 (human immunodeficiency) virus pushes out part of the infected cell's membrane and detaches itself. The viruses are then thought to leave hundreds of tiny holes in the cell's membrane. The cell's contents leak out and it dies.*

VITAMINS AND MINERALS

▼ *Volcanoes are made up of layers of ash, dust, and lava (1). The volcano's vent (2) goes down to molten rock,* magma, *beneath the Earth's crust (3). Other vents cut through the volcano (4). Sheets of magma squeeze through the rock to form* dikes *(5). Horizontal sheets of solidified magma are called* sills *(6). When magma is forced up but fails to reach the surface, dome-shaped mounds are formed (7). Often the craters of extinct volcanoes are filled with water (8). Lava sometimes streams out of cracks in the ground (9). In some volcanic regions there are geysers (10).*

activities to produce new virus particles. The new viruses leave the cell and can infect other cells. Some viruses destroy cells. Other viruses cause cells to reproduce rapidly.

The body has its own natural defense against diseases, which is called the immune system. This can be strengthened artificially by injections or by swallowing a prepared liquid. Vaccines are usually prepared from weakened or killed viruses. Through vaccination, our natural defense system helps us overcome such viruses as polio, smallpox, and measles.

The AIDS virus, on the other hand, is both deadly and unique because it attacks and cripples the immune system—the very system intended to battle disease. So with AIDS, the victim is left with no defense at all against any infection.

In the 1980's, the disease has spread rapidly to the Western world from developing countries. It is spread chiefly through sexual contact and exchanges of blood (as with drug users sharing infected needles). In the mid-1980's, it was estimated that as many as 1.5 million people in the United States alone had been infected with the AIDS virus.

A cure for AIDS is still not in sight, but scientists using electron microscopes have identified the virus that causes AIDS, called the human immunodeficiency virus, or HIV–1 for short.

They already know a great deal about how it damages the immune system and how it is structured.

ALSO READ: BACTERIA; BIOCHEMISTRY; CELL; CRYSTAL; DISEASE; GENETICS; MICROSCOPE; PARASITE; PROTEIN; ZWORYKIN, VLADIMIR.

VITAMINS AND MINERALS

Vitamins are food substances that you need if you are to remain in good health. The amounts you need are only a few thousandths of an ounce of each vitamin each day. If the foods you eat daily include balanced amounts of meats, eggs, cheese, butter, milk, fruit, and cooked and uncooked vegetables, you are probably getting all the vitamins you need. If you do not eat meats, you can still get all the vitamins you need, so long as your diet is properly balanced.

Vitamins were named A, B, C, and so on in the order in which they were discovered. Then, it was discovered that what was called vitamin B is a combination of several vitamins. These were named B_1, B_2, and so on.

Minerals are also needed in small amounts. Among those needed is *calcium*, an important part of bones and teeth. You get calcium from milk, cream, and cheese. *Phosphorus* is an important part of certain compounds

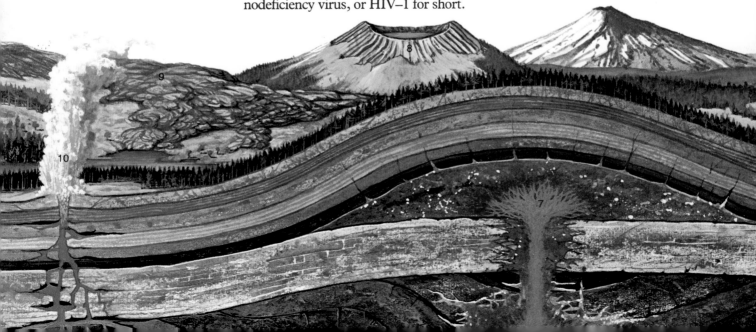

that help your body cells store and exchange energy. Your body uses *iodine* in making the thyroid hormone that regulates the pace of your body's activities. *Iron* is needed for *hemoglobin*, the matter in red blood cells that carries oxygen from your lungs to your tissues. *Sodium*, *potassium*, and *chlorine* are minerals needed to regulate the amount of water in tissues as well as to ensure the proper activity of nerves and muscles.

ALSO READ: BLOOD, HORMONE, MINERAL, NUTRITION.

VOICE see ANIMAL VOICES, SPEECH.

VOLCANO A volcano is a mountain that has an opening through which gases, ashes, and molten (melted) rock are forced. Underneath the Earth's rocky crust is hot, molten rock, called *magma*. The magma that pours out onto the Earth's surface is called *lava*.

Magma contains large quantities of gases, including steam (water vapor). When the magma rises close to the Earth's surface, the gases escape. They push outward with great force, blowing a hole in the surface. The outrushing gases carry huge amounts of dust and ashes up into the air. The tons of ashes form a cone around the hole in the Earth. Lava pours out of the hole and runs down the ash cone. In this way, a volcano is built. The outpouring of lava, gas, and ashes is called an eruption.

Most of the world's volcanoes were formed several million years ago. However, some have formed much more recently. On February 20, 1943, a farmer near Particutín, Mexico, saw a wisp of smoke rise from a field he was plowing. A few hours later, dense clouds of smoke were pouring out of a crack in the ground. Ashes shot out of the crack and began to form a cone. Two days after the eruption began, lava started to flow out of an opening in the cone of ashes. By the time the volcano stopped

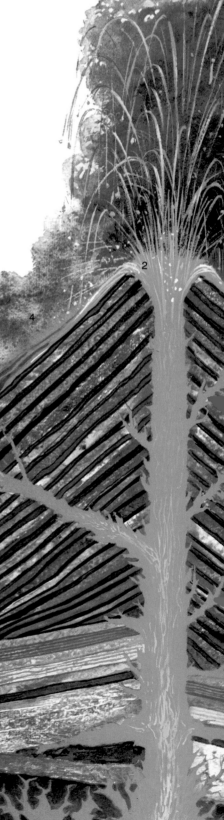

▲ *A stream of red-hot lava flows down the side of a volcano on a small island near Sicily, in the Mediterranean Sea.*

The largest volcano on Earth is Mauna Loa in the Hawaiian Islands. It measures 74 miles (119 km) across its base.

▶ *A fountain of molten lava shoots skyward from the vent of Kilauea, a volcano in Hawaii.*

erupting, in 1952, the ashes and lava had built a cone about 2,000 feet (610 m) high. The volcano was named Mount Particutín.

Most of the Earth's volcanoes are found in regions called *volcanic belts*. The Pacific Ocean is surrounded by the biggest belt of active volcanoes: the "Ring of Fire." These belts correspond to the edges of the *plates* of which the Earth's crust is made up. Also, there is volcanic activity along the underwater mountain ranges in the oceans (*midocean ridges*), where magma wells up from beneath to become new areas of the Earth's crust.

Not all volcanoes shoot forth smoke and ashes. Some simply pour out lava. Mauna Loa in Hawaii is one of these. The Hawaiian Islands are the upper parts of volcanoes that erupted on the bottom of the Pacific.

In about 1500 B.C., in the Mediterranean Sea, the volcanic island of Thēra (now called Santorini) erupted. The explosion created tsunamis ("tidal waves") that washed over Crete, another Mediterranean island. The great Minoan civilization that had sprung up on Crete was smashed. This disaster probably gave rise to the legend of the "lost continent" of Atlantis.

The ancient Roman towns of Pompeii, Herculaneum, and Stabiae once

stood at the foot of Mount Vesuvius, Italy. In A.D. 79, this volcano erupted and buried the towns and their inhabitants. Since then, Vesuvius has erupted many times.

In 1883, the volcanic island of Krakatoa in Indonesia blew up, causing widespread destruction and the deaths of about 35,000 people. When Mount St. Helens, in the state of Washington, erupted in 1980, spewing volcanic ash over much of the Pacific Northwest, only 65 people lost their lives, but the climate of much of the world was affected for a year.

ALSO READ: EARTH; EARTH HISTORY; EARTHQUAKE; GEOLOGY; GEYSER; GREECE, ANCIENT; MOUNTAIN; PLATE TECTONICS; POMPEII.

VOLGA RIVER One of the best-known Russian folk songs is the "Song of the Volga Boatmen." It is a rhythmic chant once sung by Russian workers as they used ropes to pull heavy boats along the Volga River.

Although it is frozen during the long Russian winter, the Volga River has always been an important transportation route. It is 2,292 miles (3,688 km) long—the longest river in Europe. It flows entirely within the Soviet Union. (See the map with the article on SOVIET UNION.)

The land on either side of the Volga is the most heavily populated and highly industrialized area in the Soviet Union. The cities of Moscow, Gorky, Kazan, and Volgograd are located on the Volga and its branches. Besides providing a means of transportation, the river serves the Soviet people as a source of electric power and water.

ALSO READ: SOVIET UNION.

VOLLEYBALL Volleyball is a game played indoors or outdoors, on a court 59 feet (18 m) long and 29 feet 6 inches (9 m) wide. The court is split in half by a net, the top of which is set 8 feet (2.43 m) from the ground for men, and 7 feet 4 inches (2.24 m) from the ground for women. Players use their open hands or fists to hit an inflated rubber or leather ball, about 26 inches (66 cm) in diameter, back and forth over the net.

There are six players on each team. The three closest to the net are *forwards*. The three in the back row are *backs*. The right back always *serves* (starts the play). The server has only one chance to hit the ball into the opposing team's court. After the ball is served, the opposing team usually uses three hits to return it across the net. The first person to hit the ball is called the *receiver*. The receiver passes it to a second player, who in turn passes it to a forward. This forward returns the ball over the net as hard as possible, so that the opposing team will not be able to return the ball.

The ball may not touch the ground. The ball may not be caught or held. A team may hit the ball no more than three times before returning it over the net. A player may not hit the ball twice in a row but may give the first and third hits.

Only the team that serves the ball may score. If the opposing team cannot return the serve, the serving team scores one point. If the serving team does not return the ball, no points are lost, but the other team takes over the serve and gets a chance to score. When a team loses the serve, every person moves one position clockwise. The first team to score 15 points is the winner, unless the other team has 14 points. In this case, they play on until one team has a two-point lead over the other.

A special set of rules has been made for boys and girls. Juniors may use a net 7 feet (2.1 m) high. They get two serves instead of one. There is no limit to the number of hits juniors may have before the ball goes over the net. Even a serve may be assisted over the net.

VON BRAUN, WERNHER (1912–1977)
Wernher von Braun was largely responsible for making the U.S. space program a reality.

Wernher Magnus Maximilian von Braun was born in Wirsitz, Germany (now Wryzysk, Poland). He became interested in science at an early age. In 1930, von Braun was one of a group of members of the German Rocket Society who did a number of successful experiments with small rockets. In 1932, when he was only 20, he was put in charge of the German army's rocket program. In 1940, von Braun joined the Nazi party.

Von Braun's research team developed the V-2 rocket, a type of flying bomb. It was first used in 1944, during World War II. It would have been used much earlier, but Hitler had interfered with the program—at one stage, he had even had von Braun imprisoned because he suspected him of disloyalty.

After World War II, von Braun surrendered to U.S. forces and came to the United States where he continued his work on rockets. He became a U.S. citizen in 1955.

In 1957, the Soviet Union launched the first artificial satellite, Sputnik 1. U.S. politicians and scientists were dismayed because they had assumed that Soviet science was years behind U.S. science. A crash program to launch a U.S. satellite was put through, and on January 31, 1958, a team headed by von Braun launched into orbit the first U.S. satellite, Explorer 1.

Von Braun was involved with almost all U.S. spaceflight projects. He became deputy associate administrator for NASA in 1970. In 1975, he founded the National Space Institute.

ALSO READ: MISSILE, ROCKET, SATELLITE, SPACE RESEARCH, WORLD WAR II.

▲ *People playing volleyball; the ball has just been hit over the net.*

▲ *Wernher von Braun as a young man. He worked on missiles for the Nazis but after World War II came to the United States to work on missiles and the space program.*

VOTING see ELECTION.

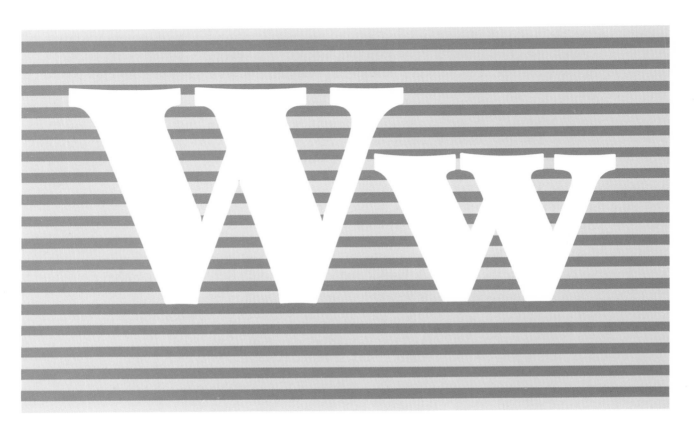

▲ *Richard Wagner, the German composer.*

WAGNER, RICHARD (1813–1883)

Wilhelm Richard Wagner was a German composer whose music brought about great changes in the art of opera composition. Wagner was born in Leipzig. As a boy, he became interested in the theater, but later he decided to study music. Operas at this time were written mainly to show off the voices of the singers. The story was not important. But Wagner believed that an opera should be a "music drama," vividly expressed in the music, the words of the singers, and the scenery. Wagner wrote his own *librettos* (scripts) for his operas.

His first opera, *Rienzi* (1842), was about Cola di Rienzo, who led an uprising in Rome in 1347. On a stormy sea voyage in 1837, Wagner had an idea for an opera about a ghostly sea captain. This opera, *The Flying Dutchman*, was produced in 1843 in Dresden, Germany, where Wagner was court music director. *The Flying Dutchman* and his next opera, *Tannhäuser* (1845), were not nearly so popular as *Rienzi*. Wagner's powerful music had few of the conventional tunes that people were used to hearing in operas.

In 1848, Wagner took part in a political revolution in Germany. Many of the rebels were arrested, but Wagner escaped to Switzerland. In a little cottage near Zurich, he began to write his greatest work, *The Ring of the Nibelung*. This work consists of four music dramas based on old German legends. They tell the story of a magical ring and the adventures of the hero, Siegfried, and the beautiful Brunnhilde. Wagner represented each person or idea in the operas with a different musical theme, called a *leitmotiv*. For example, every time Siegfried is seen or spoken about, "Siegfried's Theme" is heard in the music. These themes give the music great dramatic meaning.

Wagner was allowed to return to Germany in 1861. At Bayreuth, he designed a festival theater especially for his operas. *The Ring of the Nibelung* premiered there in 1876.

ALSO READ: MYTHOLOGY, OPERA.

WALES The principality of Wales is part of the United Kingdom of Great Britain and Northern Ireland. Wales occupies a broad peninsula to the west of England on the island of Great Britain. (See the map with the article on the BRITISH ISLES.) The island of Anglesey off the northwest coast is also part of Wales. The coast of Wales is bordered on the north by the Irish Sea, on the west by Saint George's Channel and Cardigan Bay, and on the south by the Bristol Channel. Wales has been joined with England for almost 450 years, but the Welsh people have kept many of their own traditions.

The Cambrian Mountains run north to south through most of Wales. In the northwest, the great Snowdon peak rises to 3,560 feet (1,085 m)—the highest point in England and Wales. Many of the most beautiful Welsh valleys are in the southeast, such as those of the River Usk and the River Wye. Wales has a mild climate, but the rainfall is heavy.

Nearly 3 million people live in Wales, mostly in the cities such as Swansea, Newport, and Cardiff, the capital. English is the official language, but about one-quarter of the people also speak Welsh, and a few people speak only Welsh, not English.

The Welsh are a very musical people. Nearly every village or town has its own choir. Every year, poets, painters, musicians, and other artists from all over Wales enter competitions at a national festival, or *Eisteddfod*.

Coal mining is a major occupation. Most of the mines are in the valleys of south Wales. Steel is manufactured in the cities of the south. Tourism is another important industry. People travel from all over Britain to enjoy the Welsh mountains and beaches.

Among the earliest settlers in Wales were a small, dark-haired people, who may have come from south-west Europe. Around 600 B.C., Wales was overrun by tall, fair-haired Celts from central Europe. These two types of people can still be seen in Wales.

Until the 1200's, Wales was ruled by a series of princes and chieftains. Some traditions tell that the legendary British hero, King Arthur, lived in Wales. In 1282, an English king, Edward I, defeated the great Welsh prince, Llewellyn ap Gruffydd. Edward made his eldest son Prince of Wales. Since then, it has been the tradition that the eldest son of the British monarch has the title "Prince of Wales." In the early 1400's, a Welsh rebellion led by Owen Glendower was put down by the English. Later, during the Wars of the Roses (1455–1485), a Welshman named Henry Tudor became leader of the English House of Lancaster. Henry defeated the reigning English king, Richard III, and became King Henry VII. The political union of England and Wales was brought about by King Henry VIII between 1536 and 1542.

ALSO READ: ARTHUR, KING; BRITISH ISLES; EDWARD, KINGS OF ENGLAND; ENGLISH HISTORY; HENRY, KINGS OF ENGLAND; RICHARD, KINGS OF ENGLAND; UNITED KINGDOM.

WALLACE, ALFRED RUSSEL (1823–1913) Alfred Russel Wallace was a British naturalist who worked out an idea of how plants and animals evolve slowly over millions of years into new varieties. Wallace and another British naturalist, Charles Darwin, both developed this idea (*natural selection*) at the same time.

Wallace was born in Monmouthshire, Wales. He became interested in botany and started collections of plants. When he was 25 years old, he and another naturalist went on an expedition to South America to collect plants and animals. Wallace wrote a book about his travels.

▲ *Fishguard, in southern Wales.*

Wales has its own special festivals called "eisteddfodau," which promote Welsh music, literature, and language. The most famous of these is the Royal National Eisteddfod of Wales, which is performed entirely in the Welsh language.

▲ *Alfred Russel Wallace, the British naturalist and explorer who arrived at the theory of evolution by natural selection at about the same time as did Charles Darwin.*

From 1854 to 1862, Wallace studied plants and animals in the islands of Malaysia. He noticed basic differences between the animals of Asia and those of Australia. He began thinking about a theory of natural selection. He wrote a paper expressing his thoughts and sent it to Darwin. Darwin's own ideas of evolution, which were like those of Wallace, were ready to be published. Parts of the manuscripts (papers) of both men were published in July 1858.

Although most people talk about Darwin as the discoverer of the idea of natural selection in evolution, scientists call Darwin and Wallace codiscoverers of the theory.

ALSO READ: DARWIN, CHARLES; EVOLUTION.

WALL STREET see STOCKS AND BONDS.

WALRUS The walrus belongs to the same order of animals as the seal does. The walrus and seal look much alike, but the walrus is bigger than all but the largest seals. The walrus is also fatter. Both the seal and the walrus have a layer of fatty blubber under the skin, but the walrus's layer is thicker. The blubber holds in warmth. The walrus has no fur, so it needs more blubber. The blubber also provides energy when food is scarce.

A walrus can be most easily recognized by its tusks. The tusks are a pair of upper canine teeth that never stop growing. Some walruses have tusks 3 feet (90 cm) long. The walrus uses its tusks to dig mussels and clams from the floor of the ocean. It cracks the shells of the mussels and clams with its blunt back teeth. The walrus also uses its tusks to move about on land. The name of the walrus genus (*Odobenus*) means "those who walk with their teeth."

The male walrus is called a *bull*. A full-grown bull may be 12 feet (3.7 m) long and weigh over 2,000 pounds (910 kg). The female, or *cow*, is about two-thirds the size of a bull. A baby walrus is a *pup* or *calf*. Usually only one pup is born at a time, and it stays with its mother for about two years. Walruses become mature at five or six years and may live to be 40 years old.

The Eskimos hunt walruses with harpoons and with bows and arrows made of bone. They eat the meat and blubber, burn the blubber in lamps, and make clothes from the walrus's skin. They use the bones to make weapons, and they make artistic carvings of the tusks. In recent years, the hunting of the walrus with guns has put the animal in some danger of extinction.

ALSO READ: ANIMAL, ARCTIC, MAMMAL, POLAR LIFE, SEALS AND SEA LIONS.

WAR There are few nations in the world that have not been at war at one time or another. A war is an armed conflict between nations or groups within a nation.

People go to war usually in an effort to increase their power—over their own lives or country or perhaps over

▼ *Walruses live in large families on beaches and ice floes.*

the lives or countries of other people. Revolutions and civil wars are started by discontented groups who try to overthrow the existing government and establish a new one. In such wars, the aggressors are usually trying to increase their power by gaining more freedom and control over their own lives. The American and French revolutions are examples of this type of war.

Wars between nations are frequently started by one nation (the aggressor) that wants to gain territory owned by another nation. Imperialism—the policy of acquiring colonies around the world—has led to many wars. From the ancient Roman Empire to the British Empire of the early 1900's, imperialism was a major factor in wars between nations. Economic interests, such as business and trade advantages, are also major factors in wars. Economic and territorial interests are often tied together, since more land usually means a wealthier nation.

ALSO READ: GUERRILLA WARFARE, INTERNATIONAL RELATIONS, LEAGUE OF NATIONS, NORTH ATLANTIC TREATY ORGANIZATION, NUCLEAR ENERGY, REVOLUTION, TREATY, UNITED NATIONS, WARSAW PACT, WORLD WAR I, WORLD WAR II.

WAR OF 1812 In the late 1700's and early 1800's, a state of war existed between Great Britain and France. The policy of the United States was to remain neutral (not to take sides), but both the British and the French ignored the rights of neutrals. U.S. merchant ships were stopped on the high seas and U.S. crews were impressed (forced) into military service on British naval vessels. Any U.S. ship trading with France was seized by the British, and any U.S. ship trading with Britain was seized by the French. Britain took more U.S. ships than did France.

Relations between the United States and Britain worsened. Two U.S. Congressmen—Henry Clay of Kentucky and John C. Calhoun of South Carolina—charged that British army officers in Canada were equipping and encouraging Indian raids across the U.S. frontier. Clay and Calhoun became known as the "War Hawks." They wanted the United States to declare war on Britain in order to defeat the Indians and their British supporters. The War Hawks claimed that a British defeat would keep Britain from seizing U.S. trading ships. The United States might also be able to acquire British territory in Canada.

Congress declared war on Britain on June 18, 1812. Three military invasions were begun against the British in Canada, their goal being to take the city of Montreal. All were defeated by the British.

Beginning in August of 1812, several sea battles resulted in victories for the United States. The frigate U.S.S. *Constitution* captured the British frigates *Guerrière* and *Java*, and the U.S.S. *United States* captured the British ship *Macedonia*. Both U.S. ships were armed with 44 guns, which were faster and more accurate weapons than the 38 guns on the British ships.

By the spring of 1813, a U.S. fleet commanded by Oliver Hazard Perry had been organized on Lake Erie. William Henry Harrison had moved his Kentucky militia into Ohio. There, he successfully defended Fort Meigs and Fort Stephenson against British and Indian attacks. Perry's ships heavily defeated the British in a battle on Lake Erie, capturing the entire fleet. Harrison's troops were then able to invade Canada, where they defeated British and Indian forces. The famous Indian chief Tecumseh died while fighting with the British against Harrison's forces.

In the spring of 1814, Britain defeated France and began to send rein-

MAJOR WARS

Some of the most important wars fought since the Fall of the Roman Empire in A.D. 476.

1337–1453	Hundred Years' War
1455–1485	Wars of the Roses
1618–1648	Thirty Years' War
1642–1651	English Civil War
1701–1713	War of Spanish Succession
1740–1748	War of Austrian Succession
1756–1763	Seven Years' War
1775–1783	American Revolution
1792–1815	Napoleonic Wars
1812–1814	War of 1812
1854–1856	Crimean War
1861–1865	American Civil War
1870–1871	Franco-Prussian War
1898	Spanish-American War
1899–1902	Boer War (South Africa)
1914–1918	World War I
1936–1939	Spanish Civil War
1939–1945	World War II
1950–1953	Korean War
1957–1975	Vietnam War
1973	Yom Kippur War
1980–1988	Iran-Iraq War

U.S. armed forces suffered heavier casualties in World War II than in any other war. There were 1,078,162 killed or wounded. In the Civil War there were 646,392 casualties; in World War I, 320,710; in the Korean War, 157,530 killed or wounded; in the Vietnam War, 50,000 killed and more than 300,000 wounded.

forcements to fight the United States. The British fleet set up a blockade of U.S. ports. A British landing force came ashore, moved inland, and burned the city of Washington, D.C., including the Capitol and the White House.

In the summer of 1814, the British sent ships and troops to the Lake Champlain area (between Vermont and New York State). A U.S. fleet was anchored across the entrance to Plattsburg Bay at the north end of the lake, so the more powerful British ships could not reach open water. The British attacked on September 11, 1814. The wind was so light that the British sailing ships could not move about and had to drop anchor. The British ship *Confiance* fired furiously for two hours at the U.S. ship *Saratoga* and knocked out all the *Saratoga*'s guns on one side. The *Saratoga*'s captain turned the ship around, bringing a whole set of fresh guns to fire on the *Confiance*. The British could not move without wind in their sails, and so they surrendered and retreated back into Canada the next day.

On January 8, 1815, about 8,000 British troops landed in New Orleans, Louisiana, and attacked the 5,000 troops under the command of General Andrew Jackson. In only 25 minutes of fighting, the British lost over 2,000 soldiers, while Jackson's forces lost only 71. The British immediately retreated and left the country.

The Battle of New Orleans actually took place after a peace treaty had been signed between Britain and the United States. Negotiators had met at Ghent in Belgium and concluded the Treaty of Ghent on December 24, 1814. The treaty gave no new territory to either side and left many other issues unsettled. However, the war had forced the United States to defend itself for the first time as a unified nation.

ALSO READ: ADAMS, JOHN; AMERICAN HISTORY; CALHOUN, JOHN C.; CANADA; CLAY, HENRY; HARRISON, WILLIAM HENRY; JACKSON, ANDREW; MADISON, JAMES; PERRY, MATTHEW; PERRY, OLIVER HAZARD, TECUMSEH.

WARSAW PACT The Warsaw Pact, or Eastern European Mutual Assistance Treaty, is a military alliance among the Communist nations of Bulgaria, Czechoslovakia, Hungary, Poland, Romania, and the Soviet Union. It was formed during WWII on May 14, 1945 when these nations plus Albania (which withdrew in 1968) and East Germany (which united with West Germany in 1990) signed the Warsaw Treaty for mutual defense.

After World War II, a number of European nations and the United States and Canada formed a military alliance called NATO (the North Atlantic Treaty Organization). The purpose of NATO was to protect Western Europe from attack by an enemy nation. When West Germany joined NATO in 1955, Eastern European nations reacted by forming the Warsaw Pact for their own defense.

In 1956, the people of Hungary rebelled against Soviet domination and left the Warsaw Pact. Soldiers from the other Pact countries forced them to return. The same thing happened to Czechoslovakia in 1968. In 1990 the countries of the Warsaw Pact signed a treaty with the NATO countries.

ALSO READ: NORTH ATLANTIC TREATY ORGANIZATION, WORLD WAR II.

▼*General Andrew Jackson, his sword triumphantly raised. He led the U.S. forces to victory over the British in the Battle of New Orleans on January 8, 1815. The War of 1812 had already ended, but news of the peace had failed to reach New Orleans.*

WARS OF THE ROSES The Wars of the Roses were a series of civil wars fought in England during the 1400's between two great families—the House of Lancaster and the House of York. Both claimed to be rightful rulers of England. The name of the wars comes from the badges used by the two houses—the red rose of Lancaster and the white rose of York.

Henry VI was only a few months old when he became king of England in 1422. In 1454, he went mad for a short time, and the country was ruled in his place by Richard Plantagenet, Duke of York. Henry and Richard were both descended from the same king, Edward III. Richard was descended from the third son of Edward III, so he claimed that he had more right to be king than Henry, who was descended from Edward's fourth son. Richard formed a league of several great nobles in England. In 1455, civil war broke out, and Henry was captured by the Yorkists at a battle near Saint Albans. In 1455–1466, Henry was again insane, and again Richard ruled in his place.

However, the queen, Margaret of Anjou, supported the rights of her son, Prince Edward, and in 1460 defeated the Yorkists at the Battle of Wakefield. Richard of York was killed during the battle. But in 1461, his son (also called Edward) was proclaimed king as Edward IV. In 1470, Edward IV was overthrown by forces led by Margaret and by the Earl of Warwick (known as the "Kingmaker" because he was so influential). Henry was briefly restored to the throne. But the following year, Edward IV completely routed the Lancastrians at the Battle of Tewkesbury. Prince Edward was murdered by Richard's men, and, later, so was Henry VI.

Edward IV was succeeded by his son, Edward V, in 1483. The new king was only 13, and his uncle, Richard, Duke of Gloucester, was cho-sen to rule the kingdom. Richard imprisoned both Edward and his younger brother in the Tower of London, and the two "Princes in the Tower" were never seen again. Richard proclaimed himself King Richard III. He made many enemies by this act. When Henry Tudor (the young leader of the house of Lancaster) marched into England with an army, many people supported him. The Yorkists were beaten at the Battle of Bosworth Field in 1485. Richard III was killed during the battle, and Henry was crowned as King Henry VII. He later married Elizabeth, heiress of the house of York, and the rival families of York and Lancaster were finally united, establishing the house of Tudor.

ALSO READ: EDWARD, KINGS OF ENGLAND; ENGLISH HISTORY; HENRY, KINGS OF ENGLAND; RICHARD, KINGS OF ENGLAND.

WASHINGTON The state of Washington was named in honor of the first President of the United States. It is the only state named for a President. It is also called the "Evergreen State" because of the many forests of evergreen trees that grow on the slopes of its high mountains.

The inhabitants of Washington live close to natural beauty. Green islands lie in Washington's blue Puget Sound. Forests and meadows of wild-flowers are found in the state's national parks. There are many lakes and rivers. And the great Columbia Plateau stretches for miles under a cloudless sky.

The Land and Climate Washington lies in the Pacific Northwest. North of it is the Canadian province of British Columbia. To the east is Idaho. The Columbia River forms most of Washington's southern border with Oregon. On the Western shore of Washington, the Coast

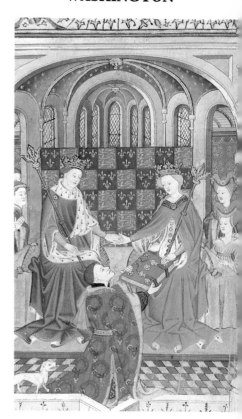

▲ *Margaret of Anjou and her husband, Henry VI of England. Her enmity toward Richard of York, whom she saw as a threat to the succession of her son Prince Edward was one of the causes of the Wars of the Roses.*

▲ *The modern skyline of Seattle, a major trading center for the United States and the Orient. The snowy volcanic peak of Mt. Hood rises in the distance.*

In 1980, Mount St. Helens, a volcano dormant for 123 years, erupted in the Cascade Range in southwestern Washington. The top of the volcano was blown off, leaving the 9,677-foot (2,950-m) peak only about 8,300 feet (2,530 m) high and forming a 2-mile (3-km) long crater.

Range rises on the Olympic Peninsula. The Olympic Mountains are the highest part. Their name comes from that of the tallest mountain in the range, Mount Olympus—7,965 feet (2,428 m). Glaciers, lakes, and waterfalls are found in these mountains.

East of the Coast Ranges is the Puget Sound lowland. The sound is an arm of the Pacific Ocean. Large oceangoing ships sail past its islands to Seattle and Tacoma. The lowland is a long, broad, fertile valley.

The Cascade Range separates the green and often rainy western part of the state from the drier eastern part. Many cascades, or waterfalls, are formed by water pouring over rocks in the streams. Mount Rainier, at 14,410 feet (4,392 m), is the highest peak in the Cascades. A beautiful national park stretches around tall Mount Rainier.

Eastern Washington is mainly made up of the Columbia Plateau. Nature made the plateau brown and dry. But irrigation with river water and modern farming methods have made it a rich farming region. It is called the "Inland Empire," with Spokane as its major city. Wheat is grown by *dry farming*. Such farming uses the rain of two years, collected in the soil, to grow *one* crop. Eastern Washington produces a huge amount of wheat by dry farming. North of the Columbia Plateau are the forested mountains of eastern Washington.

Rain makes all the difference in Washington. Precipitation is heavy in the western part of the state and light in the eastern part. The Columbia Plateau receives little rain. West winds bring moisture from the Pacific Ocean. When they reach the Coastal Ranges, the winds turn upward to cross the mountains.

The winds continue eastward. When they reach the high Cascade Range, the air rises and is chilled. Much rain falls. On the eastern side of the Cascades, the winds turn downward. The air grows warmer. What-

ever moisture is left in it is unlikely to fall as rain. Eastern Washington has rather warm summers and cold winters. West of the Cascades, the climate is milder.

History Indian tribes with greatly differing ways of life once lived in what is now the state of Washington. West of the Cascade Range were two groups of tribes. One was on the Pacific Coast. The other lived farther inland, beside rivers and bays. On the coast were the Quinault, the Quilleute, and the Makah. These Indians were bold ocean fishermen. They even hunted whales in their dugout canoes. Inland tribes such as the Chinook and Puyallup fished in calmer waters. The Klickitat Indians of central Washington were known as good traders.

East of the Cascades, on the dry Columbia Plateau, food was scarce. The Sahaptian Indians gathered berries and dug the bulbs of wild plants. But they had animal foods, too. They fished for salmon in the Columbia and Snake rivers. They hunted deer and elk in the mountain forests. Nez Percé and Cayuse Indians lived in the southeast.

Spaniards reached the coast of Washington in the 1770's. British seafarers were only a few years behind them. In 1792, a British naval officer, George Vancouver, explored Puget Sound. That same year, Captain Robert Gray of Boston discovered the great river of the Northwest. He named it "Columbia," after his ship.

The first North Americans to come by land reached Washington in 1805. They were led by Meriwether Lewis and William Clark. The explorers floated down the Snake River to the Columbia. Fur trading was the earliest business of the Northwest. At first, the traders came by ship. Later they came by land and followed the route of Lewis and Clark. The first permanent settlement was Tumwater, which is on a river near the south-

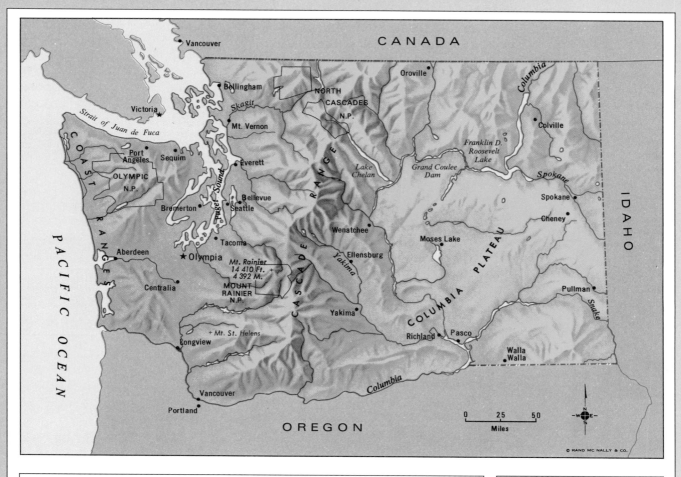

STATE EMBLEMS

Rhododendron

Western Hemlock

Willow Goldfinch

WASHINGTON

Capital
Olympia (27,000 people)

Area
68,192 square miles
(176,616 sq. km)
Rank: 20th

Population
4,648,000
Rank: 18th

Statehood
November 11, 1889
(42nd state admitted)

Principal river
Columbia River

Highest point
Mount Rainier;
14,410 feet (4,392 m)

Largest city
Seattle (492,000 people)

Motto
Alki ("Bye and Bye")

Song
"Washington, My Home"

Famous people
Bing Crosby, Mary McCarthy, General Jonathan M. Wainwright

▲ *A view of the Pacific shoreline in Washington state.*

▲ *The Space Needle dominates the skyline of Seattle, the largest city in the state of Washington. The tower, built for the 1962 World's Fair, has an observation deck at the top.*

ern end of Puget Sound. This point was the end of the long Oregon Trail.

As the white population increased, the Indians of the region felt threatened. Some tribes fought small, hopeless wars. The white people had the advantages of numbers and better weapons. A large council of many tribes, the Walla Walla Council, met in 1855 and ceded land to the United States through several treaties. Tribes were moved to reservations. One tribe, the Palouse, refused ever to live a reservation life. In the 1950's, the Nez Percé Indians asked and finally received more payment from the Federal Government for lands ceded in the 1800's.

Washingtonians at Work The Puget Sound lowland is Washington's most thickly settled area. Most of the state's manufacturing is done here. Among the most important industries are aircraft and missiles, shipbuilding, chemicals, food-processing, metals, and machinery.

Agriculture is the second biggest business. Crops earn more money than livestock. Wheat is the leading crop. In western Washington, dairying is the main livestock industry. Beef cattle are raised in the east. The fertile valley of the Yakima River has been called the "Fruit Bowl of the Nation" because of the apples and other fruits grown there.

Tourism is another lively business.

The lakes and mountains of the national parks and forests attract people for boating, fishing, and skiing. The great forests of Washington have made it one of the top lumbering states. Sawmills—mostly on the shores of Puget Sound—turn logs into lumber. The state has a big fishing industry, with salmon the most important catch.

ALSO READ: COLUMBIA RIVER, FUR, IRRIGATION, LEWIS AND CLARK EXPEDITION, OREGON TRAIL, WESTWARD MOVEMENT.

WASHINGTON, BOOKER T. (1856–1915) Booker Taliaferro Washington was born a slave. He grew up to play an important part in helping blacks improve their economic and social lot.

Booker T. Washington was born on a plantation near Hale's Ford, Virginia. From the age of nine, he worked in the coal mines all day and taught himself to read and write at night. At the age of 20, he graduated from Hampton Normal and Agricultural School, where he later became an instructor.

In 1881, Washington was asked to establish a new school for black students in Tuskegee, Alabama. He founded and became the first president of Tuskegee Institute. Under his direction, Tuskegee Institute became famous as a vocational, industrial, and agricultural training school. In 1900, Washington founded the National Negro Business League to help blacks succeed in business. He also wrote a number of books, including *Up from Slavery* (the story of his life) and *The Future of the American Negro*.

Washington believed that black people would advance best through having greater opportunities in education and in business. He placed less emphasis on social and political equality. Although many other black people have disagreed with him, Washington is still remembered for his achievements at the Tuskegee Institute and his efforts to provide better opportunities for black people to live with dignity in a largely white society.

ALSO READ: BLACK AMERICANS.

WASHINGTON, D.C. see DISTRICT OF COLUMBIA.

WASHINGTON, GEORGE
(1732–1799) Few leaders have ever served their country more unselfishly or in more different ways than did George Washington. After the American Revolution, he was so popular that he might easily have made himself king or dictator. But he wanted no reward, he said, except the "affection of a free people."

Washington was born on a farm in Virginia. His father died when George was 11 years old, and Lawrence, his older half brother, became like a second father to him. Lawrence was the owner of a plantation named Mount Vernon, and George was a frequent visitor there. George received little formal schooling, but he studied surveying and practiced measuring the fields around Mount Vernon. He drew such accurate maps that Lord Fairfax, the

owner of a neighboring plantation, was much impressed.

Fairfax, who had recently come from Britain, had inherited thousands of acres of land west of the Blue Ridge Mountains. He decided to send out some surveyors to map the land. George Washington was asked to be a member of the surveying team. He was only 16 years old.

When he was 21 years old, Washington was asked by Robert Dinwiddie, governor of Virginia, to deliver a message to the French commander of a fort in the Ohio Valley. The message warned the French to withdraw from land claimed by the British. The refusal of the French helped to bring on the French and Indian War that lasted from 1754 to 1763. In that conflict, Washington served first as a lieutenant colonel and then as a colonel in command of troops from Virginia.

When Lawrence died in 1752, Colonel Washington became the owner of Mount Vernon. Seven years later, he married a beautiful and wealthy widow, Martha Custis, and took her and her two young children to Mount Vernon to live. Washington became a successful farmer, but this happy, peaceful life was not to last. When the American Revolution broke out in 1775, Washington was asked by the Continental Congress to

▲ *Booker T. Washington, U.S. educator, who promoted education and training for blacks.*

George Washington always thought that farming was the most pleasant pursuit. He said that a farmer's life was "honorable, amusing, and, with superior judgement, profitable." He liked to be thought of as the "nation's first farmer."

In the past, doctors used to take blood from their patients, thinking that this would cure almost any illness. In 1799, George Washington was probably bled to death by his doctors.

GEORGE WASHINGTON
FIRST PRESIDENT   APRIL 30, 1789–MARCH 4, 1797

Born: February 22, 1732, Pope's Creek (later called Wakefield), Westmoreland County, Virginia
Parents: Augustine and Mary Ball Washington
Education: Attended local country schools at intervals, then studied surveying
Religion: Episcopalian
Occupation: Surveyor, farmer, army officer
Political Party: Did not join a political party
Married: 1759 to Mrs. Martha Dandridge Custis (1731–1802)
Children: One stepson and one stepdaughter
Died: December 14, 1799, Mount Vernon, Virginia
Buried: Mount Vernon, Virginia

▲ *This painting of Mount Vernon, George Washington's home in northern Virginia, is by an unknown artist. The painting is in the National Gallery of Art, Washington, D.C., gift of Edgar William and Bernice Chrysler Garbisch.*

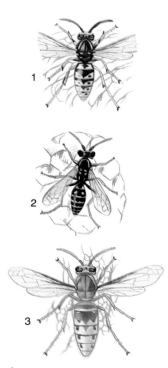

▲ *Three types of wasps you may come across: (1) the common wasp, (2) the paper wasp, and (3) the hornet.*

command the colonial army. Few generals ever faced greater difficulties. Washington served without pay, except for his expenses. He sometimes found it hard to collect enough money from Congress to pay his soldiers. It was often hard to get food for his troops, and the soldiers lacked adequate clothing. Washington's army spent a terrible winter (1777–1778) at Valley Forge, suffering from hunger and freezing cold. But General Washington managed to keep an army together until the colonies won their freedom. In 1783, a treaty was signed with Great Britain, recognizing the independence of the United States. Washington then returned to Mount Vernon, expecting to spend the rest of his life there. But his country still needed him.

As chairman of the Constitutional Convention that met in Philadelphia in 1787, he helped to draft the Constitution of the United States. The Constitution stated that the head of the government should be a President. Washington was the person everyone trusted to get the new government started. On the first election day, every vote was cast for General Washington.

On April 30, 1789, Washington walked out on the balcony of Federal Hall in New York, the city that had been chosen as a temporary capital. Beside him stood Robert R. Livingston, Chancellor of New York State,

holding an open Bible. George Washington repeated the oath of office in which every President since has promised to "preserve, protect, and defend the Constitution of the United States."

In 1790, the capital was moved to Philadelphia, Pennsylvania, where the business of government was carried on during the next ten years. In the meantime, President Washington was helping to plan a new capital city (which one day would be named "Washington" in his honor).

After serving as President for a term of four years, he was elected to a second term and continued to try to give the nation a strong central government. When France and Britain went to war, President Washington issued a Proclamation of Neutrality in 1793. The proclamation stated that the United States would not take sides. Washington believed that it would be neither wise nor safe for a new nation that was still weak to become involved in another war. The President was severely criticized by those citizens who favored France. Most citizens hoped that Washington would run for a third term, but he refused. Washington died two years after his retirement. He was buried at Mount Vernon. In a speech delivered before Congress, General Henry ("Lighthorse Harry") Lee paid tribute to his former commander in these words: "He was first in war, first in peace, and first in the hearts of his countrymen."

ALSO READ: AMERICAN REVOLUTION; CONSTITUTION, UNITED STATES; CONTINENTAL CONGRESS; DISTRICT OF COLUMBIA; FRENCH AND INDIAN WAR; PRESIDENCY.

WASPS AND HORNETS Wasps are usually thought of as large insects that sting. All wasps have slim bodies with a narrow connection between the front and back parts. Two transparent wings (called *membranous* wings) with veins in them are attached to each side of the front part of the body. Two smaller wings are fastened to the back edge of the front pair. The stinger is at the rear tip of the wasp. Only queens and other females have stingers. The males have none.

Some wasps live in communities and are called *social wasps. Hornets* are one common type. A community of hornets may include hundreds, or even thousands, of hornets. The colony is made up of a queen, a few males or drones, and a large number of female workers. The hornets' communities are in nests made of paper. The hornets make paper by chewing bits of woody plant material until the fibers that make up the wood are broken apart and thoroughly mixed with the hornets' saliva. Some nests are built hanging from tree limbs, and some are attached under eaves of roofs. Another social wasp, the *yellow jacket*, often burrows into the ground to make a nest.

Unlike hive bees, most hornets die in winter. But a few of the eggs laid by the old queen become queen hornets, and they survive the cold weather. In spring, each queen builds small containers or cells. She lays an egg in each cell, puts food in, and seals the cell. In about 14 days, female worker hornets come out of the cells. The workers build more cells and hunt for food. The queen's main task is to lay eggs.

Solitary wasps do not live in communities, but a few may make small nests close together. Some solitary wasps are larger than hornets, while others are only ¼ inch (6 mm) long. One kind of solitary wasp is the *mud dauber*, which builds small nests by sticking mud to beams in barns or under eaves. *Digger wasps* hollow out holes in the ground for nests. The *potter wasps* (or *mason wasps*) make nests of clay.

Among solitary wasps, the female feeds her young by stinging an insect and sealing it into a chamber with one or more eggs. The insect is paralyzed and lives until the eggs hatch into larvae. The larvae then eat the insect the female has provided. Almost every kind of solitary wasp hunts a different kind of insect. Among these are caterpillars, flies, beetles, cockroaches, crickets, grasshoppers, cicadas, and ants. Wasps also eat spiders (which are not insects) and feed on fruits.

ALSO READ: BEE, INSECT, SPIDER.

WATCH see CLOCKS AND WATCHES.

WATER Water is one of the most vital and "peculiar" substances on Earth. Its importance is obvious—without it, nothing could live. About 71 percent of the Earth's surface is covered with water. The human body is about 65 percent water. All living organisms are at least half water.

Its peculiarity is less obvious but is one reason for its importance. Water is peculiar in two important ways. One is that it can absorb (soak up) and hold a tremendous amount of heat. More heat is needed to raise the temperature of water one degree than is needed to raise the temperature of most other substances by the same amount. But once water has absorbed heat, it loses it very slowly. The water in seas, lakes, and rivers changes temperature more slowly than does the land around it, and this affects climate.

Another peculiarity is that water expands (swells up) when it freezes. Most substances shrink when they freeze. Because water expands when it freezes, ice is less dense (lighter) than liquid water. Because ice is less dense, it rises to the surface, or floats, while the denser warm water stays near the bottom of the seas, lakes, and rivers. If the ice did not float, the warm water would flow to the top,

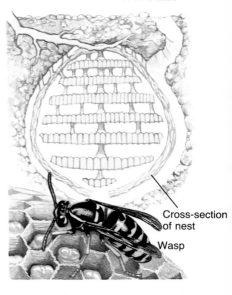

Cross-section of nest

Wasp

▲ *Wasps use paper to construct their complicated nests. They make the paper by mixing chewed wood with saliva.*

On average, a person takes in about 20,000 gallons (76,000 liters) of water during a lifetime.

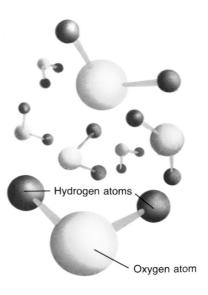

Hydrogen atoms

Oxygen atom

▲ *A single molecule of water has two atoms of hydrogen and one atom of oxygen.*

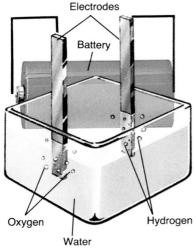

Electrodes

Battery

Oxygen

Water

Hydrogen

▲ *Water can be separated into hydrogen gas and oxygen gas by passing an electric current through it.*

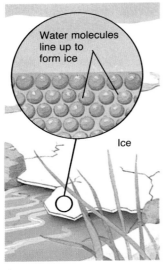

Water molecules line up to form ice

Ice

▲ *If the temperature is low enough, water freezes to form a solid substance, ice. This is because the colder it is, the less the water molecules can move around. At freezing point—32°F (0°C)—the molecules line up in rows to form solid crystals.*

give off its heat, and freeze. The oceans could freeze completely, and the plants and animals in them would die. But, because this is not so, fish do not freeze in very cold weather. This peculiar expansion of freezing water has made life in the ocean possible, and thus it has made all life on the Earth possible.

Pure water is a clear, very slightly blue, odorless, tasteless liquid at ordinary pressures and temperatures. It freezes at 32°F (0°C) and boils at 212°F (100°C).

Pure water contains only the elements hydrogen and oxygen. Each water molecule has two hydrogen atoms joined to one oxygen atom, so the chemical formula for water is H_2O. But water is rarely pure. Water dissolves many different substances. Drinking water, for example, often has a definite odor, taste, or color because of the substances dissolved in it. The beverages we drink are mostly water. Other substances dissolved in the water add color and flavor.

"Hard water" is water that has dissolved large amounts of certain minerals. "Soft water" contains few minerals. It is difficult to wash with hard water because it does not readily form soapsuds. Water softeners are frequently added to remove the minerals and make hard water softer.

Heavy water is not really heavy. It gets its name because, instead of hydrogen atoms, it has atoms of an unusually heavy form of hydrogen, called *deuterium*. Heavy water is used in scientific research and in the production of nuclear energy.

For further information on:
Bodies of Water, *see* LAKE, OCEAN, RIVER, WELLS AND SPRINGS.
Properties, Forms, and Effects of Water, *see* BUOYANCY, CHEMISTRY, CLIMATE, CLOUD, CONSERVATION, DISTILLATION, EARTH HISTORY, ECOLOGY, FLOOD, FROST, GEYSER, GLACIER, GULF STREAM, HURRICANE, HYDROGEN, ICE AGE, ICEBERG, LIQUID, OXY-

▲ *Water can exist as a liquid, a solid (ice), or a vapor (steam). Here, hot water is being poured onto ice. You can't see the steam, but you can see water droplets forming as the hot steam cools.*

GEN, QUICKSAND, RAIN AND SNOW, RAINBOW, SEACOAST, SURFACE TENSION, TIDE, WATER CYCLE, WATER POLLUTION, WAVE, WEATHER.
Uses of Water, *see* BOATS AND BOATING, DIVING, ELECTRIC POWER, FIRE FIGHTING, FISHING INDUSTRY, HARBORS AND PORTS, IRRIGATION, NAVIGATION, NAVY, PLUMBING, SAILING, SCUBA DIVING, SHIPS AND SHIPPING, SUBMARINE, SURFING, SWIMMING, WATERSKIING, WATER SUPPLY.

WATER BIRDS More than 600 different species of birds live in streams, ponds and marshes, and along the banks of rivers and the shores of oceans. These water birds spend much of their time swimming or wading. They eat plants and animals that grow in and near the water. They often build nests on or near the water.

Swimming Water Birds Ducks, geese, and swans are the best-known swimming birds. They have webbed feet and wide, flat "duck bills." Oil from special glands waterproofs their feathers. A typical duck is about 2 feet (60 cm) long and has a short neck. A goose is larger and has a longer neck. A swan is even larger and has an even longer neck.

A loon looks like a large duck with a sharp bill. Loons have solid, heavy bones, which prevent them from floating well. A loon often swims with only its head and neck above water. It dives below the surface to catch fish. Grebes are similar to loons but are smaller and have longer necks. Grebes are excellent divers but poor fliers. Both loons and grebes are awkward on land and rarely go ashore. Grebes even build floating nests.

Cormorants are large, dark, diving birds with webbed feet and hooked bills. Cormorants swim low in the water like loons, but cormorants are more likely to be seen perched on rocks and buoys. The anhinga, or snakebird, is similar to the cormorant, but has a long, snakelike neck. The anhinga rarely swims. However, it lives near water and eats by diving and spearing fish with its sharp, pointed bill.

Wading Water Birds Herons, ibises, storks, and cranes are some of over 100 species of wading birds.

▼ *A great-crested grebe sitting watchfully on its grassy nest.*

These birds often have long legs and long necks. Their long legs are useful in wading in deep water, and their long necks are useful in scooping food from under water.

Herons, egrets, and bitterns are all members of the heron family. The largest heron is the great white heron, a pure white bird 4 feet (1.2 m) tall with a yellow beak and yellow legs. The great blue heron is slightly smaller and is blue-gray in color. The American egret and the snowy egret are white herons with black legs. The white feathers of egrets were once used to decorate hats. So many egrets were killed for their feathers that they almost became extinct. It is now illegal to kill them. Night herons and bitterns are smaller and shorter-necked than other herons.

Cranes are birds that look much like large herons. But herons fly with their necks pulled back on their shoulders, while cranes fly with their necks stretched out. Cranes also have a very distinctive trumpeting call.

The only stork in North America is the wood ibis, a large, white wading bird with a dark, featherless head, black feathers under the wings, and a long, curved bill. The white ibis is much smaller, has a feathered head, and has black only at the wing tips. The roseate spoonbill is related to the ibis but is pink and has a curious, spoon-shaped bill.

▲ *Statuesque greater flamingos standing in the weedy shallows of a lake. These water birds are about 4 feet (120 cm) high.*

▲ *A scarlet ibis of tropical America.*

Continental form

Atlantic form

▲ *The cormorant is an expert fish-catcher. It can stay underwater for more than a minute.*

▼ *In the water cycle, the sun's heat makes water evaporate from the sea and land. Cooled vapor falls back down (precipitates) as rain or snow. Water precipitated onto the land flows through streams and rivers to the sea.*

Another remarkable pink wading bird is the flamingo. The flamingo has very long, slender, stiltlike legs, a long neck, and a hooked bill. Flamingos nest in large groups in the marshes of southern Florida.

Shore birds are small wading birds that feed along the shore. The plover is a plump shore bird with a short bill. Sandpipers, curlews, and godwits have long, slender bills. The curlew's bill curves downward, the godwit's curves upward.

Today, water birds are disappearing because their marshes have been drained to get land for farming and building, and shorelands have been taken to provide sites for homes and factories. Birds are driven from their homes and crowded together in areas too small to support them. Those birds that do survive run the risk of being shot by hunters. The whooping crane, the tallest of U.S. birds, is an example of how quickly a bird can be driven to the edge of extinction. In the 1800's, there were huge numbers of these birds, but by the early 1900's almost all had been killed. The hunting of whooping cranes was made illegal in 1916, but these birds number only about 50 today.

ALSO READ: BIRD, CRANE, DUCKS AND GEESE, SEABIRDS, STORK.

WATER CYCLE Water is continuously moving among the oceans, the air, and the land. This movement is called the water cycle. The water cycle is made up of three natural processes: *evaporation*, *condensation*, and *precipitation*.

There is always some water in the air. The water is in a gaseous form called *water vapor*. Water vapor is made up of water molecules that have separated from the surface of water. This separation process is called evaporation.

■ LEARN BY DOING

Warm water evaporates faster than cold water. You can prove this by putting a quarter-inch (0.5 cm) of water into each of two pie pans. Place one pan on a sunny window sill or on a radiator. Set the second pie pan in a cool place indoors. Examine both pie pans after several hours. Which pie pan has less water—the warm one or the cool one? ■

Water evaporates from the surfaces of oceans, lakes, ponds, rivers, streams, and puddles. More water evaporates in warm weather and warm climates than in cold. Water also evaporates or *transpires* from the leaves of plants. Roots take up water from the soil. The water rises through the plant to the leaves. It evaporates through tiny holes in the undersides of the leaves.

Condensation is the opposite of evaporation. In condensation, a gas changes to a liquid. For example, water vapor changes to water. When the water vapor at the mouth of a teakettle spout comes into contact with cooler air, the hot water vapor condenses to form a visible cloud of water droplets (steam). Blow your breath on a mirror. The water vapor in your warm breath condenses on the cool surface of the mirror, making the mirror cloudy.

Cool air cannot hold as much water vapor as warm air can. Therefore, when warm air cools, some water vapor must leave the cooling air. The water vapor condenses. When con-

Rain and snow

Sun

Water vapor

Water vapor

Water vapor

Water flows back to sea

densation takes place high above the Earth's surface, clouds form.

The tiny droplets of water that make up a cloud bump into each other as air currents move through the cloud. The bumping droplets join and form larger droplets. This joining goes on, and the droplets become larger and larger. Finally, after about a million tiny droplets have joined, a raindrop has formed. The raindrop is heavy enough to overcome the upward push of the air currents, and it falls out of the clouds. If the air is cold enough, snowflakes, sleet, or hailstones are formed. The forming and falling of raindrops, snowflakes, sleet, and hailstones is *precipitation*.

Rain falling on the land runs into streams or soaks into the ground. The streams may flow into lakes and ponds, or join and form rivers. The rivers flow into the oceans or lakes. Some of the water that soaks into the ground runs into underground streams, and some is taken up by plants. Evaporation from water surfaces and transpiration from plants produce water vapor, which condenses and forms clouds. Precipitation falls from the clouds. This circular, never-ending process is the water cycle.

ALSO READ: CLOUD, DISTILLATION, FOG, HUMIDITY, RAIN AND SNOW.

WATERFALL When a stream or a river plunges over a cliff, it forms a waterfall. This often occurs where a stream passes from hard rock to soft rock. The running water erodes (wears away) the soft rock faster than it erodes the hard rock. The channel in the soft rock becomes lower than the channel in the hard rock. A cliff and a waterfall are formed.

As water continues to pour over the waterfall, it may cut under the cliff. After a while, the cliff is undermined. It breaks off, and the waterfall moves upstream a short distance. This is happening at Niagara Falls, where the Horseshoe Falls have been mov-

ing upstream about one yard (a meter) each year. The smaller American Falls have moved upstream 2 to 3 feet (60–90 cm) a year. After a long time—thousands of years—falls may wear down to become *cataracts* or *rapids*, a series of low falls.

Yosemite Falls in California (which is made up of two falls) is the highest waterfall in North America. The upper falls is 1,430 feet (436 m) high, the lower falls 320 feet (98 m). The water plunges into the valley of the Yosemite River. Yosemite is a *hanging-valley* waterfall. During the last ice age, glaciers cut the valley of the river. A small glacier cut a shallower valley that joined the Yosemite Valley. When the glaciers melted, they left behind the small "hanging valley" opening into the deep valley of the Yosemite River. Water from the stream in the small valley plunges to the valley, forming a waterfall.

The highest waterfall on Earth is Angel Falls in Venezuela. It is 3,212 feet (979 m) high, with one long drop of 2,648 feet (807 m).

ALSO READ: DAM, EROSION, GLACIER, HYDROELECTRICITY, ICE AGE, NIAGARA FALLS.

WATERLOO Waterloo is the name of a small town in Belgium. The French emperor, Napoleon Bonaparte, was defeated near there at the Battle of Waterloo on June 18, 1815.

The battle was fought after Napoleon escaped from the island of Elba, where he had been imprisoned since 1814. On June 16, 1815, Napoleon attacked a Prussian (German) army under General Gebhard von Blücher near the Belgian town of Charleroi. Believing that he had crushed the Prussians, Napoleon then marched northward with about 125,000 soldiers. At Waterloo, on June 17, he met British and Dutch armies commanded by the British general, the Duke of Wellington. These armies

▲ *The highest waterfall in the world is the Angel Falls, on the Carrao River, in Venezuela, South America.*

The great Victoria Falls on the Zambezi River is more than 350 feet (107 m) high and about a mile (1.6 km) wide. Nearly 30 million gallons (100 million liters) of water plunge over this drop every minute. If all this power could be used, there would be enough energy to supply all the electricity used by 5 million people.

together numbered about 93,000 soldiers. Heavy rains prevented Napoleon from moving his big guns, and he did not attack that day. The following morning, Wellington arranged his foot soldiers in a line across the battlefield. The French cavalry charged repeatedly, but they could not break the line.

Meanwhile the Prussians had recovered from the attack at Charleroi and were marching toward Waterloo. By the later afternoon, Wellington's troops were just beginning to weaken when Blücher arrived. The Prussians attacked fiercely, and the French were routed. Napoleon escaped from the battlefield but later surrendered to the British. During the battle, the French lost about 40,000 soldiers. Allied losses numbered about 22,000.

ALSO READ: ENGLISH HISTORY; FRENCH HISTORY; NAPOLEON BONAPARTE; WELLINGTON, DUKE OF.

▲ *The Battle of Waterloo, 1815, marked the final defeat of Napoleon and his French troops. Here, British Life Guards charge through the French infantry line.*

WATER PLANT see ALGAE, MARINE LIFE, POND LIFE.

WATER POLLUTION Small amounts of natural wastes are present in almost all water. These wastes include silt washed out of the soil, the waste products of plants and animals, and the remains of dead plants and animals. Water can cleanse itself of most natural wastes through the action of oxygen and bacteria. However, when human beings add large amounts of artificial wastes, the water becomes overloaded and can no longer cleanse itself thoroughly. The wastes pile up and the water becomes polluted.

Millions of tons of acid from coal mines run into the rivers of the eastern United States. Paper mills, chemical plants, and other factories empty wastes into streams. Power plants use huge quantities of fresh water to cool and condense steam. This water becomes hot, and, if hot water is dumped into streams or lakes, it kills the fish and plants that live in these places.

Many cities are growing so fast that they cannot give their sewage proper treatment. As a result, harmful sewage is poured into the rivers. Some laundry detergents contain phosphates, which cannot be eliminated by sewage treatment. Phosphates act as fertilizers. When phosphates get into rivers or lakes, they increase the growth of certain water plants, and this robs the water of oxygen for fish and other water life.

Lake Erie is a good example of what pollution can do to a body of water. This lake is dying because millions of tons of sediment, sewage, and chemical wastes are poured into the lake every year. Some parts of Lake Erie have so little oxygen that very little life can exist there.

With increasing population, there is a growing demand for clean water for drinking, cooking, bathing, irrigation, fishing, and other uses. An increased population can also cause increased pollution. To have enough clean water, the dumping of indus-

▼ *A trawler boat, adapted for cleaning up oil slicks, combs over polluted areas. Chemicals are sprayed onto the water to disperse pollutants.*

trial wastes and untreated sewage will have to be stopped. Although some businesses and cities are making efforts to halt water pollution, many of them are not. It takes money to clean up pollution, and many people don't like to spend money. But water is essential to life and health.

ALSO READ: AIR POLLUTION, LAKE, MARINE LIFE, POLLUTION, SANITATION, SOAPS AND DETERGENTS, WATER, WATER SUPPLY.

WATERSKIING Waterskiing is the art of skimming over the water on skis while being pulled by a rope attached to a motorboat.

Water skis are made of fiberglass, aluminum, or wood. They are usually about 5 to 7 inches (13–18 cm) wide and 5 to 6½ feet (1.5–2 m) long. The skis are not connected to the boat. Instead, the water-skier grips a wooden tow bar, which is attached to a rope going to the boat. The skier's feet are inserted into rubber binders mounted on the skis. Many water-skiers use only a single ski, with two rubber binders for the feet.

Waterskiing events can be divided into three main categories—trick riding, slalom, and jumping. Trick riding includes turning around on the skis and skiing sideways or backward. In the slalom, the water-skier weaves in and out between a series of markers, riding on one or two skis. Ski racing is also becoming popular. A number of people have waterskied nonstop for about 200 miles (320 km) from Nassau in the Bahamas, to Miami, Florida. Jumping involves skiing upward over a waxed, wooden platform. Some skiers attach themselves to kites and use the ski jump to get them high enough into the air for flying. Aquaplaning, a sport similar to waterskiing, is also performed at water shows. Aquaplaners ride on a broad platform attached to a boat by ropes.

Most of the boats used in waterskiing have motors of 40 horsepower (30,000 W) or more. They should be capable of speeds of 20 miles (32 km) an hour. In addition to the operator of the boat, there should be at least one other person aboard, for safety purposes. This person faces to the rear and watches the skier.

A water-skier starts by bending the knees and holding the arms straight ahead with the hands gripping the tow bar. The ski tips are up and out of the water. As the boat begins to pick up speed, the water-skier rises to a standing position. All skiers should wear life belts or life jackets.

One of the best-known waterskiing areas is Cypress Gardens, Florida.

ALSO READ: SPORTS, SWIMMING.

WATER SUPPLY There are about 364 billion billion (quintillion) gallons (13.8 billion billion cu. m) of water on the Earth. Less than 3 percent is fresh water. The rest is the salt water of the oceans. Of the small amount of fresh water, much is frozen as ice, and some is too deep underground to be easily obtainable. Only about one-tenth of the fresh water is available for human use.

About 1,200 billion gallons (45.4 billion cu. m) of water are available in the United States each day. Over 300 billion gallons (11.4 billion cu. m) a day are used. Industry uses about half of this. More than a third irrigates farms. About 20 billion gallons (0.75 billion cu. m) are used for drinking, washing, sanitation, and fire fighting.

Rain is the source of most of our water supply. Most of the rain falling on a city runs into a sewer, then usually into a river. In open country, some of the rain runs off the surface of the land into small streams. The streams join and flow into a river. Some of the rainwater evaporates, and some soaks into the ground. The groundwater may be taken up by

▲ *Waterskiing is a popular sport at DeSoto Bend on the Missouri River in Nebraska. All water-skiers should wear life preservers in case they fall.*

▲ *An expert water-skier gets extra lift with a kite at Cypress Gardens in Florida, where waterskiing shows are held daily.*

plant roots or drain into underground streams. It can be tapped by wells.

Ocean water can be converted to fresh water by *desalinization*—removing the salt. This is most often done by *distillation*—evaporating and condensing the liquid so that the salt and water are separated. Brackish (slightly salty) water can be desalinated by *electrodialysis*—using an electric current to separate the salt. Freezing methods may eventually provide the cheapest way of desalinating salt water. When salt water is frozen, the salt does not become part of the ice. If the ice and salt could be easily separated, fresh water could be obtained.

A farmhouse or a small town can be supplied by nearby sources of water, such as lakes, ponds, or wells. A large town or a city usually needs more water than is available from nearby sources, so water must be brought from far away. Often a river is dammed to form a lake or *reservoir*. An *aqueduct* is a pipeline, canal, or tunnel that carries water from a reservoir to a town or to farmland for irrigation.

Water Treatment Although many rivers and lakes are sources of water supply, they are used also for dumping sewage and industrial wastes. This dumping pollutes the water and makes it unfit for human use. Polluted water can be made clean and pure through several processes.

In a typical treatment plant, the water is first *aerated*—sprayed into the air. The aeration improves the taste and helps in the removal of certain minerals through the purifying action of air and sunlight. Then the water is *coagulated*—chemicals are added that cause small particles to lump together. The water passes into a *sedimentation* tank where the particles are allowed to settle to the bottom. The water is then filtered and chemicals are added. Almost all water is *chlorinated* (chlorine is added in very small amounts) to kill bacteria. In most parts of the United States, water is *fluoridated*—fluorine is put into the water to help prevent tooth decay.

ALSO READ: WATER, WATER CYCLE, WATER POLLUTION, WELLS AND SPRINGS.

WATT, JAMES (1736–1819) James Watt was a Scottish inventor and engineer. The electric unit of power, the watt (W), was named in his honor.

Watt was born in Greenock, Scotland. His father was a merchant. When he was 18 years old, Watt went to London to learn how to be an instrument maker. When he returned to Scotland, he became the instrument maker for the University of Glasgow. In 1764, Watt was asked to repair a small model of the Newcomen atmospheric engine, a machine used to pump water out of mines. While repairing the engine, Watt noticed that it worked very slowly. He began to experiment with the engine, trying to find ways to make it work faster. In 1769, he patented a steam engine that could work faster and do

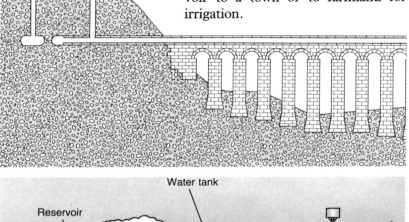

▼ Below: *In the days of ancient Rome, water was carried to towns by aqueducts. Workers drove shafts down to where there was water, and then dug a slightly sloping tunnel so that the water ran out into the aqueduct, which looked rather like a bridge.* Bottom: *Today, our water usually comes from a large reservoir fed by rain and a river. Water from the reservoir goes to the water works to be purified.*

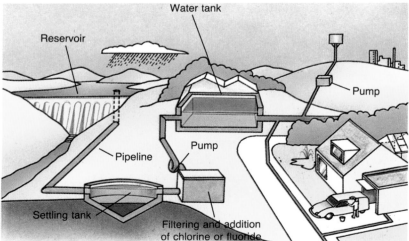

Reservoir

Water tank

Pump

Pipeline

Pump

Settling tank

Filtering and addition of chlorine or fluoride

more varied work than the Newcomen engine.

In 1775, Watt went into business with an engineer named Matthew Boulton. They began manufacturing steam engines, and Watt became very wealthy and successful. His steam engines were used in many factories in Europe and the United States.

Watt spent the rest of his life inventing and improving machines. He developed a new type of propeller for boats, an improved copying press, a machine for reproducing statues, and many other mechanical devices. He is credited with introducing the word "horsepower" as a unit of power.

ALSO READ: ENGINE, ENGINEERING, INVENTION.

WAVE When a stone falls into a pond of water, it pushes molecules of water out of the way. These molecules push against surrounding molecules and bounce back. The pushed molecules in turn push against more molecules. In this way a wave moves across the surface of the water. The wave carries no water with it. If you drop a piece of paper in the water as the wave moves past, the piece of paper will usually move only up and down, not across the water.

A water wave is a *transverse* wave—the molecules move up and down and at right angles to the direction that the wave is moving. Sound waves are *longitudinal* waves—the molecules move in the same direction as the wave, squeezing tightly together and then spreading apart.

What makes waves? Energy does. When a stone is thrown into the water, the moving stone has *energy*. If a stone is thrown at a piece of fragile glass, for example, the glass breaks when the stone hits it. This is because of the energy the stone has as it moves through the air. The heavier the stone, and the faster it is moving, the more energy it has. When a stone hits water, the energy in the stone is transferred to the water in the form of waves moving out across the water from the point where the stone hit.

A wind blowing across a body of water also has energy. Some of the energy in the wind is transferred to the water. The energy of the wind is changed into waves. These waves travel in the same direction as the wind. The stronger the wind blows, the larger the waves. A hurricane can make waves 50 feet (15 m) high. The *tsunamis* ("tidal waves") formed by underwater earthquakes are larger.

Light, X rays, radio waves, and infrared and ultraviolet radiation are all types of *electromagnetic* waves. The energy is carried by changing electric and magnetic fields. They do not have to move through matter but can travel for billions of miles through space.

▲ *James Watt, Scottish inventor and engineer.*

The highest recorded *tsunami*, "tidal wave," appeared near the Ryukyu Islands, Japan, in 1971. It was estimated to be 278 feet (85 m) high.

▼ *Passing waves set stacks of water particles circling. When the water becomes less than half a wavelength deep, the circles flatten out to form ellipses. The waves slow down and crests pile up. Then the crests break on the shore as surf.*

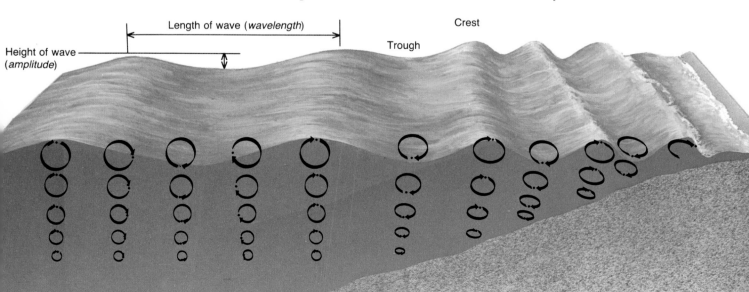

Length of wave (*wavelength*)

Crest

Trough

Height of wave (*amplitude*)

▲ *The very life-like figure of pop singer Michael Jackson is made entirely of wax and stands in Madame Tussaud's wax museum in London, England.*

▲ *Honeybees produce beeswax, which they use to build combs to hold their honey and eggs.*

Electromagnetic waves can be thought of as peaking and troughing like waves in water. When waves all peak and trough together, they are described as *in phase* or *coherent*. When they peak and trough every which way, they are called *out of phase*.

ALSO READ: LASERS AND MASERS, LIGHT, OCEAN, RADIATION, RADIO, RADIO ASTRONOMY, SOUND, SPECTRUM, TELEVISION.

WAX Wax is a moldable, solid substance that has a dull luster. It has a somewhat greasy texture and softens gradually when heated.

Wax is produced both naturally and artificially. It comes from animal, vegetable, and mineral sources. Beeswax is perhaps the best-known type of animal wax. It comes from the abdomen of the worker bee and is used to construct the honeycomb. Lanolin, used in polishes, is a wax taken from the fat that coats the wool of sheep.

Vegetable waxes cover the leaves, nuts, and berries of many plants. The berries of the wax myrtle tree provided the early colonists with wax for candle-making.

Mineral waxes are found in the Earth's crust. They include paraffin, petrolatum, and ozocerite. Paraffin is derived chiefly from the distillation of petroleum and is used for candles, as a preservative, as a fuel, and for waterproofing. Petrolatum, sometimes called petroleum jelly, is a greasy substance used in making ointments, cosmetics, and medicines. Ozocerite is obtained from shale and is used in commercial polishes and candles. Synthetic wax is made from ethylene glycol, a colorless alcohol obtained from petroleum.

People have made faces, figures, and other objects out of wax since earliest times. They discovered that wax can easily be molded when it is soft, and can be tinted by adding coloring. In 1721, a presentation of wax models of the human body was given in Hamburg, Germany. It was the first real waxworks show.

The most famous name in waxworks is that of Madame Marie Tussaud. She operated a waxworks museum in Paris during the French Revolution. In 1802, she went to Britain and opened a waxworks in London. There are now many waxworks exhibits throughout the world.

ALSO READ: BEE, CANDLE, COSMETICS.

WAYNE, ANTHONY (1745–1796) Anthony Wayne was a general in the Continental Army during the American Revolution. He gained the nickname "Mad Anthony" for his daring and valor in combat.

Anthony Wayne was born on the family farm near Paoli, Pennsylvania. His father owned a prosperous leather tannery, which Wayne managed after his father died.

When the American Revolution began in 1775, Wayne became a colonel in the Continental Army. He fought in the battle at Three Rivers, in Canada. He was a brigadier general in the battles of Brandywine, Germantown, and Stony Point. His leadership in the Battle of Stony Point won him a medal from Congress. Wayne was at Valley Forge with George Washington. He also served in Georgia, where the British surrendered to him at Savannah.

After the war, Wayne retired from the military. In 1783, he was given an 800-acre (320-hectare) rice plantation in Georgia, but he could not make a success of it. He represented Pennsylvania in Congress in 1791.

In 1792, President Washington appointed Wayne major general in command of troops on the old northwest frontier. This land was east of the Mississippi River, north of the Ohio River, and west of Pennsylvania.

Other generals had already tried to defeat the Indian tribes of the Wabash and Maumee Rivers. They had failed. Wayne used careful military planning and strategy and trained his troops well before he sent them into combat. On August 20, 1794, he met and defeated a confederation of Shawnee, Ottawa, Chippewa, and Potawatomi Indians in the Battle of Fallen Timbers near what is now Toledo, Ohio. This battle, followed by the Treaty of Greenville, brought peace to the Ohio territory and opened it to white settlement.

ALSO READ: AMERICAN REVOLUTION.

WEAPONS Our earliest African ancestors must have looked very weak and defenseless. All around were animals with "natural weapons," such as large teeth, claws, or tusks. Other animals could run fast to escape from their enemies or climb up to the branches of a tree. Human beings, in comparison, were small creatures with weak hands and small teeth, who could seldom outrun their enemies. But they had a better brain than any of the other animals, and they survived because they were able to make weapons. From the beginning, these weapons were as important to human beings as claws were to a tiger or speed to a gazelle. In the course of a few thousand years, human weapons have developed from the battle-ax to the nuclear bomb. Weapons used to attack an enemy have become known as *offensive* weapons. Those used to ward off enemies or to destroy the enemy's weapons are called *defensive* weapons.

Stone Age hunters learned that they could throw a weapon much farther if they fastened it to the end of a long wooden shaft, to make a spear. They also invented the bow, which could hurl a weapon farther than a person could throw it. The early hunters used their weapons mainly to

kill animals for food and to defend their territory against other bands of hunters. After the first farmers learned how to domesticate (tame) animals, weapons were used more and more against other people, to defend or seize territory. People began to build *fortifications*, or walls, around their settlements. *Siege* weapons, such as battering rams and catapults, were developed for attacking, or *besieging*, fortifications. Defenders on the walls often hurled down rocks or poured boiling oil onto the attackers. The invention of metalworking, first in copper and bronze and then in iron, meant that much sharper and stronger weapons could be made. A deadly weapon called the *crossbow* was invented; it could fire an arrow with great force.

The invention of gunpowder brought about great changes in the history of weapons and warfare. Guns were first used in Europe in the 1300's. They rapidly became the major weapons of war. In the late 1700's, a U.S. manufacturer, Eli Whitney, invented the method of "interchangeable parts," which allowed guns to be mass-produced.

By the time of World War I (1914–1919), new types of explosives, made with chemicals, had been invented. Chemical explosives were

▲ *"Mad Anthony" Wayne and his officers talk with defeated Indian leaders near Greenville. The discussions resulted in the Treaty of Greenville in 1795.*

▼ *Weapons and tools made of stone were used in the early Stone Age. The stones were pebbles and pieces of flint chipped and flaked to make sharp points and edges.*

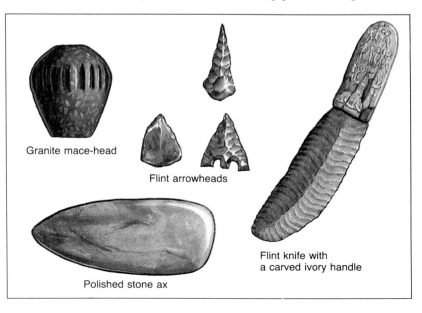

Granite mace-head

Flint arrowheads

Polished stone ax

Flint knife with a carved ivory handle

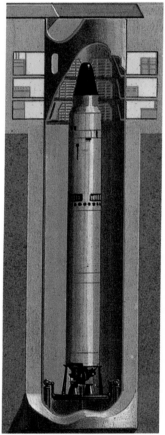

▲ *Weapons have increased vastly in destructiveness over the centuries. The crossbow of the Middle Ages* (top) *could usually kill only one person at a time and took a long time to reload. A Minuteman III missile* (above) *of the late 20th century, shown here in its silo, is capable of killing millions of people.*

used in new weapons, such as bombs, mines, hand grenades, and torpedoes. Special types of vehicles were designed to carry weapons. These included bomber airplanes, battleships, armored tanks, and submarines. During World War II (1939–1945), scientists developed the first atomic bombs (A-bombs). An even more deadly weapon, the thermonuclear or hydrogen bomb (H-bomb) was invented soon after. Warfare is no longer limited to hand-to-hand fighting on the battlefield. Soldiers using modern weapons are often miles away from one another. Rockets carrying nuclear missiles can be fired at targets thousands of miles away and guided by remote control.

ALSO READ: AIR FORCE; ARMOR; ARMY; BOW AND ARROW; EXPLOSIVES; FORTIFICATION; GUNS AND RIFLES; MISSILE; NAVY; ROCKET; SUBMARINE; SWORDS AND KNIVES; TANK; WAR; WHITNEY, ELI.

WEASEL The weasel is a small, meat-eating mammal. It lives in parts of Europe, Asia, and North and South America. In Europe, one kind of weasel is called a stoat. The weasel has a slender body from 6 inches to 2 feet (15–60 cm) long and short legs.

The weasel is a very fast, active animal. It kills by biting its prey at the base of the skull. Weasels are fierce fighters and have been known to kill animals much larger than themselves. They usually eat rabbits, snakes, birds, and rodents such as mice and squirrels.

A weasel has soft underfur with stiff, shiny guard hairs. The fur is usually reddish brown on its back and head, and white on its belly, throat, and feet.

Weasels that live in cold regions turn white when winter comes. Their white fur serves as protective coloring in the snow. One of these weasels is the *ermine*. The tip of its tail is black.

People hunt the ermine for its beautiful fur.

Weasels nest in rocks, trees, or in burrows in the ground. The female may have as many as five to ten young in one litter. Young weasels are able to hunt when they are about eight weeks old.

Minks, martens, ferrets, and polecats belong to the weasel family and are similar in appearance and behavior. Badgers, wolverines, and skunks are also related to weasels but are less similar. Badgers have heavy bodies, thick skin, short legs, and short tails. They have strong front claws and use them to dig elaborate, comfortable burrows. Badgers sleep in their burrows during the day and hunt at night. Wolverines are larger and darker than badgers. A large wolverine weighs about 50 pounds (23 kg) and a badger about 25 pounds (11 kg). Both animals are very strong for their size and are almost fearless.

Skunks are small, gentle animals with attractive black-and-white coats. The skunk is noted for the foul-smelling liquid produced by scent glands under its tail. When a skunk is threatened, it stamps its feet and lifts its tail. If the enemy does not back off, the skunk turns and sprays. The skunk's aim is accurate, and if the

▼ *The weasel has a long, slim body and very sharp teeth.*

male

liquid hits an eye it can cause temporary blindness. After having its scent glands removed, a skunk can be tamed as a pet. The scent glands' liquid is used in making perfume. Clothing has been made from skunk fur.

ALSO READ: MAMMAL, PROTECTIVE COLORING, RODENT.

WEATHER

WEATHER Weather is the condition of the air above a particular place on Earth at a particular time. It varies from place to place and from time to time. Climate is the weather pattern at a particular place over a long period of time. If it rains tomorrow, that affects the weather but does not affect the climate.

Weather is essentially a product of sunlight, air, and water. The sunlight heats the Earth, the water wets the Earth, and the air moves the heat and water around.

The Sun The sun shines for at least a few hours every day on most places on Earth. The Earth receives heat and light from the sun. The amount of heat and light each place receives depends on the angle of the sun's rays and how long the sun shines. The equator becomes very hot because the sun's rays hit it directly. The North Pole is always cold, because even when the sun's rays strike the pole, they strike it at an angle.

Air The air around the Earth is constantly moving. The movement of the air is caused primarily by heat. When air becomes warmer, it expands. The molecules move farther apart, the air becomes lighter, and the air pressure falls. When air becomes cooler, the molecules move closer together, the air becomes heavier, and the air pressure rises. The light, warm air rises, and the heavy, cool air falls. When warm air rises from a place, cool air moves in. This movement of warm

and cool air is *wind*. Winds usually blow from cool places to warm places.

Wind results whenever one place on Earth becomes hotter than another. Sea breezes usually blow in from the ocean during the day because the land is hotter than the water. Land absorbs heat more quickly than water does and gives it off more quickly. So, during the day the air above the land heats up more than the air above the water. The warm land air rises and the cool sea air blows in. In the nighttime, the land cools off more quickly than the water, so a breeze blows from the land out to sea.

These air movements occur also on a large scale. The equator receives much more heat than the poles. As the warm air above the equator rises, the cool air from the poles moves towards the equator. The path of these large-scale air movements is affected by the rotation of the Earth. The rotation causes winds in the Northern Hemisphere to bend to the right (clockwise) and winds in the Southern Hemisphere to bend to the left (counterclockwise). It changes the large-scale air movements into prevailing winds. This bending of the winds (and waters) of the Earth is named the *Coriolis effect*.

The air rising from the equator begins to sink back toward the Earth at about 30 degrees latitude. Part of this sinking air mass moves back toward the equator. Another part continues towards the poles. The Earth's rotation bends the path of the air mass moving toward the equator to form the *trade winds*. These winds blow almost constantly from below 30 degrees latitude to near the equator. In the Northern Hemisphere, the trade winds blow from the northeast, and in the Southern Hemisphere, they blow from the southeast. The path of the air mass that continues moving towards the poles is also bent by the Earth's rotation. This air mass forms the prevailing winds called *westerlies*.

▲ *Badgers do not look much like weasels, but they are in fact from the same family.*

▼ *Some instruments used in weather stations. Anemometers measure wind speeds. Vanes show wind directions. Hygrometers measure humidity. Thermometers record air temperatures. Changing air pressures can be recorded on a rotating drum by barographs.*

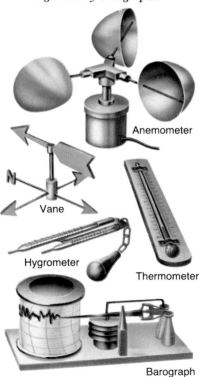

Anemometer

Vane

Hygrometer

Thermometer

Barograph

▲ *Swirling clouds photographed from a satellite. Photographs and TV pictures taken from satellites orbiting (going around) the Earth help meteorologists study the weather.*

▲ *You have probably seen weathercocks on towers and church spires. They are vanes shaped like roosters, which indicate the wind direction.*

In the Northern Hemisphere, the westerlies blow from the southwest. In the Southern Hemisphere, they blow from the northwest.

Water Nearly three-fourths of the Earth's surface is covered with water. This water is in constant motion. Water from the oceans evaporates to form water vapor in the air. The water vapor collects to form clouds. The wind blows the clouds around. Some of the clouds dump their water on the land. The water soaks into the land or runs through streams and rivers to the ocean. Some of the water that has soaked into the land is taken up by plants. The plants give off water vapor (they *transpire*), and this collects with water that has evaporated from the surfaces of rivers, oceans, and so on to form new clouds. These clouds are blown around by the wind until they drop their water back onto the land or into the ocean. This process, the *water cycle*, goes on constantly.

Clouds bring rain when they have more water than they can hold. The amount of water a cloud can hold depends mainly on the temperature of the air in the cloud. Warm air can hold more water vapor than cold air can. The warm air rising from the Earth contains a certain amount of water vapor. As the warm air rises, it becomes cooler. As the air becomes cooler, it can hold less water vapor. Eventually the air reaches the *dew point*, the temperature at which it contains all the water vapor it can hold. Below the dew point the water vapor begins to *condense* (change from gas to liquid), forming drops of water. These drops of water collect to form clouds. As the air in a cloud becomes increasingly cooler, more and more water vapor condenses to form more and larger drops of water. Eventually some of the drops become so large that the air rising under them can no longer support them. These drops fall to the Earth as rain.

Weather Patterns The movements of heat, air, and water across the Earth's surface produce certain characteristic weather patterns. These major patterns vary from place to place.

Near the equator, the air is always warm and is therefore always rising. At about 30 degrees latitude, the warm air that rose from the equator begins to sink back to Earth. So at this latitude, the air is always falling. These two areas (30 degrees north and 30 degrees south) have very calm weather. The area around the equator, called the *doldrums*, has calm, wet weather because of all the water vapor condensing from the rising warm air. The belts around 30 degrees latitude are called the *horse latitudes*, supposedly because so many horses died there on sailing ships stranded by the lack of wind.

The *temperate zones* of the Earth are the areas between 23½ degrees latitude and 66½ degrees latitude, north or south. The weather in these areas ordinarily forms at the *polar fronts*—the lines where the prevailing westerlies collide with the cold air moving from the poles. These air masses move alongside each other for a while. But then the cold air mass begins to cut under the side of the warm air mass. This movement forms a *cold front*. At the same time the front edge of the warm air mass rises over the cold air, forming a *warm front*.

This movement of the warm and cold fronts forms a *cyclone*, a circular movement of air around a low-pressure area. The low-pressure area is the tip of the warm air mass. In the Northern Hemisphere, cyclones move counterclockwise, and in the Southern Hemisphere they move clockwise.

Air also moves around high-pressure areas. This movement is called an *anticyclone*. In the Northern Hemisphere, anticyclones move clockwise. In the Southern Hemisphere they move counterclockwise.

Cyclones and anticyclones result

from, first, the effects of large-scale air movements between high- and low-pressure areas and, second, the Coriolis effect. Air tends to move from high-pressure areas to low-pressure areas, and the Earth's rotation causes the air to move in curves rather than straight lines.

In a low-pressure area, the wind blows towards the center and the air rises, forming clouds and rain. The weather can change suddenly and unpredictably. In a high-pressure area, the weather is usually calm, with light winds, few clouds, and little rain.

Local Conditions Even with the same large-scale air movements, different places can have different weather because of local conditions. Mountains, forests, and large bodies of water are some of the local conditions that can affect the weather.

Air masses moving in from the ocean carry a great deal of water vapor. In order to pass over mountains, the air masses have to rise. If the mountains are high enough, the rising air becomes so cool that its load of

water vapor condenses to form clouds and rain. The rain falls on the ocean side of the mountains. The wind that passes over the mountains has given off all its moisture and is dry, so the land on the other side of the mountains receives little rain. This is why, for example, the western part of the state of Washington is wetter than the eastern part.

Plants hold heat and release it gradually. Because of the lack of plant growth, deserts absorb heat rapidly and give it off rapidly. Although deserts are very hot during the daytime, they cool off very quickly at night. Forested areas have more even temperatures.

Meteorology Meteorology is the study of the atmosphere and of weather. Meteorologists use various instruments to study and forecast the weather. A *barometer* is used to measure the air pressure, a *hygrometer* to measure the humidity (amount of moisture in the air), a *weather vane* to measure wind direction, and an *anemometer* to measure wind speed. A *radiosonde* carried aloft by a balloon

The highest surface wind speed ever recorded was on Mount Washington, New Hampshire, on December 4, 1934. A speed of 231 mph (372 km/hr) was measured. In the upper atmosphere, much higher wind speeds take place. Jet streams of more than 400 mph (640 km/hr) have been recorded at heights of over 150,000 feet (46,000 m).

▼ *A depression occurs when a wedge of warm air is enclosed between areas of cold air. The advancing cold air on the left, bordered by a cold front, undercuts the warm air. Beyond the warm front, warm air rises over the cold air and clouds form.*

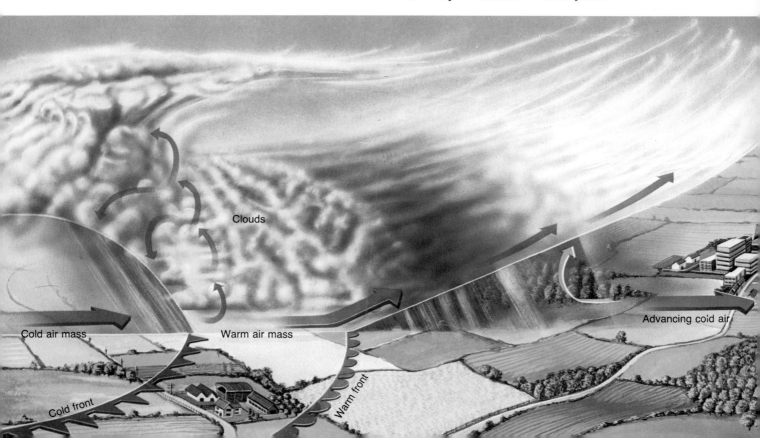

Clouds

Cold air mass

Warm air mass

Advancing cold air

Cold front

Warm front

▲ *Daniel Webster, U.S. statesman.*

"The Devil and Daniel Webster" is a story by Stephen Vincent Benét. The story tells how Daniel Webster was such a clever speaker and lawyer that he saved a man's soul from the devil.

▲ *Noah Webster, who compiled the first dictionary of the English language as used in the United States.*

measures the weather conditions at high altitudes. Today, weather satellites orbit the Earth, sending back pictures of cloud movements and weather disturbances across the Earth's surface.

To know what the weather is going to be like in one place, a meteorologist must have weather reports from many different places. The United States Weather Bureau receives reports from every major station every hour. Smaller stations report every three to six hours. These reports are combined, and meteorologists at individual stations can use this information to forecast the weather in their areas.

For further information on:
Climate, *see* ANTARCTICA, ARCTIC, AUTUMN, CLIMATE, DESERT, GULF STREAM, JUNGLE, LATITUDE AND LONGITUDE, SEASON, SPRING, SUMMER, TUNDRA, WINTER.
Meteorology, *see* ATMOSPHERE, BAROMETER, EARTH, GEOLOGY, PHYSICS, SATELLITE, SCIENCE, SPACE RESEARCH, TEMPERATURE SCALE, THERMOMETER.
Weather Conditions, *see* AURORA, CLOUD, DROUGHT, ECLIPSE, FLOOD, FOG, FROST, HAIL, HURRICANE, LIGHTNING AND THUNDER, MONSOON, RAIN AND SNOW, TORNADO, WIND.
Weather Features, *see* AIR, AIR PRESSURE, HEAT AND COLD, HUMIDITY, LIGHT, SKY, SUN, WATER, WATER CYCLE.

WEAVING see SPINNING AND WEAVING.

WEBSTER, DANIEL (1782–1852) Daniel Webster was a U.S. statesman who served his country as a senator and as secretary of state during the first half of the 1800's. He was a fine public speaker whose speeches helped preserve the Union before the Civil War.

Webster was born in Salisbury, New Hampshire. He was a graduate from Dartmouth College and later became a successful lawyer. A member of the Federalist Party, he was elected to Congress in 1812. In 1816, he moved to Boston, Massachusetts, and was appointed to the U.S. Senate in 1827.

In speaking in the Senate and in arguing cases before the Supreme Court, Webster spoke eloquently for a strong Constitution and strong national government. He had an impressive physical appearance and a fine speaking voice.

John C. Calhoun and other Southerners said that state governments had the right to nullify (cancel) federal laws. In a debate with Senator Robert Y. Hayne of South Carolina in 1830, Webster attacked this idea. The words, "Liberty *and* Union, now and forever, one and inseparable," are often quoted from his speech in the Webster-Hayne debate.

In 1840, Webster became secretary of state under President William Henry Harrison. He completed an agreement with Great Britain, known as the Webster-Ashburton Treaty (1842), which settled the northeast boundary dispute between the United States and Canada. He returned to the Senate in 1845, and in a famous speech he supported the Compromise of 1850. Webster's argument for compromise between the North and the South probably put off the Civil War for ten years. In 1850, he became secretary of state under Millard Fillmore.

Webster wanted the Whig nomination for the Presidency in 1852, but he did not receive it. He died on October 24 of that year.

ALSO READ: CALHOUN, JOHN C.; CIVIL WAR; FILLMORE, MILLARD; HARRISON, WILLIAM HENRY.

WEBSTER, NOAH (1758–1843) Noah Webster was a U.S. educator and writer. He wrote the first U.S.

dictionary, which became known as "Webster's Dictionary." Besides the usual English words, it included some words that had come into usage in the United States from North American Indian languages, from African tongues, and from several European countries.

Webster was born in West Hartford, Connecticut. He was educated at Yale College and later studied law, supporting himself by teaching school. Webster found that few U.S. textbooks were being used in the schools. The United States had only recently won its independence, and teachers were still using British books. Webster wrote three textbooks using U.S. words and stories. The most successful of these was his *Elementary Spelling Book*, which was used for many years.

Webster practiced law for several years and later worked as editor of two newspapers. He was knowledgeable about many subjects, including science, medicine, and history. Webster published his first dictionary in 1806, after working on it for three years. He then made a more detailed study of the English language and traveled to Britain and France to consult other scholars. In 1828, he published his greatest work, *An American Dictionary of the English Language*. This dictionary established set forms of spelling and pronunciation in the United States. It included words that were particularly North American. It has since been revised many times and is still on sale.

ALSO READ: DICTIONARY.

WEED see GARDENING.

WEIGHT Every object pulls every other object toward it—even two pencils at rest on a desk. This pull is called the gravitational force. The size of the gravitational force depends on two things—the mass (quantity of matter) of each object and the distance between them.

Unless an object is very massive, its gravitational pull is not very large. The Earth is large enough to have a noticeable gravitational pull on the objects on its surface. The gravitational pull of the Earth on an object is called the *weight* of that object.

The weight of an object can change in three ways. If the object gains mass, it becomes heavier; and, if it loses mass, it becomes lighter. If the object moves closer to the Earth's surface, it becomes heavier; and, if it moves away from the Earth, it becomes lighter. If an object were to be moved from the Earth to a more massive planet, such as Jupiter, it would become heavier. If it were moved to a less massive planet, such as Mercury, it would become lighter.

In outer space, far enough from other objects so that their gravitational pull is very slight, an object becomes almost weightless. Astronauts traveling from Earth to the moon experience weightlessness.

ALSO READ: GRAVITY AND GRAVITATION, MATTER, MEASUREMENT.

WEIGHT LIFTING Weight lifting is a sport in which people lift heavy weights according to certain rules. Many people lift weights for exercise or recreation. Others compete in contests to see who can lift the heaviest weights. Weight lifting has been an Olympic sport since 1920.

The standard equipment for weight lifting is a *barbell* and *weights*. A barbell is a straight steel rod, and a weight is a metal disk with a hole through the center. Weights of different sizes are slipped onto the barbell and attached with clamps. Different numbers and sizes of disks produce different weights for lifting. A *dumbbell* is a short metal bar with a weight permanently attached at each

▲ *Instruments called balances are used to measure weights. This analytical balance, patented by F. Sartorius in 1870, could detect a difference of weight of about 3½ millionths of an ounce (one-tenth of a milligram)— outstanding for an instrument of that time. Modern balances are even more sensitive.*

If something weighs 440 pounds (200 kg) on Earth, it will weigh 70 pounds (32 kg) on the moon, 170 pounds (77 kg) on Mars, 400 pounds (180 kg) on Venus, and 1,200 pounds (540 kg) on Jupiter.

▲ *Precious McKenzie, a flyweight weight lifter. Olympic flyweights weigh no more than about 114 pounds (52 kg), but regularly lift more than four times their bodyweight.*

▲ *The first Duke of Wellington, British soldier and statesman.*

▲ *H.G. Wells, British novelist and historian.*

end. Dumbbells are used for exercise.

The events in a weight-lifting competition are: the *press*, the *snatch*, and the *clean-and-jerk*. The weight lifter begins each lift by crouching slightly in front of the barbell and gripping the bar firmly with both hands. At the peak of the lift, the lifter stands with legs straight, arms fully extended and locked, and the weight under control. In the press, the weight lifter lifts the barbell to shoulder height in one motion, then pauses, and, with a second motion, raises the barbell overhead. The weight lifter cannot move the feet or bend the legs during the second motion of the press.

In the snatch, the weight lifter lifts the barbell from the floor straight overhead in one motion. He or she can move the feet and bend the legs during the lift.

The clean-and-jerk is similar to the press in that the weight is lifted to the shoulders with one motion and then overhead with a second motion. The weight lifter can gain added power by moving the feet and bending the legs.

The winner of a competition is the lifter who has the highest total for the three lifts. The best superheavyweights may lift a total of over 1,350 pounds (614 kg) in three lifts.

ALSO READ: EXERCISE, MUSCLE.

WELLINGTON, DUKE OF (1769–1852) Arthur Wellesley, the first Duke of Wellington, was one of Britain's greatest military generals. He was a strict commander and is often known as the "Iron Duke."

Arthur Wellesley was born in Dublin, Ireland. He was sent to school in England and later attended a military academy in France. At the age of 18, he became an officer in the British army. From 1796 to 1805, Wellesley served in India, where he defeated the armies of several local princes and was made a general.

When Wellesley returned from India, Napoleon had conquered much of Europe and was threatening to invade Britain. In 1808, Wellesley was sent with an army to attack Napoleon's forces in Spain and Portugal. By 1814, the British had driven the French out of these regions. As a reward for this victory, Wellesley was given the title "Duke of Wellington."

In 1815, Napoleon escaped from the island of Elba, where he had been imprisoned, and raised another army. Wellington was put in command of the British and Dutch armies in Belgium. With the help of a Prussian (German) army under General Gebhard von Blücher, Wellington finally defeated Napoleon at Waterloo. Wellington served as prime minister of Britain from 1828 to 1830.

ALSO READ: WATERLOO.

WELLS, H. G. (1866–1946) Herbert George Wells was a British writer of science fiction and history. He was born in Bromley, England, and studied science at the University of London. He was a clerk, usher, teacher, and journalist, before becoming a writer.

Wells is probably best known for his science-fiction novels. His book *The Time Machine* (1895) is about a scientist who invents a marvelous machine that takes him into the future. *The War of the Worlds* (1898) is a frightening story of an attack on Earth by creatures from Mars.

Wells's scientific studies helped him to write about many ideas and inventions not known in his day.

ALSO READ: SCIENCE FICTION.

WELLS AND SPRINGS In most places, if you dig a deep enough hole, you will hit water. A hole dug for the purpose of finding water is a well. In some places, water flows freely from a small opening in the ground. This natural flow of water is called a spring. Springs with water warmer than body temperature are called hot springs. Hot Springs, Arkansas, is noted as a health resort because of the waters there.

The water that flows from wells and springs comes from the groundwater held beneath the Earth's surface. Rainwater soaks into the ground and sinks until it hits rock. If the rock is cracked, the water will continue to sink until it reaches a level where the rock is unbroken. If the rock is *porous* (has many small holes in it, like sandstone), water will sink through it until the water reaches a layer of rock that is not porous. The nonporous layer holds the water in an area called the *saturated zone*. The upper level of water in the saturated zone is called the *water table*. In order to provide water for use aboveground, a well must be dug down to the water table.

The distance from the Earth's surface down to the water table depends not only on how deep the nonporous layer of rock is, but also on the amount of underground water. After heavy rains or after snow melts in the spring, there will be more groundwater, and the water table will be higher. In dry periods, the water table will be lower, or it will disappear altogether, because no water is soaking into the ground. When the water table gets too low, the well runs dry.

In some places, a layer of porous rock is sandwiched between two layers of nonporous rock. If these layers of rock follow the shape of a hill, then there are two water tables. One is on top of the upper nonporous layer; the other is between the two nonporous layers. If you dig a well through the upper layer and into the sandwiched porous layer, water will flow out of the top of the well. If the rainwater enters the porous layer near the top of a high hill, and if the well is dug at the bottom of the hill, the water may shoot from the well high into the air.

The weight of the water flowing downhill produces the pressure that makes the water shoot out. This kind of well is an *artesian well*.

A hot spring is usually formed when water is heated by rocks deep underground. If the water becomes hot enough, it boils and forms steam, and the water can shoot into the air. This is called a *geyser*. One well-known geyser is Old Faithful in Yellowstone National Park.

A river cutting a valley may cut through a water table and the nonporous rock beneath it. The part of the water table left behind is called a *perched water table*. Rainwater flows down to the nonporous layer of rock, and then it flows sideways to where the river cuts through the rock layers. The water then flows out of the side of the valley to form a spring. Springs may dry up during periods of little rain. In ancient times, when no one understood what made a spring flow, springs were worshiped as gifts of the gods.

Wells can be drilled, dug, or driven, depending on the soil and rock and the height of the water table. The bottom of the well, below the water table, is lined with porous material so the water can seep through. The upper part of the well is lined with nonporous material to keep out soil and surface water that may be contaminated. A well should always be located uphill from a sewage system and far from any source of contamination, such as waste depositories or barnyards.

ALSO READ: GEYSER, WATER, WATER SUPPLY.

▲ *Steam from geysers in New Zealand's North Island is piped to a geothermal power station, where the heat is used to generate electricity.*

▼ *Artesian wells are wells whose water gushes to the surface under its own pressure. They occur where there is a layer of porous rocks through which water can flow (the layer is called an aquifer), and where the uppermost level of the underground water (the water table) is above the surface of the land. If you dig down to the aquifer, water comes from your well because of the water pressure.*

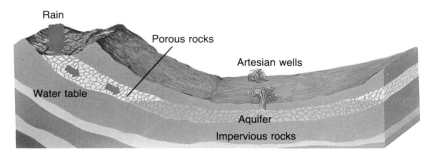

Rain

Porous rocks

Artesian wells

Water table

Aquifer

Impervious rocks

▲ *Charles Wesley, one of the founders of the Methodist Church.*

WEREWOLF see ANIMALS OF MYTH AND LEGEND.

WESLEY, JOHN AND CHARLES

The Wesley brothers were British religious leaders. John Wesley (1703–1791) was the founder of the Methodist Church, one of the largest Protestant churches. Charles Wesley (1707–1788) is best known for his hymns. The Wesleys were the sons of Samuel Wesley, a minister of the Church of England.

The brothers were born in Lincolnshire, England, and attended Oxford University. While at Oxford, Charles Wesley and some of his friends formed a religious society called the Holy Club. John Wesley returned to Oxford to teach in 1729 and became a member of the club. Its members studied the Bible and did good works. They practiced religion in such an orderly and methodical way that other students mocked the members of the club, calling them "Methodists."

In 1738, within a few days of one another, the Wesley brothers each had religious "awakenings" that changed their lives. They both became *evangelists*, or traveling preachers. Charles Wesley's hymns include "Jesus, Lover of My Soul" and the popular Christmas carol, "Hark, the Herald Angels Sing." John Wesley

traveled widely throughout the British Isles, riding on horseback over 5,000 miles (8,000 km) a year. He taught that people can be saved through faith in Jesus Christ. John Wesley formed many Methodist societies in the places he visited. He did not actually intend to start a new church. He wanted mainly to renew people's interest in the Church of England.

The Church of England, however, strongly opposed John Wesley's emotional way of preaching. The Methodists began to train their own preachers and gradually formed their own church. A personal difference between the brothers caused Charles Wesley to withdraw from active leadership in the Methodist societies. In 1784, John Wesley announced that the Methodist societies operated independently from the Church of England. Methodist missionaries then traveled to many parts of the world, including the United States. The Methodist Church in the United States today has about 13 million members.

ALSO READ: EVANGELIST, PROTESTANT CHURCHES.

WESTERN SAMOA see PACIFIC ISLANDS, POLYNESIA.

WEST GERMANY see GERMANY.

WEST INDIES The West Indies are a long chain of islands stretching about 2,000 miles (3,200 km) from Mexico and Florida to South America. The islands separate the Atlantic Ocean from the Caribbean Sea and extend a little into the Gulf of Mexico. Their total land area is about 91,000 square miles (235,700 sq. km), and their population is around 30 million people.

When Columbus discovered the

▼ *John Wesley preaching to Indians in Georgia.*

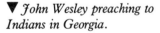

Americas in 1492, he came first to the West Indies. He thought he had found islands just east of India, so he called them the Indies Islands. They were later referred to as the West Indies to distinguish them from the East Indies, which lie between Asia and Australia.

Early mapmakers often marked on maps imaginary islands called Antilia. Some people thought the new islands found by Columbus might be Antilia, so they named them the Antilles. Today, the islands of the West Indies (excluding the Bahamas) are sometimes called the Antilles. The four large westernmost islands in the West Indies—Cuba, Jamaica, Hispaniola (shared by Haiti and the Dominican Republic), and Puerto Rico—are the Greater Antilles. The smaller islands curving south from Puerto Rico are referred to as the Lesser Antilles, which are divided into the Leeward Islands and the Windward Islands. ("Leeward" means away from the wind.) The French and the Dutch share one of the Leeward Islands, St. Martin (in French) or St. Maarten (in Dutch). The islands of Barbados and Trinidad and Tobago are in the southeastern part of the Lesser Antilles. The Netherlands Antilles are Dutch islands just north of Venezuela in the southern Caribbean, where huge refineries process much of Venezuela's oil. Curaçao, Aruba, and Bonaire are the largest Dutch islands. Willemstad, a city on Curaçao, is the capital of the Netherlands Antilles.

The Bahamas are a scattering of islands between Florida and Hispaniola. Much farther north, and not really a part of the West Indies, are the islands of Bermuda.

Geographers believe the islands of the West Indies may be the tips of an underwater mountain chain that once formed a bridge of dry land between North and South America. Many of the islands were formed by volcanic eruptions. Some islands consist only of coral and sand built up on sub-merged peaks or on land that sank beneath the waves.

Climate and Resources The West Indies are in the hot tropics. But because they are surrounded by the sea, the ocean breezes help to cool them. Hurricanes often occur in late summer, causing great damage when they sweep overland.

The crops best suited to these islands are sugar, tropical fruits, tobacco, cacao (for chocolate), coffee, cotton, and sisal (for rope). Offshore fishing is a common occupation. Textile mills, furniture making, and handicrafts provide some employment. Industry has grown in Puerto Rico because of tax benefits given to manufacturers and because of the development of electric power.

The islands are not rich in minerals, but there are nickel and iron ore in Cuba, bauxite for aluminum in Jamaica, and oil and natural asphalt in Trinidad. Tourism is an important industry in many of the islands. Airplanes bring in thousands of visitors from the chilly parts of North America during the winter months. In general, however, the West Indies are poor. Wages are low and luxuries few. Without major industries or large farms, there cannot be the

▲ *Sugar is the chief product of the island of Martinique, in the West Indies. The island was settled by the French in 1635.*

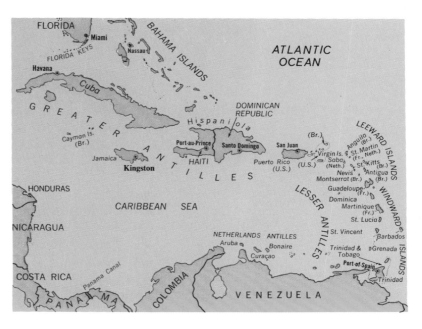

ANTIGUA AND BARBUDA

Capital City: Saint John's.
Area: 171 square miles (442 sq. km).
Population: 100,000.

BAHAMAS

Capital City: Nassau.
Area: 5,380 square miles (13,935 sq. km).
Population: 200,000.

BARBADOS

Capital City: Bridgetown.
Area: 166 square miles (431 sq. km).
Population: 300,000.

CUBA

Capital City: Havana.
Area: 44,218 square miles (114,515 sq. km).
Population: 10,105,000.

DOMINICA

Capital City: Roseau.
Area: 290 square miles (751 sq. km).
Population: 100,000.

DOMINICAN REPUBLIC

Capital City: Santo Domingo.
Area: 18,816 square miles (48,734 sq. km).
Population: 6,200,000.

profits and savings of mass production. Populations are too large for many of the smaller islands, and unemployment is widespread.

The People Most West Indians are black or of mixed ancestry, the descendants of black slaves brought over from Africa in earlier days to work on the plantations and in the mines. Cuba, Puerto Rico, and the Dominican Republic have a high proportion of people of European descent. Many people in Trinidad are descendants of workers brought from India.

Virtually no descendants survive of the first inhabitants of the islands, the Arawak and Carib Indians. Their ancestors were almost entirely wiped out by diseases brought by Europeans or through mistreatment by early colonizers.

Nations of the West Indies There are now 13 independent nations in the West Indies. Some islands or groups of islands remain territorial possessions of Great Britain, France, the Netherlands, and the United States.

Cuba is the largest island nation of the Antilles. It was a Spanish colony until the U.S. war with Spain in 1898. When the United States won, it insisted that Cuba be free and that Puerto Rico become a part of the United States. The last parts of the Spanish empire had won their freedom. (See the articles on CUBA and PUERTO RICO.)

Haiti occupies the western third of the island of Hispaniola. The name Haiti is an Arawak Indian word meaning "many mountains." Haiti was the first West Indian nation to become independent. In the late 1700's, a daring man named Toussaint l'Ouverture led a revolt of Haitian slaves against the French. He was tricked and captured, but his follower, Jean-Jacques Dessalines, called "the Tiger," continued the struggle. At last, in 1804, Haiti de-

clared its independence, the first black republic in the world.

Unfortunately Haitians, as slaves, had never been educated nor had the chance to learn the art of government. After their first strong leaders died, the country was plagued by civil war and banditry. U.S. Marines occupied Haiti from 1915 to 1934 to try to maintain order. In 1957, François Duvalier (called "Papa Doc") was elected president. He organized a cruel secret police service called the *Tontons Macoutes* and made himself dictator. His son, Jean-Claude Duvalier (called "Baby Doc"), succeeded him in 1971 but was forced to flee the country in 1986.

The Dominican Republic occupies the other two-thirds of Hispaniola. Christopher Columbus's brother, Bartholomew, founded the capital city of Santo Domingo as early as 1496. The country became independent in 1844. It, too, suffered from political turmoil. When the Dominicans refused a U.S. demand to establish a stable government in 1916, U.S. troops occupied the country and remained until 1924. A military leader named Rafael Trujillo Molina was elected president in 1930 and ruled until he was killed in 1961.

In 1962, Juan Bosch, a Dominican politician with supposed Communist sympathies, was elected president. The following year a small group of

▼ *A scene in Dominica. Stems of bananas are ferried out to the refrigerated ship for transport all over the world.*

▲ *The warm Caribbean Sea is ideal for all sorts of water sports—sailing, swimming, scuba diving, and windsurfing.*

military officers seized power. In 1965, a revolt began with the object of putting Bosch back in power. U.S. troops were sent to help evacuate U.S. citizens and to prevent a Communist takeover of the country. In 1966, Joaquín Balaguer defeated Bosch for president. In 1978, Antonio Guzmán was elected president. He was succeeded in 1982 by Jorge Blanco.

Jamaica is an Indian word meaning "island of springs." Now an independent country, Jamaica was a Spanish colony from 1494 until the British captured it in 1655. It became a British pirate base and the main slave market of the Caribbean.

Most of the British colonies in the Antilles joined to form a West Indies Federation in 1958. But a union of such scattered islands proved unworkable. Jamaica and Trinidad and Tobago decided to become separate, independent countries in 1962. Jamaica's capital and largest city is Kingston, an important Caribbean seaport.

Jamaican farmers grow sugar, bananas, oranges, and grapefruit. Jamaica produces excellent ginger and much of the world's allspice. The island is a leading source of the aluminum ore called bauxite. But the chief source of income is tourism.

Barbados, which means "bearded," was named by the Portuguese for the long wisps of fiber hanging from the island's fig trees. It is the most densely populated of the West Indies with an average of more than 1,800 people living on each square mile (700 people on each sq. km). The most eastern of the West Indies, Barbados is almost entirely surrounded by coral reefs. It became independent in 1966.

Trinidad and Tobago are two islands, but one country. Trinidad is best known for its colorful capital, Port-of-Spain, and for a huge lake of liquid asphalt almost two miles (3 km) around. The calypso (story-telling) music of Trinidad developed from African and Spanish rhythms. The two islands lie near the coast of Venezuela. Tobago, the smaller island, has a neighboring small island known as Bird of Paradise Island. It is the home of these unusual birds.

The Bahamas, off the Florida coast, consist of some 700 islands and more than 2,000 reefs and keys of rock or coral. Columbus landed in 1492 at San Salvador in the Bahamas. The islands were a British colony from 1717 to 1973, when they became independent.

Grenada, the southernmost of the Windward Islands, is called the "spice isle" because of the nutmegs, cloves, cinnamon, and cacao that grow abundantly there. It became independent in 1974, after more than 200 years of British control. In 1983, the United States and other countries invaded Grenada to remove its Marxist government. Other British possessions in the Windward Islands have recently gained independence: Dominica in 1978 and St. Lucia and St. Vincent (including its dependent islands, the Grenadines) in 1979. Antigua and neighboring Barbuda, both in the Leeward Islands, became an independent nation in 1981, and St. Christopher and Nevis (St. Kitts-

GRENADA

Capital: Saint George's.
Area: 133 sq. mi. (344 sq. km).
Population: 100,000.

HAITI

Capital City: Port-au-Prince.
Area: 10,714 sq. mi. (27,750 sq. km).
Population: 5,800,000.

JAMAICA

Capital City: Kingston.
Area: 4,244 sq. mi. (10,991 sq. km).
Population: 2,300,000.

SAINT CHRISTOPHER AND NEVIS

Capital City: Basseterre.
Area: 101 sq. mi. (262 sq. km).
Population: 40,000.

SAINT LUCIA

Capital City: Castries.
Area: 238 sq. mi. (616 sq. km).
Population: 100,000.

SAINT VINCENT AND THE GRENADINES

Capital City: Kingstown.
Area: 150 sq. mi. (388 sq. km).
Population: 100,000.

TRINIDAD AND TOBAGO

Capital City: Port of Spain.
Area: 1,981 sq. mi. (5,130 sq. km).
Population: 1,200,000.

See also the article on CUBA.

▲ *The uniforms of the police in the Bahamas are a reminder of the nation's years as a British colony.*

▼ *Westminster Abbey in London, England, where many British monarchs and statesmen are buried.*

Nevis) became independent in 1983. The Cayman Islands, the Turks and Caicos Islands, Montserrat, and the British Virgin Islands remain under the control of Great Britain.

The U.S. Virgin Islands in the Lesser Antilles once belonged to Denmark. The United States bought them in 1917 for 25 million dollars. St. Croix, St. Thomas, and St. John are the three main islands. The sunny climate and lovely beaches bring many tourists there. Charlotte Amalie on St. Thomas is the capital of the U.S. Virgin Islands. In 1956, the Virgin Islands National Park opened on St. John. The park has lush plants, colorful birds, and undersea coral.

Bermuda is a group of some 300 coral islands, of which 20 are inhabited. The coral formed on the peaks of huge underwater mountains that almost reach the surface of the sea. Bermuda is about 570 miles (920 km) east of North Carolina. Easter lilies are raised for export. The beautiful scenery and beaches and the moderate climate attract many tourists. Bermuda was discovered by a Spanish sea captain, Juan de Bermúdez, but settled by the British. Its parliament dates from 1620. Hamilton is the capital and main port.

Guadeloupe and Martinique are French possessions in the West Indies. Guadeloupe consists of two main islands—Basse-Terre and Grande-Terre—and several small dependencies. The volcano, La Soufrière, on Basse-Terre erupted violently in 1976 and 1977, causing thousands of people to flee to Grande-Terre. Guadeloupe's capital is Basse-Terre, located on the island of the same name. Its largest city is Pointe-à-Pitre. Martinique has a volcano, Mont Pelée, which erupted in 1902 and destroyed the city of Saint-Pierre. Fort-de-France is Martinique's capital.

ALSO READ: CARIBBEAN SEA, CORAL, CUBA, ISLAND, NORTH AMERICA, PUERTO RICO, VOLCANO.

WESTMINSTER ABBEY Westminster Abbey stands close to the Thames River in the city of Westminster, London, England. The kings and queens of England, and later of Britain, have been crowned in Westminster Abbey since 1066 (except Edward V and Edward VIII). Many of the greatest men and women in British history are buried in the abbey.

Westminster Abbey was founded in about 1050 by King Edward the Confessor. It was called an abbey because the earlier churches on the site had been part of a monastery. The main part of the abbey was built between the 1200's and the 1500's. The church is shaped like a giant cross. The *nave*, or main hall, is 531 feet (162 m) long. Near the eastern end of the church another hall, called a *transept*, crosses the nave at right angles to form the short arms of the cross. The southern part of the transept is known as Poets' Corner. Many great British poets are buried there, including Chaucer and Tennyson. In the chapel of Edward the Confessor stands the ancient coronation chair of the British monarchs.

ALSO READ: BRITISH ISLES, EDWARD THE CONFESSOR, ENGLISH HISTORY.

WEST POINT see UNITED STATES SERVICE ACADEMIES.

WEST VIRGINIA Most of West Virginia lies in a vast coal region that stretches from Alabama to Pennsylvania. Only Kentucky produces more coal each year than West Virginia does.

Coal brings West Virginia hundreds of millions of dollars every year. It also presents problems that are hard to solve. There are two kinds of coal mines in West Virginia. One is the underground mine. The other is

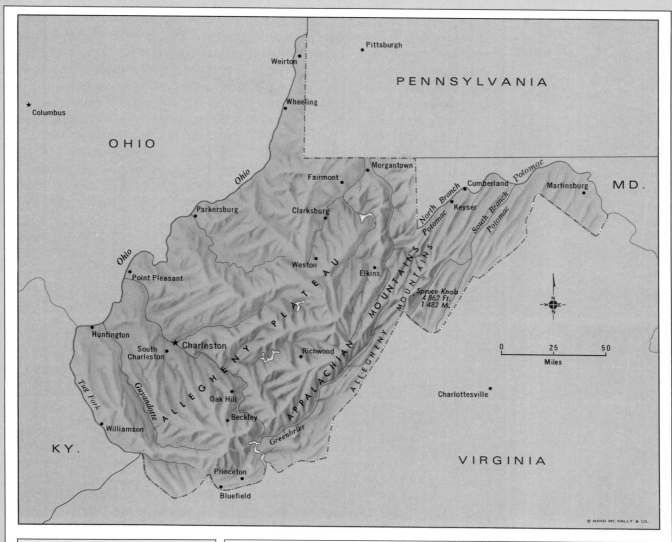

OHIO

PENNSYLVANIA

★ Columbus

Weirton

Pittsburgh

Wheeling

Morgantown

Cumberland

Potomac

Martinsburg

MD.

Fairmont

Clarksburg

Parkersburg

North Branch Potomac

Keyser

South Branch Potomac

Ohio

Weston

Elkins

Spruce Knob
4,862 Ft.
1,482 M.

ALLEGHENY MOUNTAINS

ALLEGHENY MOUNTAINS

APPALACHIAN MOUNTAINS

ALLEGHENY PLATEAU

Point Pleasant

Ohio

Huntington

★ Charleston

South
Charleston

Richwood

Charlottesville

Tug Fork

Guyandotte

Oak Hill

Beckley

Greenbrier

VIRGINIA

Williamson

KY.

Princeton

Bluefield

N
W—E
S

0   25   50
Miles

© RAND MC NALLY & CO.

WEST VIRGINIA

Capital and largest city
Charleston (64,000 people)

Area
24,181 square miles (62,629 sq.
km) Rank: 41st

Population
1,876,000
Rank: 34th

Statehood
June 20, 1863
(35th state admitted)

Principal river
Ohio River

Highest point
Spruce Knob; 4,862 feet (1,482 m)

Motto
Montani Semper Liberi ("Moun-
taineers Are Always Free")

Song
"The West Virginia Hills"

Famous people
Pearl Buck, General Thomas
"Stonewall" Jackson

STATE EMBLEMS

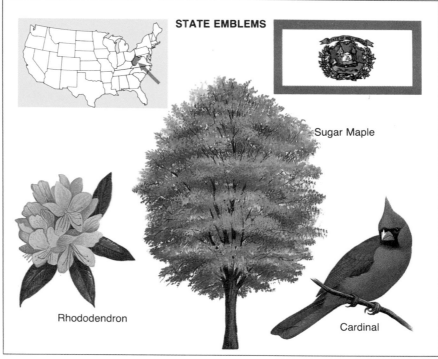

Sugar Maple

Rhododendron

Cardinal

▲ *A commanding lookout over the scenic West Virginian countryside from Hawk's Nest.*

the strip mine, or surface mine. Underground mines are dangerous. In spite of safety rules and new machines, accidents still happen. When they do, miners may be killed.

Strip mines are safer. In these mines, large power shovels dig coal that lies near the surface. Miners work by daylight in the open air. Strip mining costs less than mining coal underground, but it leaves wide, ugly holes in the ground. Sometimes mining companies turn these holes into lakes, or they spread topsoil in them and plant trees. But strip mining has ruined much beautiful country. A West Virginia member of Congress has said it should be forbidden by law. Many people agree, but many do not.

The Land and Climate The shape of West Virginia might make you think of a strange, thick-bodied animal. Look at the map of the state. The pointed nose is pushed between Pennsylvania and Maryland. One foreleg is between Ohio and Pennsylvania, and the other is between Maryland and Virginia. Notice the floppy paw at the end.

West Virginia is in the great Appalachian Highland. The eastern part of the state is in the Appalachian Mountains. But most of it is in the western part of the highland, or the Allegheny Plateau. The plateau is made up of long ridges. Westward from the mountains, the ridges become lower.

Except in the state's northeastern leg, all rivers flow toward the Ohio River. The rivers show the directions in which the land slopes.

Because West Virginia is very mountainous, its river valleys are unusually important. All of the state's main roads and railroads follow rivers. The larger rivers are used for water transportation. Tow-boats pull heavy barges up and down the Kanawha, the Ohio, and other rivers. Most of the level farmland is in the river valleys. Good cropland and good

transportation made people want to live and work in the valleys, and so most of West Virginia's towns grew up there.

West Virginian weather depends upon the altitude. The climate of Spruce Knob, the highest point—4,862 feet (1,482 m)—is very different from that of the lowest, on the Potomac River—247 feet (75.3 m). In general, West Virginia has hot summers with plenty of rain. The higher parts have less heat and more rain than the lower areas. Winters are rather cold. In the lowlands, however, snow is likely to stay only three or four days before melting. High in the mountains, it may last through most of the winter.

History Not many Indians lived in what is now West Virginia. Some Tuscaroras, Shawnees, and Delawares had villages on the edges of the area, but most Indians came only to hunt and fish in the wooded mountains. Many obtained salt from salty springs.

West Virginia's written history begins with the coming of Europeans. But until the Civil War, that history is part of Virginia's. West Virginia lay within the boundaries of Virginia. In the 1700's, this section was frontier country. It was settled after 1731 by men and women from Pennsylvania and Maryland.

This northwestern part of Virginia was different from eastern Virginia. The northwestern farms were small. Farming was done by the owners and their families. The large and rich eastern plantations were worked by slaves. Easterners played a bigger part in governing Virginia. In western Virginia, therefore, people were discontented. They remained remote and dissatisfied after the American Revolution. Many of them talked about having a state of their own.

The Civil War gave such people the chance they wanted. In 1861, Virginia decided to leave the Union. The northwestern counties were strongly against the move. They separated themselves from the rest of Virginia and formed a new state. Virginian troops tried to hold West Virginia. There was hard fighting. Union forces fought on West Virginia's side, and they won. In 1863, West Virginia became the 35th state. Wheeling was the first capital. Charleston has been the capital since 1885.

West Virginians at Work Before the Civil War, nearly all the people of northwestern Virginia were farmers. But there were other occupations. Some people produced salt from the waters of salty springs, and others mined coal. Some people ran small mills that wove woolen cloth.

Today, manufacturing is the big industry of West Virginia. The leading manufacture is of chemical products. Both salt and coal are used in manufacturing them. Next in importance are iron and steel. West Virginian coal provides fuel for the furnaces. The state is also known for its glassware and pottery.

Mining coal is the state's second biggest business. Not all the coal is used in West Virginia. A large amount is sold elsewhere. And power produced from coal goes outside the state. Coal is burned in West Virgin-

▲ *Lush grasslands and tree laden hills stand before the Seneca Rocks in rural West Virginia.*

ian electric-power plants. Cables take the electricity to cities and factories far away. West Virginia also has valuable deposits of oil, natural gas, limestone, and sandstone.

Agriculture is well behind mining in dollars earned. Milk, beef, chickens, and eggs are the main livestock products. Hay, wheat, peaches, and apples are the leading crops.

The region known as Appalachia, of which West Virginia is a part, is one of the poorest in the United States. Unemployment is a serious problem and has forced many people to leave the state. Recently, however, coal companies have invested more money in mining and have found new markets at home and overseas for their product.

Tourism is increasingly popular in the state, whose forested mountains offer many pleasant places for recreation. State parks, such as Blackwater Falls and Hawks Nest, and historical spots, such as Harpers Ferry (where John Brown's raid took place in 1859), are visited by many people.

ALSO READ: APPALACHIAN MOUNTAINS; BROWN, JOHN; JACKSON, THOMAS JONATHAN "STONEWALL"; VIRGINIA.

▼ *Colonial days are re-enacted by these volunteers in period costume at the restored site of Picketts Port, West Virginia.*

Harpers Ferry, West Virginia, is where John Brown led his infamous raid on the U.S. Armory in 1859 and so became the folk hero of the song "John Brown's Body." The town is now restored to its Civil War days as the Harpers Ferry National Historic Park and attracts many visitors.

WESTWARD MOVEMENT In 1775, at the outbreak of the American Revolution, the United States was made up of 13 sparsely populated colonies strung along the eastern seaboard from New England to Georgia. During the next 75 years, thousands of people traveled westward from those colonies, settling areas of wilderness land from the Appalachian Mountains to the Pacific coast. In 1775, Spain and France held most of the territory west of what is now Ohio. French land in the Midwest became part of the United States through the Louisiana Purchase of 1803. Lands in the far West extending to the Pacific Ocean were ceded to the United States through the Treaty of Guadalupe-Hidalgo after the Mexican War. By 1850, the land area of the United States was about 35 times larger than it had been in 1775.

Beyond the Mountains   In the early 1700's, people in the colonies were already venturing westward. Recent immigrants and former indentured servants who had little money settled along the frontier (then at the eastern foothills of the Appalachian Mountains) where land was cheap.

Most settlers were totally unprepared for wilderness living. Few had any knowledge of the North American Indians, and they did not know how to deal with them. For years, they suffered attacks from wild animals and raids from Indians. Many times they had to flee settlements that were burned by the Indians. The settlers pleaded for army garrisons to protect them, but no army was provided.

Finally, these backwoods people began fighting back against the dangers of the wilderness. By 1775, strong leaders were beginning to emerge who were not afraid of the frontier and its dangers but considered it an exciting challenge. These leaders were hunters and trappers who liked the loneliness of the wilderness. They ventured westward into ever more distant areas to seek animals for food and for trade. Others followed to settle the lands these people had explored. These early westward pioneers became known as "frontiersmen." One of the best known was Daniel Boone, who blazed a trail—called the Wilderness Road—through the Cumberland Gap in the Appalachian Mountains. Through the Cumberland Gap streamed hundreds of new settlers, the first white and black inhabitants of Kentucky. John Sevier was another early frontiersman. He opened the area that is now Tennessee.

During the American Revolution, George Rogers Clark, a frontiersman and army general, led the fight against the British to put the Northwest Territory under American control. Indians in the Northwest Territory went on the warpath and in 1789 attacked and burned hundreds of pioneer settlements. These Indian raids were put down by troops under the command of General Anthony Wayne.

The Midwest   In 1803, President Thomas Jefferson purchased the Louisiana Territory and the city of New Orleans from France. He assigned Meriwether Lewis and William Clark to explore the Louisiana Territory between the Missouri River and the Pacific Ocean. They returned with tales about great forests, fertile plains, wild animals and birds, rivers, lakes, and giant mountains in the West. The imagination of many people was aroused, and they began to dream of an independent life in the "wide open spaces." But the War of 1812 with Britain brought on more Indian raids and temporarily slowed

▼ *Thousands of pioneers packed all their belongings into wagons and set off for the West during the westward movement of the late 19th century.*

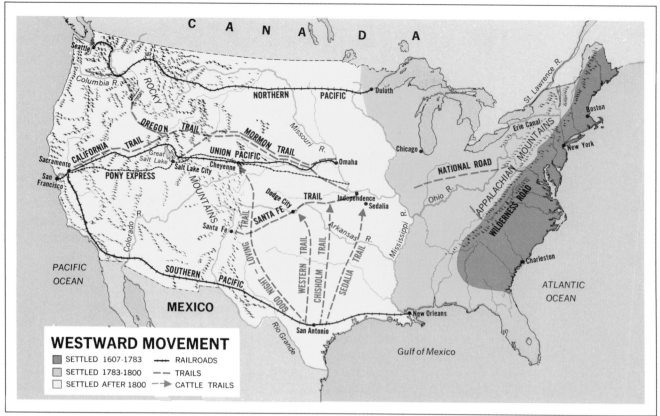

WESTWARD MOVEMENT

- ■ SETTLED 1607-1783 ┄┄► RAILROADS
- ■ SETTLED 1783-1800 ┄ ┄ TRAILS
- ▢ SETTLED AFTER 1800 ┄ ► CATTLE TRAILS

the westward movement. Shortly after the war, people moved west by the thousands. Farmers settled in the midwestern territories—in Illinois, Ohio, Indiana, and Missouri. The completion of the Erie Canal in 1825—connecting the Hudson River and the Great Lakes—helped people get to the Midwest.

The Far West The Far West was a rugged, unknown land. The idea of crossing mountains and deserts to find homes in a dangerous wilderness appealed to people seeking adventure. Whole families piled their belongings into *Conestoga (covered) wagons* and began the hard journey into the unknown. Long trains of wagons creaked across the midwestern plains, struggled up mountainsides, and floated across rivers. These pioneers suffered the blazing heat of summer days and the freezing winds and snow of winter nights as they pushed westward, on and on through 2,000 miles (3,200 km) of territory.

These pioneers often came into conflict with the Indian inhabitants, who saw their lands being taken away from them. Foreign powers who owned land on which the pioneers settled tried to prevent their passage. The Spanish in Mexico owned Texas and California, and the British claimed Oregon. U.S. citizens settled in these areas and later won control of them. The Santa Fe Trail from Missouri to New Mexico opened the West to trade with the Spanish. Texas became independent after a revolt by U.S. settlers against Mexico in 1836. Farmers in the Northwest found the Oregon country to be fertile land, and, in the 1840's, thousands of people traveled over the Oregon Trail to settle there.

Settlers began crossing the Sierra Nevada Mountains into California in the 1840's. By 1848, the treaty ending the Mexican War added California to U.S. territory. In that same year, gold was discovered at Sutter's Mill in Coloma, California. When the news arrived, people by the thousands sold their homes and businesses in the

The California Gold Rush of 1849 greatly spurred the western migration from the eastern and central states. Over 100,000 gold prospectors rushed to California in that year. One year later California became a state.

▲ *A wagon train of pioneers makes its way westward through the Rocky Mountains. Pioneers had to face the hazards of Indian attacks and treacherous terrain.*

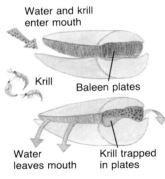

Water and krill enter mouth

Krill — Baleen plates

Water leaves mouth — Krill trapped in plates

▲ *Some of the largest sea creatures are baleen whales, and they feed on some of the smallest, shrimplike animals called krill. In place of teeth, baleen whales have plates of hornlike baleen that act like huge sieves.*

East and headed west to get rich. The Gold Rush was on. In California, a village called San Francisco became a boom town.

After the Civil War ended in 1865, thousands of veterans went west where they were given free lands, called *homesteads*, on which to settle. Homesteaders raised crops of wheat, oats, corn, and fruit. Others raised herds of cattle and sheep. To make way for white settlers, Indians were killed by the hundreds of thousands or pushed into reservations by the government. In almost all cases, the Indians were robbed of their freedom and the lands on which they had lived for centuries.

In California, the Central Pacific Railroad Company began laying railroad track toward the east. In Nebraska, the Union Pacific Railroad began laying track westward. On May 10, 1869, the two sets of track were joined together at Promontory Point, Utah. People could now travel by train from New York to San Francisco. Thousands of families bought land near railroad depots, and new towns began to spring up all across the country. Trains provided transportation for grain and livestock that midwestern farmers shipped to eastern and western markets. The trains also brought in supplies from both directions.

The "Wild West" was being tamed and settled. One by one, its territories became states of the Union. The explorers blazed the trails, and the pioneers with the courage to follow settled the West and formed a nation stretching from the Atlantic to the Pacific Ocean.

For further information on:

Geography, *see* APPALACHIAN MOUNTAINS, BADLANDS, CONTINENTAL DIVIDE, GREAT LAKES, GREAT PLAINS, MISSISSIPPI RIVER, ROCKY MOUNTAINS, SIERRA NEVADA.

History, *see* AMERICAN HISTORY; FUR; GOLD RUSH; INDIANS, AMERICAN; LEWIS AND CLARK EXPEDITION; LOUISIANA PURCHASE; MEXICAN WAR; OREGON TRAIL; PIONEER LIFE; SANTA FE TRAIL; WAR OF 1812; WAYNE, ANTHONY; WILDERNESS ROAD.

Pioneers, *see* BOONE, DANIEL; CLARK, GEORGE ROGERS; CROCKETT, DAVY; JACKSON, ANDREW; YOUNG, BRIGHAM. *For individual states, see article at name of state.*

WHALES AND WHALING

Whales are the largest animals on Earth. A large blue whale may be over 100 feet (30 m) long and weigh over 200 tons (180 metric tons). However, not all whales are this large. Some whales are only about 5 feet (1.5 m) long and weigh less than 50 pounds (23 kg).

Whales are mammals that live in water. They are thought to have descended from mammals that once lived on land. Whales are warmblooded and they breathe air, as do all mammals. They give birth to live young, and the mother nurses the young with milk.

Although whales are really mammals, they look much like fish. They have an almost completely hairless, fish-shaped body. Their limbs have developed into flippers. They have a tail fin called a *fluke*, but the fluke runs sideways, unlike the up-and-down tail of fish. Using its tail and fluke, a whale can swim at up to 25 miles (40 km) an hour. The fishlike characteristics of the whale have

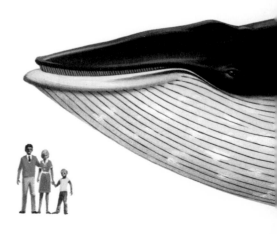

adapted it for life in the water.

The whale is also unlike other mammals in that its nostrils open on top of its head, through an opening called the *blowhole*. Toothed whales have one blowhole, and other whales have two. The whale breathes in air through the blowhole before diving beneath the surface of the water. A whale can dive several hundred feet deep and stay underwater for almost an hour. When it comes back to the surface, it blows the old air out of the blowhole and takes in fresh air. When the warm breath from its body strikes the cold air, it forms a "spout" of water droplets, like the cloud that comes from your mouth in very cold weather.

The skin of most whales is as thin as paper. Under the skin is a thick layer of fat called *blubber*. The blubber keeps the thin-skinned, hairless whale warm.

The whale has a very sharp sense of hearing, even though its ear openings are as small as a thumbtack. A whale can move through pitch-black water by using a kind of *sonar*—bouncing sounds off objects and listening to the echoes. Most whales have fairly good eyes but a poor sense of smell. Toothed whales have no sense of smell at all.

Many whales are extremely intelligent animals, perhaps as intelligent as human beings.

The two main types of whale are the baleen whales and the toothed whales (including dolphins).

Baleen Whales　Blue whales, right whales, and humpback whales are all baleen whales. Baleen whales have strips of *baleen* in their mouths instead of teeth. Baleen is often called whalebone, but it is not actually bone. It is a horny substance similar to the stuff of which your fingernails are made. A right whale has about 350 baleen strips along each side of its upper jaw. Each strip is up to 12 feet (3.7 m) long and usually less than an inch (2.5 cm) wide. The outer surface of the baleen strip is smooth but the inside is fringed.

A baleen whale eats small crustaceans called krill that it catches in the fringed baleen. The whale fills its mouth with water containing krill. The whale then closes its mouth and squeezes all the water out of it mouth through the strips of baleen. The krill are caught in the fringes of the baleen and cannot escape. The whale then swallows the krill. A large whale can swallow over a ton (0.9 metric tons) of krill at one time.

Toothed Whales　The largest toothed whale is the sperm whale. The sperm whale is about 60 feet (18 m) long, much smaller than the largest baleen whales. A sperm whale can be easily recognized by its large, square, blunt head. Other whales have more pointed or rounded heads. The sperm whale's head is half-filled with fatty tissue and a liquid wax called *spermaceti*. The spermaceti has been used in cosmetics and lubricants.

▲ *A killer whale leaping in Miami's Sea World. There are many such marine amusement parks around the United States. Some people question whether such intelligent creatures should be made to perform tricks in this way.*

▼ *The largest whale, and possibly the largest creature ever to have lived on Earth, is the blue whale. The biggest ever known was 110 feet 2½ inches (33.58 m) long. Overfishing has reduced their numbers to some 12,000. Certain countries' whaling fleets continue to hunt them.*

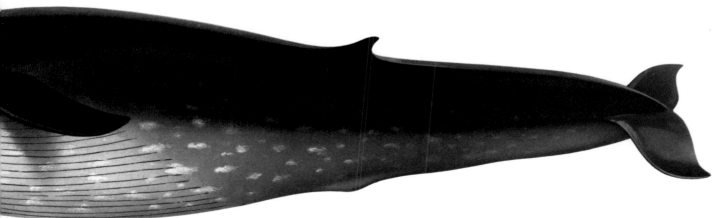

▲ *A whale being cut up in a whaling factory. Most countries have banned commercial whaling, while some countries have limited their catch.*

▲ *Wheat was brought to the Americas in the 1500's by Spanish and Portuguese explorers.*

The sperm whale has about 40 large teeth in its lower jaw and a few small, useless teeth in its upper jaw. Each lower tooth is about 8 inches (20 cm) long and weighs about 6 pounds (2.7 kg). The sperm whale eats mainly squid, octopus, and cuttlefish. Sperm whales live in groups of 15 to 20. They usually live in the tropics in the winter and migrate north and south in the summer. The white whale in Herman Melville's story *Moby Dick* (1851) was a sperm whale.

Whaling Whales were first hunted for their blubber. The blubber was heated to produce the whale oil burned in lamps. The right whale was the most hunted whale before the 1800's. It got its name because it was the "right whale" to kill. Its blubber was very oily, and its dead body did not sink. Its baleen was used to make corsets and buggy whips.

In the early 1800's, U.S. whalers began to hunt the sperm whale. The sperm whale not only provided whale oil, it also provided spermaceti and *ambergris*. Ambergris, a curious product vomited by sperm whales, was used as a fixative in perfumes. By 1840, there were about 800 U.S. whaling ships. But with the rise of the petroleum industry in the 1860's, the demand for whale oil dropped and the U.S. whaling fleet shrank to a few ships. Today, whale oil is occasionally used as a lubricating oil for fine machinery and in the manufacture of soap and margarine.

Early whalers went to sea in sailing ships. When a whale was spotted, a few sailors would chase after it in a small boat. A harpooner in the boat would try to harpoon the whale. When the whale was killed, the sailors towed its body back to the ship. The sailors cut the blubber from the whale's body with long knives. The blubber was cooked in large kettles to extract the whale oil. The oil was then put in barrels. When the ship had all the oil it could hold, it would return home. Sometimes a whal-

ing ship was at sea for two or three years before returning.

Today, whalers use fast motorboats to chase whales. They shoot explosive harpoons from special guns. The explosives blow up inside the whale and kill it. The dead whale is towed to a large factory ship. Workers on the factory ship cut the whale into small pieces. The blubber is cooked in giant kettles. The red meat may be frozen for later use as food, boiled for its oil, or ground up as meal or animal feed. The organs and bones are boiled for oil or ground up for fertilizer. A modern whale factory gets the last ounce of use from the whale's body.

So many whales have been killed that they are in danger of becoming extinct. Also, a great many people have come to believe that killing such intelligent animals is immoral. International agreements have been made in an effort to limit the number of whales that can be killed, but it is difficult to enforce such agreements. The United States banned commercial whaling in 1971. Japan and the Soviet Union, the two leading whaling nations, have limited their catch.

In 1985 the International Whaling Commission imposed a ban on commercial whaling, but Iceland, Norway, the Soviet Union and South Korea still hunt whales.

ALSO READ: DOLPHINS AND PORPOISES; FISHING INDUSTRY; MAMMAL.

WHEAT Golden stalks of wheat cover more of the world's farmland than any other crop. Wheat is the most widely grown grain crop in the temperate regions of the world. It provides millions of people with their basic food.

Wheat is a cereal grass. Its fruits are called grain, and they are used for food. A mature wheat plant grows 2 to 4 feet (60–120 cm) high. Its slender stalks have long, thin leaves. The stalks are topped by "spikes," or "ears," of grain.

Each spike contains about 40 kernels of wheat. Each kernel of wheat is divided into three main sections—germ, endosperm, and bran. The *germ* is the innermost section. If the grain is planted as seed, growth begins in the germ. Next to the germ is a starchy section called the *endosperm* (inside seed). Surrounding both the germ and the endosperm is a layer called the *bran*. It protects the kernel. The entire kernel is covered with a husk called the *chaff*.

The kernels of wheat are removed from the stalk by a process called threshing. The stalks are beaten to separate them from the grain, usually by a threshing machine. The threshing process also removes the chaff from the kernel. The kernels are then ground up for food.

The main food product made from wheat is flour. Whole wheat flour is ground from the entire wheat kernel, including the bran, the germ, and the endosperm. It has more vitamins and protein than white flour. White flour is ground from the endosperm only. Flour is used to make bread and pastries. Wheat is also used to make breakfast cereals, health foods, and some types of beer and whiskey. A hard-grained wheat, called *durum wheat*, is used in the manufacture of macaroni, spaghetti, and noodles.

There are many different varieties of wheat. Some, called winter wheats, are sown in the fall and harvested the following summer. Others, called spring wheats, are planted in the early spring and harvested in late summer after the winter wheats. Winter and spring wheats are further classified according to the color of their grain.

The leading wheat-growing countries in the world today are the Soviet Union, the United States, China, and India. The states of the United States that grow the most wheat are Kansas, North Dakota, Oklahoma, and South Dakota.

ALSO READ: AGRICULTURE, BAKING AND BAKERIES, FLOUR MAKING, GRAIN.

▲ *Combine harvesters cutting the wheat on the vast farmlands of the North American great plains.*

WHISTLER, JAMES McNEILL (1834–1903)

One of the greatest artists of the 1800's was born in the United States but spent his whole career as an artist in Europe. He was James Abbott McNeill Whistler, who was born in Lowell, Massachusetts. He became a cadet at the U.S. Military Academy at West Point, New York, but he did not do well there. He left after three years and went to work as a drafter. Whistler studied art in Paris and became known for his etchings. Perhaps his early etchings influenced his painting, because he often used black and white and grays. Whistler's pictures look almost colorless when compared with the wild colors used by some other artists.

You may have heard of the painting called *Whistler's Mother*—a profile portrait Whistler painted of his mother in 1872. It is probably the artist's most famous work. The painting's real title is *Arrangement in Grey and Black, No. 1: The Artist's Mother*. The titles of Whistler's works show his interest in color combinations for their own sake. Some of his paintings are abstract art, with the subject almost unable to be recognized. In the same year, he also did the painting shown here, *Miss Cicely Alexander: Harmony in Grey and Green*. Besides gray and green, Whistler also used much black and white and yellow in this picture.

It must have been exciting for this young girl, Cicely Alexander, to be chosen as a model for Whistler's

▲ Miss Cicely Alexander: Harmony in Grey and Green, *by James McNeill Whistler.*

▲ *The famous Presidential Oval Office in the White House, where many momentous decisions affecting U.S. history have been made. It is the nerve center for the President's day-to-day activity.*

painting. Whistler picked the dress she was to wear. He even gave instructions about how it should be laundered! Every detail mattered to Whistler. It took the artist 70 long sittings to complete the painting.

Whistler's work was also deeply affected by his study of the works of the Japanese printmakers. He adapted some of their techniques in his own art. Whistler continued to do etchings and other forms of graphic art, such as dry point and lithography. He also had a strong interest in interior decoration. Whistler never came back to his native land, but much of his art did. Most major museums in the United States have examples of his work.

ALSO READ: ABSTRACT ART, ART HISTORY, INTERIOR DECORATION, ORIENTAL ART.

WHITE, E. B. see CHILDREN'S LITERATURE.

WHITE HOUSE The White House is the official residence of the President of the United States. It is on an 18-acre (7.3 hectare) plot at 1600 Pennsylvania Avenue, N.W., in Washington, D.C. It is one of the oldest federal buildings still standing.

The White House received its name from its sandstone walls, which are painted white. However, the house has been called by several different names, including the President's Mansion and the President's House. In President Madison's time, it was known as the Executive Mansion. Theodore Roosevelt officially adopted the name "White House" in 1902.

The site for the building was chosen by George Washington. James Hoban, an Irish-born architect, made the plans for the President's home. His design was chosen over one submitted anonymously by Thomas Jefferson.

The first President to live in the White House was John Adams. He and his wife, Abigail, moved in during November 1800. The house was set on fire by British troops in 1814, during the War of 1812, and only the shell was left standing. It was restored in 1817 and has undergone many renovations since then.

The main part of the house is 175 feet (53.3 m) long and 85 feet (26 m) high. Today, the White House contains four stories and two basements. There are 132 rooms, several of which are open to the public. These include the East Room, Red Room, Blue Room, Green Room, and State Dining Room.

The Presidents have transacted official business in the White House offices for many years. Theodore Roosevelt added the West Wing in 1902 to provide additional office space. Franklin D. Roosevelt rebuilt and enlarged the East Wing in 1942.

The entire interior of the White House was rebuilt from 1948 to 1952, during Harry Truman's administration. It was reconstructed at a cost of more than 5½ million dollars. In 1961, Mrs. John F. Kennedy (now Jacqueline Onassis) initiated a program to restore the interior of the White House to its colonial appearance in the late 1700's and early 1800's. The White House Historical Association was formed to publish guidebooks and obtain historic furnishings. The White House library acquired many important books about U.S. history. Public contributions of antiques and funds have helped to redecorate the mansion.

ALSO READ: DISTRICT OF COLUMBIA, PRESIDENCY.

WHITMAN, WALT (1819–1892) Walt Whitman was one of our nation's greatest poets. He was born in West Hills, Long Island, New York. Whitman did not have much formal education. He worked as a printer, schoolteacher, and newspaperman before he began writing poetry.

In 1855, Whitman published the first edition of his life's work, *Leaves of Grass*. It was considered a shocking book at that time, mostly because of the open way in which Whitman wrote about sexuality, but also because it was written in free verse, which was then rather unpopular. Whitman believed in the brotherhood of all men and women. His poetry is very personal, but in it he also identifies with people everywhere and with nature, too. He said in "Song of Myself,"

I celebrate myself, and sing
    myself,
And what I assume you shall
    assume,
For every atom belonging to me
    as good belongs to you.

Whitman revised and added to *Leaves of Grass* many times, and nine other editions, each with more poems than the one before, were printed. During the Civil War, he worked as a nurse in army hospitals. He remained in Washington after the war and worked as a clerk for the government. Two of his best known poems, "O Captain! My Captain!" and "When Lilacs Last in the Dooryard Bloom'd," were written in memory of President Abraham Lincoln.

ALSO READ: POETRY.

WHITNEY, ELI (1765–1825) Eli Whitney was a U.S. inventor best known for his invention of the cotton gin—a machine that separated cotton fibers from seeds. He also set up one of the first mass-production assembly lines.

Whitney was born in Westboro, Massachusetts. As a boy, he liked to build things in his father's workshop. By age 11, he had set up his first business, manufacturing nails during the American Revolution. Whitney

graduated from Yale College and took a job as a teacher on a wealthy plantation in the South. There, he became aware of the problems involved in separating cotton fibers from seeds by hand. In 1794, he patented the cotton gin, a machine that did this job much faster than it had been done by hand. The cotton gin helped make the United States the world's largest cotton producer. But Whitney did not profit from it very much because other manufacturers copied his invention.

In 1798, Whitney built a factory to make rifles for the U.S. Army. Until that time, guns had been made by hand. Whitney used machines to produce the parts and hired workers to put them together on an assembly line. Because the parts were machine-made, they were interchangeable. Before, if part of a gun failed, its owner had to buy a new gun. Now, people could repair guns with a new part.

ALSO READ: MANUFACTURING.

WHITTIER, JOHN GREEN-LEAF (1807–1892) John Greenleaf Whittier was a U.S. poet. His parents belonged to the Quaker faith, and he is sometimes called the "Quaker Poet."

Whittier was born on a farm near Haverhill, Massachusetts. He read a great deal as a boy but received little formal education. Long before the Civil War, Whittier became deeply interested in freeing the slaves, and he wrote many antislavery poems. His work was first published in 1826 in an abolitionist newspaper in Massachusetts, the *Free Press*. Its editor, William Lloyd Garrison, took an interest in Whittier and helped further his writing career. Whittier also served for a year in the Massachusetts legislature. After the war, Whittier concentrated on poems about U.S. history and folklore, and about life in the New England countryside.

▲ *Walt Whitman, U.S. poet.*

▲ *Eli Whitney, inventor of the cotton gin.*

▲ *John Greenleaf Whittier, U.S. poet and hymn writer.*

▲ *Kate Douglas Wiggin,*
U.S. author and educator.

▲ *Laura Ingalls Wilder,*
author of the "Little House"
series.

▲ *Thornton Wilder, U.S.*
novelist and playwright.

"Barbara Frietchie" and "Barefoot Boy" are two of his best-known works. "Barbara Frietchie" is about a Civil War hero. "Barefoot Boy" is a happy poem about growing up in rural New England. "Snowbound" describes winter on a New England farm. Whittier also wrote several Protestant hymns, including "Dear Lord and Father of Mankind."

ALSO READ: POETRY.

WHOOPING COUGH see CHILDHOOD DISEASES.

WIGGIN, KATE DOUGLAS (1856–1923) Kate Douglas Wiggin was a U.S. educator and author. She was born Kate Douglas Smith, in Philadelphia, Pennsylvania. She grew up in New England, attending school in Andover, Massachusetts. While still in her teens, she moved to California and began teaching school.

In 1878, Wiggin and her sister, Nora Smith, started the first free kindergarten in San Francisco. They also wrote a book on kindergarten theories and, in 1880, founded a training school for kindergarten teachers. Wiggin's best-known stories are *Rebecca of Sunnybrook Farm* (1903), which was later made into a movie, and *The Birds' Christmas Carol* (1888). She also wrote *Mother Carey's Chickens* (1911). Her books were very popular with children in the early 1900's. They are sentimental, sometimes sad, tales, but they are spiced with humor.

ALSO READ: BIOGRAPHY, CHILDREN'S LITERATURE.

WILDER, LAURA INGALLS (1867–1957) Laura Ingalls Wilder wrote books for children about pioneer days in the Midwest. She began writing them when she was over 60 years old. The "Little House" series

is based on Wilder's own life in the long-ago pioneer days. She was born in Wisconsin and tells about her early childhood there in *Little House in the Big Woods* (1932). Her family later moved to Kansas, Minnesota, and the Dakotas. *Little House on the Prairie* (1935), *On the Banks of Plum Creek* (1937), *By the Shores of Silver Lake* (1939), *The Long Winter* (1940), *Little Town on the Prairie* (1941), and *These Happy Golden Years* (1943) relate Laura's growing-up and getting-married years. Another book, *Farmer Boy* (1933), is about the New York State boyhood of her husband, Almanzo Wilder. Wilder's books describe in fascinating detail the small pleasures of pioneer life and the difficult times—blizzards, droughts, wolves, and plagues of grasshoppers.

ALSO READ: CHILDREN'S LITERATURE.

WILDER, THORNTON (1897–1975) One of our country's most outstanding playwrights and novelists was Thornton Niven Wilder. He won the Pulitzer Prize three times for his work.

Wilder was born in Madison, Wisconsin. He spent much of his early life in China, where his father was in the U.S. consular service. After graduating from Yale University, Wilder studied archeology in Rome. From 1930 to 1937, he taught literature at the University of Chicago.

Wilder's first novel, *The Cabala*, was published in 1926. *The Bridge of San Luis Rey* (1927), probably his most famous novel, won the Pulitzer Prize in 1928. It tells the story of five people who are killed when a footbridge collapses in Peru. The lives of these people are examined in detail, showing how they lead to the bridge. Chance and fate are important elements in the novel.

Our Town (1938), Wilder's most noted play, received a Pulitzer Prize in 1938. It is the story of several generations of people who live in Grover's Corner, New Hampshire. The beauty and meaning of life are seen in ordinary people. *The Matchmaker* (1954), another play, was adapted into a successful Broadway musical called *Hello Dolly!* (1964). *The Skin of Our Teeth* (1942), a play about human survival and folly, also received the Pulitzer Prize.

ALSO READ: DRAMA, LITERATURE.

WILDERNESS AREA An area of wilderness consists of an undisturbed natural landscape that has remained unspoiled by mankind. Only a few hundred years ago, almost all the land in what is now the United States was a wilderness area. Today, only a small part of the nation's land area consists of wilderness areas.

Certain general conditions must apply to an area before it can be considered a wilderness. It should contain no public roads. Visitors can come to a wilderness area only on foot, by horse, or by canoe. They must bring their own camping equipment, for there are no stores, hotels, or even established campsites in a wilderness area. Also, a wilderness area should exist as a single unit. It should not be broken up by developed areas. Lastly, it must show no significant past or present disturbance by human activities. Livestock grazing, hunting, and fishing, however, may be permitted in some wilderness areas. Also, forest rangers may take measures to put out forest fires.

Wilderness areas provide a safe home for many different species of plants and animals. Scientists can study the life patterns of these living things in their natural surroundings. Both air and water are kept almost free from pollution in wilderness areas. Young and old people can enjoy the feeling of being alone and can experience the challenge of surviving in a natural setting.

The Wilderness Act, passed by Congress in 1964, established 87 official wilderness areas, covering about 10½ million acres (4.25 million hectares) of public land. All of these wilderness areas are located inside national forests, national parks, or wildlife refuges. Monomoy Island, off the coast of Massachusetts, is a favorite wilderness area for beachcombers and bird-watchers. The Great Swamp Wilderness Area in New Jersey is used mainly for wildlife research and education. Boundary Waters Canoe Area in northern Minnesota is a beautiful, isolated area for camping and canoeing.

ALSO READ: CONSERVATION, ECOLOGY, NATIONAL FOREST, NATIONAL PARK.

WILDERNESS ROAD The Wilderness Road was the main path of the pioneers as they traveled westward through the mountains of Kentucky. Daniel Boone cleared and marked an early Indian trail to connect the East with the frontier west of the Appalachian Mountains.

The Wilderness Road started at a point in southwestern Virginia called the Block House. Feeder trails from the North through Virginia and from the South through the Carolinas joined the trail there. At the Block House, travelers waited to band together. They formed groups to protect each other from Indian attacks as they traveled along the trail. When a party was completed, it began the perilous journey

▲ *Herons and egrets keep absolutely still as they wait for unsuspecting fish to pass by in a wilderness area deep in the Florida Everglades.*

▲ *Bulls Island, a wilderness area near Charleston, South Carolina, is a mecca for bird-watchers. Hundreds of species of birds may be found here.*

▲ *Daniel Boone, the American pioneer, blazes an old buffalo and Indian trail to make the Wilderness Trail at the time of the American Revolution.*

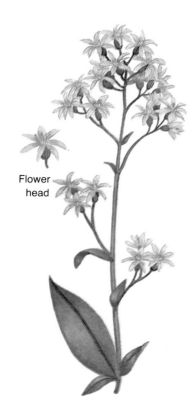

Flower head

▲ *Goldenrod is a wildflower native to North America.*

westward. It traveled by way of the Cumberland Gap through the rugged Appalachian Mountains. The states of Virginia, Tennessee, and Kentucky meet at the gap, which is a narrow, natural pass with steep sides. The travelers followed the Wilderness Road through central Kentucky, on to the Ohio River and beyond. One branch of the road led to Nashville, Tennessee. The other branch, which had been blazed by Daniel Boone, ended at a new settlement, Boonesborough, on the Kentucky River. This second branch at first was just a foot and horseback trail, but it soon became the most important wagon trail west.

After Kentucky became a state, gates or turnpikes were built across the road. Tolls were collected. More blockhouses were built to protect travelers from attack. For more than half a century after Boone first marked it, the Wilderness Road was the main route to the frontier. It still exists as part of U.S. Route 25, now known as the Dixie Highway.

ALSO READ: BOONE, DANIEL; WESTWARD MOVEMENT.

WILDFLOWER A flower that grows without being planted or cared for by people is called a wildflower. Wildflowers survive without care because they are well adapted to their environment. Most of them are native flowers. They first developed in the

▲ *Daisies are among the most common wildflowers and are found in grasslands all over Europe and Asia.*

area that is now their home, so they have adapted well to conditions of soil, light, and temperature.

More than 25,000 types of wildflowers live in different surroundings throughout North America. Some grow in forests, meadows, prairies, or deserts. Others are found on the banks of streams, the sides of roads, and even on mountaintops.

Wildflowers of the Woodlands Most wildflowers that grow in the woods bloom in the early spring, before the leaves of the trees shade the ground. Flowers that bloom in early spring get moisture from melting snow and spring rain. Among the earliest of woodland flowers is hepatica, of the buttercup family, with its white, pink, or lavender petals. White trillium and blue, white, purple, and yellow violets appear slightly later. Dutchman's breeches and forget-me-nots are other early woodland flowers.

After the forest trees have grown leaves, wildflowers that do not need much sunlight begin to grow. Some have stored up food in their roots. They use the stored food to provide energy for growing. Jack-in-the-pulpit is one of these flowers.

Meadow Wildflowers These wildflowers are able to get plenty of sunlight. They grow quickly, and they may produce several generations in one growing season. Among the first meadow flowers are daisies, buttercups, and wild roses. In midsummer, Queen Anne's lace and yellow daisies with black centers—called black-eyed Susans—begin to bloom. Autumn brings goldenrod and purple asters to the meadows.

Mountain Wildflowers Mountain, or alpine, wildflowers usually get plenty of sunlight, but they have to withstand lower temperatures than flowers that grow in meadows. They also grow in thinner soil. Mountain wildflowers include the alpine harebell, edelweiss, the mountain lady's-slipper, the Indian paintbrush, and the Rocky mountain columbine.

Prairie Wildflowers Prairie flowers also get much sunlight. On prairies of the United States are yellow California poppies, blue or purple verbena, and Texas bluebonnets. Many prairie flowers have large underground roots that help the plants survive prairie fires.

Swamp and Water Wildflowers Perhaps the most familiar water

▼ *Forget-me-nots can be anywhere from 2 inches (5 cm) to 2 feet (60 cm) in height.*

Flower

flowers are white and yellow waterlilies, which blossom on the water's surface. Yellow marsh marigolds, red cardinal flowers, and pinkish Venus's-flytraps brighten the edges of ponds and marshes. A few water wildflowers, such as the sea wrack, bloom underwater.

Desert Wildflowers Desert plants must be able to survive with very little water and in much heat. They have thick, fleshy stems that hold water. Desert plants may have no leaves or very thin, spinelike leaves that give off little water. They have hard seeds that lie on the sand until a rare rain wets the desert, and then they grow quickly. Desert flowers may bloom only during the rainy season and disappear afterward. Cactus flowers are often very large and striking. The flowers of the strawberry cactus are bright red, while those of the prickly pear cactus are a soft yellow with red centers. The yucca, the purple sand verbena, and the dune primrose are other common desert wildflowers.

Wildflowers and Garden Flowers All garden flowers are descended from wildflowers. They became garden flowers when people took their seeds and planted them in gardens. Plant breeders then tried to change and improve the garden-grown wildflowers. This is why most garden flowers are different from wildflowers. The ancestor of modern roses is the simple woodland rose that still can be found growing as a wildflower. After years of breeding, cultivating, and cross-pollination, modern roses are much larger, have many more petals, bloom more often, and grow in many more colors than their wild ancestor.

Some wildflowers once were garden flowers. The orange Asiatic tiger lily once was a garden flower. It was imported into the United States to be grown in gardens. Some tiger lily seeds were carried to fields—perhaps

Seed head

Lower leaf

▲ *The thistle is the national emblem of Scotland. Be careful when you touch a thistle! These plants are very prickly.*

▲ *Buttercups are common wildflowers. They are poisonous to farm animals.*

▲ *A cornfield reddened by wild poppies.*

▲ *Emma Hart Willard, a pioneer in women's education in the United States.*

by birds—and the tiger lily became a wildflower. Plants that have spread from gardens to become wildflowers are called *naturalized* plants.

Enjoying Wildflowers Wildflowers are very beautiful and can be interesting to study. Much can be learned about wild plants by observing them in their natural settings. A walk through a forest in spring, or through a field in summer, can lead to the discovery of many different varieties of wildflowers. However, some kinds of wildflowers are in danger of disappearing because so much woodland and grassland is being used for farmland, or covered by buildings and parking lots. Also, some wildflowers have been picked and uprooted so often that there are very few left. Since flowers make seeds, they must be left intact for the plant to reproduce itself. Some wildflowers have become so rare that there are laws against picking them.

■ LEARN BY DOING

You may like to grow some wildflowers around your home. Wildflower seeds are available in stores. Or you might try transplanting wildflowers. First, be sure you are not taking a rare variety. Then dig up a few of the plants on which the flowers grow. Make sure that you take plenty of soil around the roots. Put the flowers in a bag and take them immediately to where you want to grow them. Plant them with the soil still around the root, and water them well. Make sure that you plant the flowers in the same surroundings they had when growing wild. If they were in forest shade, plant them in the shade. If they were in a sunny place, plant them in full sunlight. ■

ALSO READ: ECOLOGY, FLOWER, FLOWER FAMILIES, GARDEN FLOWER, PLANT DISTRIBUTION, SEEDS AND FRUIT.

WILLARD, EMMA (1787–1870) Emma Hart Willard was a gifted teacher who did much to improve the educational opportunities for girls in the United States. She was born in Berlin, Connecticut, and at age 20 became principal of a girls' academy in Vermont. After her marriage to John Willard, she opened her own school and devised a plan "for improving female education."

She sent a copy of her plan, which called for state aid in founding schools for girls, to the governor of New York. He was impressed and suggested she open a school within his state. That school, founded in 1821, was the Troy Female Seminary, now called the Emma Willard School.

At her school, Emma Willard gave her girl students as fine an education as in any boys' school of the day. She wrote a number of school textbooks and made the school in Troy one of the best-known schools in the country. Her work did much to persuade legislators that girls deserved educational equality with boys.

ALSO READ: EDUCATION.

WILLIAM, KINGS OF ENGLAND William was the name of two kings of England and two kings of Britain.

William I (about 1028–1087), also known as William the Conqueror, was born in Normandy, a region of France. William succeeded his father as Duke of Normandy when he was only eight years old. William's cousin was Edward the Confessor, king of England. Edward had no children, and, in 1051, William claimed that Edward had named him to be the next king of England. In 1064, Harold, Duke of Wessex, the chief noble in England, was shipwrecked off the coast of France. He was captured by William, who made him promise to support the Norman claim

▲ *William I (the Conqueror), the first Norman king of England.*

to the English throne. But just before Edward died in 1066, he chose Harold to be his successor, and Harold was crowned king. William immediately invaded England with a great army. Harold was defeated and killed at the Battle of Hastings, and William was crowned on Christmas Day, 1066. William ruled England with an iron hand. He took away the lands of the English nobles and gave them to his Norman followers. William introduced the feudal system into England, under which each land-owner contributed a certain number of soldiers to the king's army. During William's reign, a great survey of all land and property in England was drawn up in a document called the *Domesday Book*.

William II (about 1056–1100) was nicknamed "Rufus" (the Red) be-cause of his ruddy skin. He became king in 1087, after the death of his father, William the Conqueror. Wil-liam II's elder brother, Richard, Duke of Normandy, tried to seize the English crown. But William defeated him and captured much of Normandy. William was not a popular king. He took money away from the English churches and forced the English peo-ple to pay huge taxes. When he was killed by an arrow on a hunting expe-dition, rumors spread that he had been murdered. William's younger brother succeeded him as Henry I.

William III ruled Britain jointly with his wife, Mary II. (See the article on WILLIAM AND MARY.)

William IV (1765–1837) was often called the "Sailor King." He was the third son of King George III. While he was still a prince, William served in the British navy and rose to the rank of admiral. He became king in 1830, after the death of his elder brother, George IV. William sup-ported the legislation called the Re-form Bill, which was passed by the British parliament in 1832. This bill reformed the voting system in Britain and gave the British merchants and

townspeople greater power in the government of the nation. William was succeeded by his niece, Victoria.

ALSO READ: EDWARD THE CONFESSOR; ENGLISH HISTORY; FEUDALISM; GEORGE, KINGS OF ENGLAND; VICTORIA; WIL-LIAM AND MARY.

WILLIAM AND MARY King William III (1650–1702), sometimes called William of Orange, was born in the Netherlands. His father, Prince William II of Orange, ruler of the Netherlands, died shortly before Wil-liam was born. William's mother was Mary, daughter of King Charles I of Britain. In 1671, William married a British princess named Mary (1662–1694), the daughter of James, Duke of York. Shortly afterward, in 1672, William bravely commanded Dutch forces against a French army that invaded the Netherlands.

Mary's father became king of Brit-ain as James II in 1685. He was a Roman Catholic and was not popular with the British people, who were largely Protestant. In 1688, a group of important British nobles asked William of Orange to lead them in overthrowing King James. William landed in England with an army, but James fled without fighting. Wil-

▼ *A medallion commemorating the marriage of William and Mary, which took place in 1677.*

▲ *Queen Mary II of England, the wife of William III.*

▲ *Roger Williams on his way into exile from Massachusetts Bay Colony.*

▲ *Tennessee Williams, U.S. playwright. His dramas often concerned family life in the Deep South of the United States.*

liam's arrival became known as the Glorious Revolution. The following year, William and Mary were crowned joint rulers of England, Scotland, and Ireland. However, the Roman Catholics in Ireland continued to support James II. William defeated James's Irish forces at the Battle of the Boyne in 1690. Protestants in Ireland still call themselves "Orangemen" after the Protestant king they supported. After Queen Mary II died, William ruled alone until his death.

ALSO READ: ENGLISH HISTORY; JAMES, KINGS OF ENGLAND.

WILLIAMS, ROGER (about 1603–1683) Roger Williams was a Christian religious leader and founder of the colony of Rhode Island. Williams was born in London, England, and educated at Cambridge University. While a student, Williams joined a religious group called the Puritans, who wanted to "purify" the Church of England. But the Puritans were persecuted by the British government. In 1631, Williams traveled to Massachusetts Bay Colony in North America, where he hoped he could worship more freely. But Williams soon quarreled with the government of the colony. He insisted that the people should be allowed to worship as they pleased and said that the government should not interfere in religious affairs. He criticized the government for seizing land from the local Indians without paying them for it.

In 1635, Williams was banished (sent away) from the colony. He went south to what is now Rhode Island and took refuge with the Narraganset Indians. In 1636, he bought land from the Indians and founded a settlement that he named Providence, for "God's merciful providence to me in my distress." Williams set up a government that allowed complete religious freedom, and many people

moved to the new settlement. In 1647, Williams joined Providence with three neighboring settlements to form the colony of Rhode Island.

ALSO READ: MASSACHUSETTS, PURITAN, RHODE ISLAND.

WILLIAMS, TENNESSEE (1911–1983) Some of the best-known plays of modern U.S. theater are those written by Tennessee Williams. His real name was Thomas Lanier Williams, and he was born in Columbus, Mississippi.

As a college student, he became interested in the theater, and his first plays were performed by local little theater groups. For two years he worked in a St. Louis shoe factory to raise enough money to continue his studies.

The play that made him famous was *The Glass Menagerie* (1944), which played on Broadway, New York, in 1944–1945 and won critical acclaim. Like many of his later plays, it was about the South, which Williams portrayed as a fading world of gentility falling into decay. Other plays by Williams are *A Streetcar Named Desire* (1947), *Cat on a Hot Tin Roof* (1955), and *The Night of the Iguana* (1962). During the 1970's, Williams was troubled by mental and physical illness, and his later plays were less successful.

Several of his plays were made into movies. Williams also wrote novels and an autobiography entitled *Memoirs* (1975).

ALSO READ: DRAMA, THEATER.

WILLIAMSBURG see AMERICAN COLONIES, MUSEUM, VIRGINIA.

WILSON, WOODROW (1856–1924) President Woodrow Wilson's great dream was to bring permanent peace to the world. He was a person who hated war. But during his administration, the United States became involved in one of the most widespread and destructive wars of all time.

Thomas Woodrow Wilson grew up in Augusta, Georgia. He was a frail, sickly child and could not attend regular school. His father, a Presbyterian minister, was his only teacher for several years. When Woodrow was 14, he moved with his family to Columbia, South Carolina, a town that had been devastated during the Civil War. Young Wilson felt sick at heart as he walked through the desolate streets, seeing the destruction that war could bring.

He graduated from Princeton University in 1889 and 11 years later returned as a professor. In the meantime, he had studied and practiced law, had taught in two colleges, and had written several books on history and government. As president of Princeton from 1902 to 1910, Wilson introduced a number of educational reforms that made him well known throughout the state of New Jersey. A Democrat, in 1910 he was elected governor of New Jersey. Wilson's accomplishments as governor became the talk of the nation, and, in 1912, he was elected President of the United States.

In his first inaugural address, Wilson said, "The great government we love has too often been made use of for private and selfish purposes, and those who used it have forgotten the people." Wilson began a program of reform. On his recommendation, Congress passed legislation to help small farmers stay in business and to prevent unfair trade practices. Under his direction, a Federal Reserve Board was set up to improve the nation's banking system. The entrance of the United States into World War I interrupted Wilson's reform program, but more legislation was passed during the first three years of his administration than at any previous time in the nation's history.

It was the sad task of Woodrow Wilson, a person who loved peace, to ask that Congress declare war on Germany on April 2, 1917. A U.S. declaration of war was necessary because ships on which U.S. citizens had been traveling had been sunk by German submarines. Many more American lives were threatened by a new German policy of unrestricted submarine warfare. "We shall fight," Woodrow Wilson told Congress, "for the things which we have always carried nearest our hearts, for democracy, for the right of those who submit to authority to have a voice in their own governments. . ."

The President considered the war, in which the United States allied itself with France and Great Britain, "a war to end all wars." At the peace conference in 1919, following the German

▲ *New Yorkers read the news of approaching war in Europe during the summer of 1914. At this time, President Woodrow Wilson was determined to keep the United States out of the war.*

Woodrow Wilson won a second term of office as President in 1916, on the slogan "He kept us out of the war"—referring to World War I. However, Wilson could not encourage the European powers to negotiate, and after American ships were sunk by the Germans, he declared war on Germany on April 6, 1917.

WOODROW WILSON
TWENTY-EIGHTH PRESIDENT   MARCH 4, 1913–MARCH 4, 1921

Born: December 28, 1856, Staunton, Virginia
Parents: Joseph and Jessie Woodrow Wilson
Education: Princeton University, Princeton, New Jersey
Religion: Presbyterian
Occupation: Teacher, college president, governor
Political Party: Democratic
Married: 1885 to Ellen Axson (1860–1914); 1915 to Edith Bolling Galt (1872–1961)
Children: 3 daughters by first wife
Died: February 3, 1924, Washington, D.C.
Buried: National Cathedral, Washington, D.C.

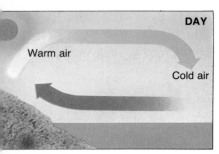

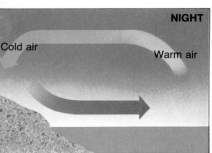

▲ *At the coast, winds often come in from the sea during the day and go out to sea at night. This is because the land heats up more quickly in the day. Warm air rises from it, and cool air comes in from the sea. At night the land cools more quickly than the sea, so the cycle works the other way around.*

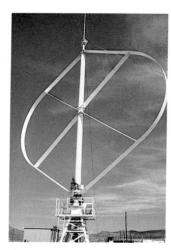

▲ *An "egg-beater" windmill in Albuquerque, New Mexico.*

surrender, Wilson insisted on a treaty that would include an international organization called the League of Nations. He believed that the League would offer nations a way to settle their disputes without going to war. A treaty to form the League of Nations was written up, and Wilson submitted it to the U.S. Senate for ratification (approval). To Woodrow Wilson's bitter disappointment, the Senate refused to permit the United States to join the League.

Wilson was so convinced that the League of Nations was necessary to world peace that he started on a cross-country speaking tour, hoping to convince his fellow citizens that the United States should join the League. "I do not hesitate to say," he told one audience, "that the war we have been through . . . is not to be compared with the war we would have to face the next time." These words were like a prediction of the future. In 1939, Europe, and later the United States, was plunged into World War II, fighting in Europe, Asia, and Africa. In the aftermath of that horrible war, people in the United States were finally convinced that an international organization was necessary. President Wilson's convictions became a reality when the United Nations was established in 1946.

During his speaking tour to promote the League of Nations, the weary President was stricken with paralysis. He was an invalid for the rest of his life.

ALSO READ: LEAGUE OF NATIONS, WORLD WAR I.

WIND Wind is moving air. This movement of air results mainly from uneven heating of the Earth's surface by the sun. When air is heated, it expands. The molecules of air move farther apart, the air becomes lighter, and the air pressure becomes lower. When air is cooled, the opposite hap-

pens. The molecules move closer together, and the air becomes heavier. The lighter warm air rises, and the heavier cool air sinks. As warm air rises from a place, cool air rushes in to fill the space left behind. Thus, air ordinarily moves from cooler places to warmer places, and winds blow from high-pressure areas to low-pressure areas.

At certain latitudes of the Earth's surface, winds blow steadily from the same direction. These winds are called *prevailing winds*. Prevailing winds are caused by large-scale air movements from cooler to warmer areas, and the effect of the Earth's rotation on these movements. The *trade winds* are the prevailing winds from near the equator to 30 degrees latitude north and south. The *westerlies* are the prevailing winds between 30 and 60 degrees.

Local winds are caused by local conditions, and not by large-scale air movements. A sea breeze is a local wind caused by local differences in heat and air pressure between the land and the ocean. During the daytime the land absorbs heat faster than the water. As the air above the land warms up, the air pressure on the land becomes lower, and a cool breeze blows in from the ocean. At night, the land gives off heat more quickly than the water. The air pressure over the ocean is now lower, and a breeze blows from the land to the water.

Local winds are often caused by air movements around mountains. The tops and sides of mountains become heated and cooled at different times. Air from the cooler areas blows into the warmer areas. During the daytime, cool air usually blows from the valleys up the mountainsides. At night, cool air blows from the mountains down into the valleys. *Mistrals* are strong, cold winds funneled down the Rhône River valley from the winter high-pressure area over central Europe. A *foehn*, *chinook*, or *Santa Ana* is a hot, dry wind caused when

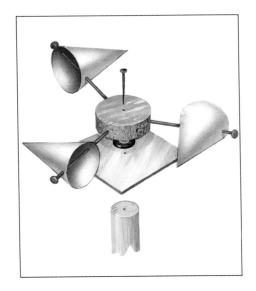

BEAUFORT SCALE OF WINDS

Beaufort Number	Description or Name of Wind	Knots (Nautical Miles) an Hour	Effects of the Wind
0	Calm	Less than 1	Smoke rises straight up
1	Light air	1–3	Smoke drifts gently
2	Light breeze	4–6	Wind felt on face
3	Gentle breeze	7–10	Leaves and twigs move
4	Moderate breeze	11–16	Small branches sway; dust blows
5	Fresh breeze	17–21	Small trees sway; waves break on lakes
6	Strong breeze	22–27	Large branches move
7	Moderate gale	28–33	Whole trees move; walking difficult
8	Fresh gale	34–40	Twigs break off trees
9	Strong gale	41–47	Loose shingles or chimneys may be blown off buildings
10	Whole gale	48–55	Trees are uprooted
11	Storm	56–63	Widespread damage
12	Hurricane	More than 64	Violent destruction

large masses of air blow down a mountainside and become heated by the pressure of their own weight. This wind is also known as the *sirocco*.

Winds are identified by the direction *from* which they blow. A wind that blows from the east is an east wind; from the west, a west wind. A weather vane indicates wind direction.

■ LEARN BY DOING

The speed of the wind is measured by an *anemometer*. You can make your own version using paper cups. Make the cups rolling sheets of paper into cones, or use empty yogurt cartons. Stick knitting needles through the cups with one end in a cork. Drill a hole in the middle of the cork so that it can rotate freely on a nail. Nail it to a board, with a washer or bead beneath it to reduce friction. Mount the board on a tall pole (away from trees if you can). The speed at which the anemometer spins will give you an idea of the wind speed. Painting one cup a different color will make counting easier. ■

In 1805, a British admiral, Sir Francis Beaufort (1774–1857), worked out a scale of wind speeds as shown in the table.

ALSO READ: BAROMETER, HURRICANE, TORNADO, WAVE, WEATHER.

WIND SURFING, or boardsailing, is a sport that began in the late 1960's in California. It is now enjoyed by water-sports fans all over the world. With a sailboard you can enjoy the fun of surfing and sailing at the same time. But you must be able to swim, and it is sensible to wear a life jacket as well.

A sailboard looks like a regular surfboard, but it has a triangle-shaped sail and a mast that fits into a mounting on the board. Running across the sail is a boom, or wishbone, and the 'sailer uses this to hold onto.

The boardsailer starts off in the water, alongside the board. He or she then climbs onto the board, standing upright and hauling the mast and sail upright. As the wind fills the sail, the board moves off, just like a sailboat. In good conditions, a sailboard can travel quite fast, and the expert boardsailer can perform jumps and other tricks.

ALSO READ: SAILING, SURFING.

WIND TUNNEL Fast-moving machines like motorcycles, automobiles, and aircraft have to push aside the air as they rush through it. Just parting the air takes some power from

▲ *Windsurfers can combine the thrill of boardsailing with the excitement of riding the crest of the wave surf-style as seen here.*

▲ *These smoke streams inside a research wind tunnel show how aerodynamics help reduce wind resistance in automobile design.*

▲ *You have to take great care to pick grapes at exactly the right moment if you want to use them to make wine.*

the engine. The designer of the machine may want it to cut through the air with less effort. It can then go faster or save energy.

To find out how a machine will behave, a model of it is made and tested in a wind tunnel. The tunnel is a shaft with a large propeller at one end. The propeller turns to blow air through the tunnel and around the model. The designer can then see how the machine will work at various air speeds. Different models can be tested.

Wind-tunnel testing is very important for aircraft. The flow of air around an aircraft—especially its wings—supports it in the air. A wind tunnel enables aircraft designers to check the air flow long before a new aircraft actually flies.

ALSO READ: AIRPLANE, FRICTION.

WINES AND WINE MAKING
Wine is an alcoholic beverage made from grape juice. It has been a popular drink for centuries and is produced in many parts of the world. There are many different types of wine, which vary according to how they are made, where they are produced, and the type of grapes used.

In the wine-making process, the juice is first pressed from whole grapes. At one time, this was done by trampling the grapes with bare feet. Today, grapes are usually pressed by machines. Grape juice contains sugar,

water, and small amounts of acid. It is gathered into vats (open tubs) to *ferment*. This means that tiny organisms called yeasts that grow on the grape skins change the grape sugar into carbon dioxide and a type of alcohol, *ethyl alcohol*. Wine that is fermented for a short time still contains some grape sugar and tastes "sweet." But if the wine is left for several weeks until most of the sugar has fermented, it tastes "dry." The wine is then stored in casks, or barrels, for *aging*. This brings out the flavor. Some wines are aged for years. After aging, the wine is bottled. Some wines are shipped immediately. Others are aged longer in the bottle.

Wines vary in color from almost colorless through greenish yellow to deep red. Red wines are colored by the skins of the grapes during fermentation. Light-colored, or "white," wines are fermented without the skins (white wines may be made from red grapes). If all the carbon dioxide released by fermentation escapes into the air before the wine is bottled, the wine is *still*. Some wines, such as champagne, are partly fermented in corked bottles, and the trapped carbon dioxide makes them bubbly, or *sparkling*.

The year of the grape harvest from which a wine is made is often marked on the bottle. This is called the *vintage*, which comes from a Latin word meaning "grape gathering." Wine fanciers like to know how long a wine was aged and if it was made in a good year.

Grapes grow best in regions with a moderate climate, abundant rain, and well-drained hillsides. The flavor of a wine depends on the soil of the *vineyard* where the grapes are grown, and the amount of sun the grapes absorb. The countries most famous for their wines are France, Germany, Italy, Spain, and the United States. Delicious wines also come from Portugal, Austria, Australia, Yugoslavia, Chile, Hungary, and Argentina. California produces by far the greatest quantity of U.S. wine.

Many wines are named after the region in which they are produced, such as Burgundy in France, or Mosel in Germany. Each wine may also be named after a particular district, village, or vineyard within the region. Other wines are named after the grapes from which they are made, such as Cabernet, Concord, or Muscatel. Many U.S. wines are named for their manufacturer. The Napa Valley in California is a well-known wine-growing region.

ALSO READ: ALCOHOLIC BEVERAGE, DISTILLATION.

WINTER Winter is one of the four seasons of the year. In the Northern Hemisphere, it begins about December 21, the year's shortest day, and ends about March 21, the spring (vernal) *equinox* (time when night and day are of the same length). Winter is the season of cold and snow. There are fewer hours of daylight and more of darkness. People need to wear warm clothing in cold winter weather. Some animals grow thicker fur. Woodchucks and chipmunks curl up in burrows and sleep the cold months away. Bears spend part of the winter in hollow trees or dens and come out sometimes in January to search for food. Squirrels, raccoons, skunks, and deer stay outdoors much of the winter. Chickadees, woodpeckers, and owls stay north for the season. Tracks of birds and small animals may be seen delicately etched on top of the white crust of the snow. In the Southern Hemisphere, people enjoy summer weather during these months of the year.

Winter has Christmas, the celebration of the birth of Christ, on December 25. Sharp-needled fir trees are brought home and decorated with rainbow-colored balls and lights and glittering tinsel. Presents are wrapped and hidden. On Christmas Eve, stockings are hung above hearths, and Santa Claus is said to visit in his reindeer-drawn sleigh. Jewish families celebrate the joyous eight-day Hanukkah Feast of Lights. New Year's Eve, December 31, is a night of cheerful parties. Some countries celebrate January 6, Twelfth Night or Epiphany, with gift-giving. January 15 is Martin Luther King, Jr.'s, birthday, and in February come George Washington's and Abraham Lincoln's birthdays, and Valentine's Day.

Winter is the time for skiing, skating, sledding, snowmobiling, snowshoeing, and making snow figures. Most years, snow falls silently from the sky in soft flakes, each different from every other. Catch a snowflake on your tongue and feel its cold, clean taste. Fall backward into a soft drift of snow, swirl your arms, and make an angel. Birch trees bend to the ground, every twig sheathed in silver ice. Frost forms exquisite patterns of lacy ferns on windowpanes. Icicles hang in transparent fringes from the eaves of houses and barns. When the sun touches them, they drip and finally fall in a tinkling, icy shatter. In March, a thaw warms the ground. The ice covering the streams cracks and melts, and the freezing water runs clear again. Tiny shoots of green appear. Spring will come soon.

ALSO READ: DECEMBER, FEBRUARY, HIBERNATION, JANUARY, RAIN AND SNOW, SEASON.

WINTHROP, JOHN see MASSACHUSETTS.

WISCONSIN Ocean freighters load and unload at the wharves of Milwaukee, Wisconsin. This city, although it is near the center of the continent, is a major seaport. Ships sail from the Atlantic Ocean through

Spain has the largest acreage of vineyards in the world, followed by the Soviet Union, Italy, and France.

▲ *A blanket of winter snow can bring out the most unusual and attractive forms of transport, such as this horse and sled in Vermont.*

Some early Wisconsin miners dug hillside caves to live in during the long, cold winter months. They came to be called "badgers," which later became the nickname of all Wisconsinites.

▼ *These young residents of Wisconsin find bicycling a good way to go places and see the countryside.*

the St. Lawrence River to the Great Lakes. They can follow this route because canals with locks take them around dangerous rapids and waterfalls.

Wisconsin borders both Lake Superior and Lake Michigan. Each coast has good harbors. At every harbor is a busy port. Lake freighters and ocean freighters tie up at the wharves. Unloaded goods are carried away by trains and trucks. Trains and trucks also bring cargoes to be loaded aboard freighters. Wisconsin's Great Lakes ports are among the busiest inland ports in the world.

The Land and Climate Water almost surrounds the state. The Menominee and Brule rivers form about half the boundary between Wisconsin and Michigan. The western boundary is formed mostly by the St. Croix and Mississippi rivers. Lake Superior and Lake Michigan cover the northern and eastern sides of the state.

Wisconsin has more than 8,000 lakes, many of which are very beautiful. You can see several lakes from the dome of the state capitol in Madison.

Wisconsin's larger rivers are used for transportation. Tugboats tow strings of barges up and down the rivers. More than two-thirds of Wisconsin's river water flows into the Mississippi River. About one-fourth runs into Lake Michigan. The rest flows into Lake Superior.

A huge, rolling plains area lies west and south of Lake Michigan and

Lake Superior. Wisconsin is in this area. Here and there, hills or ridges rise above the plains. High bluffs border the Mississippi and Wisconsin rivers.

Wisconsin has two important highlands. They are the Superior Upland and the Western Upland. Between them lies the Central Plain. The Superior Upland has thin soil. Much of it is sandy. Because of this, a large part of the highland has been left forested. But in places where the soil is good, farms have been established. The eastern end of this highland is dairying country. The Western Upland has ridges and deep valleys that make fine scenery.

In the southern region of the Wisconsin River on the Central Plain, there is a narrow valley, or gorge, called the Dells. There the river has cut sandstone into unusual shapes. Many farms are in the Central Plain.

Winters in Wisconsin are long and cold. Summers are warm. But the weather changes often. Breezes from Lake Michigan cool eastern Wisconsin in summer. In winter, the lake breezes sometimes warm the land a little.

In most years, there is plenty of rain throughout the growing season. Summers that are wet and not too hot are ideal for dairying. Grass grows well, and the cows do not suffer from the heat. Climate has helped make Wisconsin "America's Dairyland."

History During the 1600's, the Winnebago, Dakota, and Iowa tribes lived in the area that is now Wisconsin. Later, Algonkin tribes arrived from the East. The powerful Iroquois, who lived in what is now New York State, had driven them westward. Among the newcomers were the Sauk, the Fox, and the Miami. Wisconsin was a natural place for the eastern tribes to settle. Hunting and fishing were good. Rivers and lakes made it possible to travel hundred of miles in all directions by canoe.

▲ *Madison, capital of Wisconsin, at night, with the familiar dome-towered capitol all lit up.*

STATE EMBLEMS

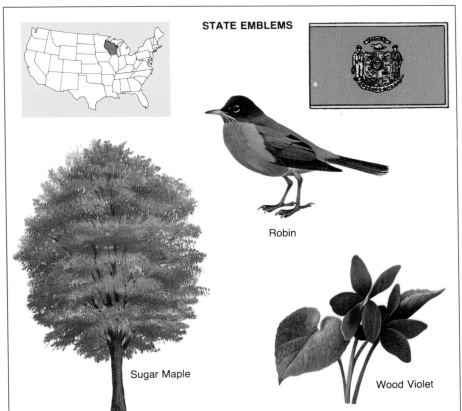

Robin

Sugar Maple

Wood Violet

WISCONSIN

Capital
Madison (171,000 people)

Area
56,154 square miles
(145,438 sq. km). Rank: 26th

Population
4,855,000
Rank: 17th

Statehood
May 29, 1848
(30th state admitted)

Principal rivers
Mississippi River
Wisconsin River

Highest point
Timms Hill; 1,952 feet (595 m)

Largest city
Milwaukee (636,000 people)

Motto
"Forward"

Song
"On, Wisconsin!"

Famous people
Senator Joseph R. McCarthy,
Thorstein Veblen, Orson
Welles, Thornton Wilder, Frank
Lloyd Wright

▲ *A grain storage building on this Wisconsin farm is passed over by flying geese.*

Witches were said to fear church bells and sometimes removed them from their belfries at night. At Canewdon in Essex, England, people said that a church bell that had been dropped in the river by seven witches could be heard ringing under the water during storms.

The Indians called the area *Wees-Konsan*, or "the meeting place of the waters."

The French were the first Europeans to reach this region. In 1634, an explorer named Jean Nicolet was sent from New France (French Canada) to find a water route to China. When he landed at the southern end of Green Bay, near a Winnebago village, he thought the Indians were Chinese. Nicolet was the first white person to see Lake Michigan. About 20 years later, other French people came. They explored and traded with the Indians for furs. The region became part of the vast area in North America claimed by France. Many French names remain on the map of Wisconsin today. La Crosse, Beloit, and Eau Claire are just a few Wisconsin towns with French names.

France lost the region to Britain in the French and Indian War. Britain lost it to the United States after the American Revolution. But the British were in no hurry to leave this good fur country. They stayed for several years and expanded their fur trade with the Northwest.

By 1830, lead mining was becoming more important than fur trading in Wisconsin. Miners and other settlers poured into the area, taking Indian land. This led to war. The Indians were finally defeated in the Black Hawk War of 1832. They continued to lose land as more white settlers arrived.

Wisconsin's worst natural disaster began on October 8, 1871. A summer drought had left the land extremely dry. Fire broke out, sweeping through northeastern Wisconsin and destroying villages and forests. Hundreds more died in Wisconsin's Peshtigo fire than died in the Great Chicago Fire of the same date.

Wisconsinites at Work "America's Dairyland" is a fitting nickname for Wisconsin, which leads the nation in the production of milk and cheese. The state ranks first in the number of milk cows. But manufacturing is the state's number-one industry. Machinery, food, and paper are three of the most important products.

Although dairying is Wisconsin's chief form of farming, cattle- and hog-raising are also important sources of farm income. The principal crops, hay and corn, are raised for feeding livestock.

Lakes, streams, and woods make much of the state an ideal vacation land. At Hayward in northern Wisconsin, the International Lumberjack and Logrolling Championship is held every July. The Winnebago Indians perform dances for tourists in the Dells region. The Circus World Museum at Baraboo, the village of Little Norway near Mount Horeb, and Taliesin (Frank Lloyd Wright's home near Spring Green) are major points of interest in Wisconsin. The state's two national forests offer excellent hunting, fishing, and skiing. Hiking is a favorite pastime for many, too.

ALSO READ: DAIRY FARMING; FRENCH AND INDIAN WAR; GREAT LAKES; ST. LAWRENCE SEAWAY; WRIGHT, FRANK LLOYD.

WITCHCRAFT Most people have heard stories on Halloween (October 31) of old, wrinkled witches who fly about on broomsticks and cast evil spells. Witchcraft is a type of magic practiced by witches, who believe that they are helped by gods and spirits. Male witches are called *warlocks* or *wizards*.

Today, most people think of witchcraft as evil and frightening. This is because most of our knowledge of witchcraft has come down to us from the Middle Ages in Western Europe. At that time, the practice of witchcraft was considered to be a terrible sin by the Christian church. Thousands of "witch trials" were held, at which people were accused of witchcraft. Probably only a few of those accused actually practiced witchcraft. But most were forced under torture to "confess" to the most ghastly practices, which were never actually proved.

Some scholars believe that witchcraft in Europe was part of a very ancient religion that existed long before Christianity. Witches were special priests of the "Old Religion." Witches gathered in large groups for *sabbats* (holy days). The most important sabbats were Candlemas (February 2), Walpurgis Night (April 30—also known as Roodmas), Lammas (July 31), and Halloween. In the old days, all the people of the neighborhood probably also gathered on the sabbats to dance and sing. In between the sabbats, smaller groups of 13 witches, called *covens*, held meetings called *esbats*.

Most witches kept some type of animal, such as a cat or a toad, as a *familiar*. Witches "told" the future by watching the behavior of their familiars. They were later accused of actually communicating with the animals. Believers in the Old Religion claimed that witches could bring rain, cure sickness, or make people fall in love. But they could also cast the "evil eye" on people and make them die. Witches were said to be able to kill a person by symbolically "killing" a wax image of him or her. Witches called on their gods for help by reciting ancient rhymes, or *spells*.

The enemies of witchcraft had many ways of "finding" witches. It was believed that witches had one spot on their bodies that could not feel pain. The accusers would prick a suspected witch with pins, trying to find the "Devil's spot." Another method was to throw the suspected witch, hands and feet tied, into a pond. If she floated, she was a witch. If she sank and drowned, she was innocent. In Europe, most accused witches were tied to a stake, strangled, and then burned. In North America, they were hanged. One of the most shocking witch trials took place in 1692, in Salem, Massachusetts, when 20 people were executed for witchcraft. They were all probably just people suffering from a mental illness called hysteria.

Witchcraft has been a basic part of the religion of many peoples of the world. The *shamans*, or "witch doctors," of the North American Indians are witches. The *voodoo* ceremonials of the people of Haiti are a form of witchcraft.

WOLF The wolf is a wild member of the dog family. Wolves once ranged all over North America, Europe, and Asia. People have long tried to kill any wolves near their settlements. Today, wolves are found only in the mountains and forests where few people live. Fearsome stories are told of wolves attacking people, but North American wolves are usually afraid of people, and no report of a wolf attack has ever been proved in North America. Ranchers claim that wolves kill their sheep and cattle. Usually only starving wolves will come close enough to human settlements to kill domestic livestock.

The most common wolf in North America is the gray or timber wolf of Canada and Alaska. This wolf may grow up to 4 feet (1.2 m) in length. It has long legs and a long bushy tail. The prairie wolf, better known as the *coyote*, is smaller and lives in the south central United States. All wolves have powerful teeth for tearing meat.

Wolves hunt in *packs*, which usually consist of a family group—the parent wolves and their *cubs* (offspring). The howling of wolves at nighttime is one of the most eerie sounds in the wilderness. Scientists believe that members of a wolf pack may signal to one another over long distances by their howls. Wolves are natural enemies of large animals, such as deer or moose. They also eat rabbits, mice, and wild fruits.

▲ *This woodcut from a German pamphlet of the 1550's shows women accused of witchcraft being burned alive at the stake. In North America, presumed witches were usually hanged. Almost all of the "witches" were innocent of any crime.*

▼ *The European timber wolf lives in northern forests, although only a few still survive. Unlike North American wolves, European wolves can be very dangerous.*

▲ *Beginning in 1903, the suffragists campaigned in Britain for women's suffrage (the right to vote). Here, a group celebrates the release of two of their members from Holloway Prison, London. Full suffrage was granted to women in Britain in 1928.*

▲ *In 1869, Wyoming became the first territory to give women suffrage. When Wyoming was admitted to the Union in 1890, it was the first state in which women voted.*

Wolves are said to mate for life. They usually have 3 to 9 cubs a year. The wolves dig a hole, or *den*, in the earth, where the cubs are born. The father wolf kills food for the family until the cubs are old enough to hunt.

ALSO READ: COYOTE, DOG, JACKAL.

WOMEN'S RIGHTS The term "women's rights" means the right of women to be full citizens, equal in every way to men under law and in society. Until this century, women did not have these rights. In many countries today, women still have no rights.

The *feminist* (women's rights) movement in the United States began early in the 1800's. At this time, women were discouraged from going to college and working. Even when women worked, they were paid less than men for the same kind of work. (This is often still true today.) Women could not hold political office. Women's earnings belonged to their husbands, and they could not own property. In fact, wives were considered to be their husbands' property under the law.

A few educated women decided that this unfair treatment must be changed. Some of the earliest feminist leaders were Lucretia Mott, Elizabeth Cady Stanton, Lucy Stone, and Susan B. Anthony. Julia Ward Howe, an early feminist, wrote "The Battle Hymn of the Republic." Sojourner Truth, a former black slave, also fought for women's rights. Some men supported women's rights. Before the Civil War, most feminist leaders also worked for abolition (ending slavery).

The first convention (meeting) for women's rights was organized by Lucretia Mott and Elizabeth Cady Stanton. It was held in Seneca Falls, New York, in 1848. Feminist leaders decided that the vote was the first, most basic step in ending sex discrimination. This meeting began the campaign for women's right to vote. After the Civil War, the suffragists (people working for women's *suffrage*, or the right to vote) found that the government would give the vote to black men but not to women of any race. In 1869, because of disagreements, feminist leaders split into the National Woman Suffrage Association and the American Woman Suffrage Association. But they agreed on the most important goal—suffrage for women—and the two groups merged again in 1890.

Suffragists were laughed at for years by many people, both men and women. Suffragists were often physically attacked or jailed for protesting unfair treatment of women. But the feminists' determined efforts finally began to be rewarded. In 1890, Wyoming became the first state to grant women the right to vote. The Nineteenth Amendment, ratified in 1919, made women's suffrage nationwide.

When suffrage was granted, the ex-suffragists formed the League of Women Voters to provide information about voting and to encourage women's participation in politics. A more recent organization, the National Women's Political Caucus, works in the United States for fairer treatment of women in politics. Since over half of the U.S. population is female, many women today feel that they should have at least half of the political power in the country. People are beginning to realize that women can be a powerful force in politics. The number of women holding political office in the United States is increasing. In some countries, such as Norway, Israel, Britain, and India, women have been elected to head the national government. But women in many other countries are not even allowed to vote.

Educational opportunities for women have increased gradually since feminists first began their work. In the United States today, few colleges will not admit women. But women still do not have the freedom men have in choosing and working at a particular occupation. For many years, women, if they had to work at all, were considered capable only of simple tasks having little authority or responsibility. For example, women were considered suited to be secretaries but not executives, nurses but not doctors.

For centuries, most of society has seen woman's role as that of wife and mother. Her only duties were to marry, keep house, bear and rear children. Women who did not marry or have children were considered failures, no matter whatever else they did. Many women today believe that marriage and a family should be a matter of choice for a woman. Marriage should not be the sole way of measuring a woman's success in life. They also believe that keeping house and caring for children should be both parents' responsibility, so that neither parent will be forced to devote all his or her time to duties at home.

In 1966, the National Organization for Women (NOW) was founded by Betty Friedan and other feminists. NOW and other groups have fought for abortion reform, equal employment opportunity, equal pay for women, and child-care facilities. Many people have worked to pass the Equal Rights Amendment (ERA) to the U.S. Constitution, which would bar sex discrimination on a national level. Some modern-day feminist leaders are Shirley Chisholm, Gloria Steinem, Germaine Greer, and Kate Millett.

More women than ever before are now working outside the family. Many have professional careers in business. In some fields the women's struggle for equality has been slow.

ALSO READ: ADDAMS, JANE; CIVIL RIGHTS; CIVIL RIGHTS MOVEMENT; HOWE, JULIA WARD; ROOSEVELT, ELEANOR; SANGER, MARGARET; TRUTH, SOJOURNER.

WOOD Wood is the tough and fibrous substance that comes from the trunks and branches of trees. It is one of nature's raw materials that is most useful to people. This page you are reading was made by processing pulpwood into paper. The chair on which you sit may be made completely or partially from wood. Your house may be constructed of wood, but even if it is made of brick or stone, some parts, such as the floors, window frames, or doors, are almost certainly made of wood. Wood is also used to make certain fabrics, fuels, cattle feed, and charcoal.

Wood is a valuable construction material because it is light but strong and durable. Wood does not rust (obviously), although it may decay if it is exposed to excessive moisture. Paint and varnish help protect wood from moisture. Insects, especially termites, and fire can also damage wood. Poisons can be used to kill these insects, and certain chemicals can be applied to wood to make it fireproof.

Woods are usually divided into two groups—*softwoods* and *hardwoods*. Softwoods come from evergreen trees. Pines, firs, and spruces are good examples. Most softwood trees are fairly fast-growing, and their leaves are in the form of needles. Softwoods are generally lighter than hardwoods. They are used chiefly in construction and in papermaking. One exception is teak, an evergreen wood that is hard and heavy. It is used to build furniture and boats.

▲ *Beautiful and intricate ancient woodwork from Nigeria, Africa.*

▼ *A section through a tree trunk. Each ring represents a year of growth. The thickness of each ring can tell you how good the weather was that year.*

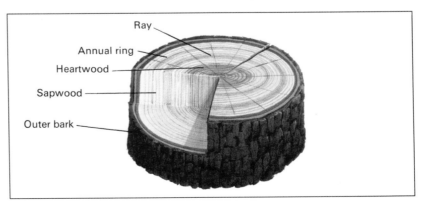

Ray
Annual ring
Heartwood
Sapwood
Outer bark

Hardwoods come from trees that have broader leaves. Hardwoods are used to make furniture, flooring, tools, and sports equipment. Maple is a handsome wood that makes very attractive furniture. Some types of maple are quite hard. Hard maple is used to make bowling alleys. Walnut and mahogany are other hardwoods that are prized for their rich appearance when finished. Hickory and ash are hardwoods used for baseball bats and ax handles.

ALSO READ: FURNITURE, LUMBER AND LUMBERING, PAINT, PAPER, TREE.

WOODWIND INSTRUMENTS

Flutes, oboes, bassoons, clarinets, and saxophones are some well-known woodwind instruments that you have probably heard played. Maybe you play one yourself. The woodwinds form one of the sections of an orchestra or band. Popular music groups frequently include a saxophone or clarinet, and sometimes a flute or oboe.

All woodwind instruments were once made of wood, but nowadays they are often made of metals and various forms of plastic. As with brass instruments, the tone of woodwind

▶ *A gentleman of the 1700's playing a flute. This was a popular woodwind in classical music of the period.*

instruments is produced by blowing or forcing a thin stream of air into the instrument.

Woodwinds are divided into two types according to how the stream of air in the instrument is made to vibrate. *Flutes* or *pipes* contain an open hole through which the air is blown. Vibration is caused by the stream of air breaking against a sharp edge (*fipple*). *Reed instruments* contain a single or double reed (a thin blade made of cane or flexible metal). Air passing around the reed causes the reed to vibrate and produce a tone.

Flutes and Pipes Modern-day flutes are called *transverse flutes* because they are held to the side and air is blown across a hole in the mouthpiece. The air strikes the opposite edge of the mouthpiece, causing a vibration of air inside the body of the flute. The player, using the fingers of both hands, presses down on keys located along the outside of the instrument. The keys open and close various holes along the body of the instrument to change the pitch. The *piccolo* is actually a small flute. It has a high pitch and a very shrill tone.

The *flageolet* is a very ancient instrument. Flageolets dating from about 700 B.C. have been discovered by archeologists. Until the 1500's the recorder, a type of flageolet, was one of the most widely played musical instruments. But in the 1600's, modern woodwinds were developed with their brilliant, powerful tone quality and wider range of pitch. Recorders have a very delicate tone that cannot be heard in a full orchestra or band. Recorders are played by blowing through a mouthpiece at one end. Along the body of the instrument are eight holes. By covering or uncovering these holes with the fingers, the player changes the pitch. Recorders come in four sizes—soprano, alto, tenor, and bass. Soprano recorders play the highest pitches, bass recorders the lowest.

Reed Instruments Oboes, clarinets, saxophones, and bassoons are the best-known modern reed instruments. Each has a mouthpiece containing either a single or a double reed. Along the body of the instrument are keys that open and close holes to change the pitch. Oboe players sometimes make their own reeds, cutting and shaping them from pieces of a special kind of cane. The oboe's double reed fits directly into the end of the instrument. The *English horn* is actually a large oboe with a lower pitch; it is often used in orchestras.

The bassoon is the lowest-pitched woodwind and, like the oboe, has a double reed. The body of the bassoon is so long that it is bent around to make it easier to handle. The double-bassoon is the lowest-pitched instrument in an orchestra. It is twice as big as the standard bassoon and can play notes that are lower than the lowest note on a piano.

The clarinet has a single reed that lies flat along one side of the mouthpiece. Like the oboe, it has keys that the player presses to produce different pitches. The most frequently used clarinet is the B-flat instrument (named for the pitch to which it is tuned). Clarinets are made also in A, C, D, and E-flat. The bass clarinet is larger and produces a much lower pitch than the B-flat clarinet. Alto clarinets are played mostly in military bands.

The saxophone is a relatively new instrument. It was invented in the 1840's by a Belgian instrument maker, Adolphe Sax. The saxophone is a single-reed instrument with a body of metal. The saxophone was played primarily in military bands until the 1900's, when it began to be used in orchestras. It has become one of the most popular jazz instruments.

ALSO READ: BAGPIPE, BRASS INSTRUMENTS, MUSIC, MUSICAL INSTRUMENTS, ORCHESTRAS AND BANDS.

WORD GAMES Word games are an entertaining way of learning new words, improving your spelling, and thinking about many different subjects. Many word games are fun because they can be played anywhere with little more than a pencil and paper.

Perhaps the most familiar word game is the crossword puzzle. The player tries to think of words of which the meaning and length are suggested by clues. He or she places the letters of each word in numbered boxes on a diagram, either downward or across from left to right. If the puzzle is solved correctly, the words written "across" will each use one or more letters of the words written "down."

For the *logophile* (word-lover), there are countless word games to play. The spelling bee is good for groups. Two teams of the same number are formed. One at a time, team members are given words to spell. Those who misspell words drop out until there is one winner.

We usually think of written language as a means of communication. But it is also a recreation. Here are some interesting ways of playing with words. See how many examples you can think of.

A *palindrome* is a word that is spelled the same backward as forward, for example, "dad," or "noon." A *reversal* is an arrangement of letters that becomes a different word when spelled backwards, for example, "ward—draw," or "ton—not." When you rearrange the letters in a word to form another word, you are *transposing*, for example, "looted—Toledo," or "unpaste—peanuts." The rearrangement of a word or phrase into an accurate description of that word or phrase is known as an *anagram*, for example, "seen as mist—steaminess." An *antigram* is a rearrangement of a word or phrase to make a word or phrase of opposite meaning, for example, "nice

▲ *The recorder is one of the easiest woodwind instruments to play.*

The longest non-scientific word in Webster's Dictionary is "interdenominationalism" which is 22 letters long. How many words can you write down that are over 12 letters?

▲ *William Wordsworth, British poet. He and his sister Dorothy were great friends of another British poet, Samuel Taylor Coleridge.*

▲ *The assassination (public murder) of the Archduke Ferdinand as he was being driven through Sarajevo, in 1914, triggered off World War I.*

love—violence."

Categories, also known as Guggenheim, is another popular word game. The players decide on a long word, such as "Guggenheim," and then make a list of categories, such as capital cities, movie stars, or poets. The players then take each letter of the long word and think of a name in each of the categories beginning with that letter. The player who fills in the most categories wins the game.

There is a game called Word Hunt in which you take a word, such as "encyclopedia," and see how many words of four letters or longer you can make using the letters of the given word. For example, from "encyclopedia" you can make:

elope	need	yield
lone	dial	cycle
lode	clod	plaid
clip	panel	place

How many more words can you think of?

ALSO READ: CODES AND CIPHERS, CROSSWORD PUZZLE, RIDDLE.

WORD PROCESSING see COMPUTER.

WORDSWORTH, WILLIAM (1770–1850) William Wordsworth was a British poet who wrote about nature and the English countryside. Wordsworth was born in Cockermouth, Cumberland. After studying at Cambridge University, he spent a year in France. He became a passionate supporter of the French people's struggle for freedom in the French Revolution. Wordsworth had begun to write poetry when he returned to Britain. He became a friend of the British poet Samuel Taylor Coleridge. The two poets published several of their works together in a collection called *Lyrical Ballads* (1798).

In 1799, Wordsworth moved to Grasmere in the English Lake District. He lived with his sister, Dorothy. Wordsworth was one of several "Lake Poets." He wrote about the beauties of the Lake District and about what nature revealed to him about God and human life. His poems clearly and simply express his love of

. . . the meadows and the woods,
And mountains; and of all that
we behold
From this green earth. . . .

Two of Wordsworth's best-loved poems are "I Wandered Lonely as a Cloud" and "Lines Composed a Few Miles above Tintern Abbey." In 1843, Wordsworth was made Poet Laureate of Britain.

ALSO READ: POETRY.

WORK see ENERGY.

WORLD'S FAIR see FAIR.

WORLD WAR I More than 25 nations became involved in the fighting of World War I, which took place in Europe, the Middle East, and northern Africa. About 65 million soldiers were sent into battle. About 9 million were killed and more than 21 million were wounded. People called it the "Great War."

The Participants The war began on August 4, 1914, as a battle between two groups of European nations. One group, called the *Allied Powers*, was made up of Great Britain, France, Russia, Belgium, and Serbia and Montenegro (both now part of Yugoslavia). The opposing group, called the *Central Powers*, included Germany and Austria-Hungary. Once the fighting began, other nations entered the field of battle. Turkey and Bulgaria joined the Central Powers. The Allied Powers were joined by Japan, Italy, Portugal, Romania, United States, Greece, Cuba, Panama, Siam (now Thailand), Liberia, China, Brazil, Guatemala, Nicaragua, Haiti, Costa Rica, and Honduras.

The important land battles were fought on two main fronts. On the *western front*, most of the fighting took place in northern France, where German forces faced the armies of France, Great Britain, Belgium, and the United States. On the *eastern front*, most of the fighting took place in what is now Poland, East Germany, Austria, and the Soviet Union, where German and Austro-Hungarian troops faced the Russian army.

Naval warfare was primarily between Germany and Great Britain. The British navy was the most powerful in the world. During the war, the British navy was able to keep the whole German battleship fleet bottled up in the Baltic and North seas. But Germany had built a sizable fleet of U-boats (submarines) to destroy shipments in the Atlantic Ocean.

The Causes World War I developed from two complex causes. One cause was the fact that all European countries had developed *conscript armies*. All adult male citizens of a nation were required to take military training, and could be called into combat at any time. Each nation had a military *mobilization plan*, a process for getting troops and equipment ready for combat with an enemy. Germany and France could complete their mobilizations in about two days. Italy and Austria-Hungary took four or five days. Russia took about 15 days. Each country had a separate war plan for every possible enemy. If one nation began mobilization, all others mobilized, too.

The second basic cause of the war was a gradual breakdown of agreements among the European nations, accompanied by changes in the balance of power among them. This was due to a lack of strong political leadership in Russia, Germany, and Austria-Hungary. The governments of these nations were being run by incompetent civilian ministers. Nations could no longer depend on each other and so became suspicious of each other. New alliances were made. In particular, France and Russia pledged to help each other in case of war with Germany.

In about 1904, Kaiser (Emperor) Wilhelm II decided to make Germany into a great naval power and began building battleships. Britain began getting nervous. In 1907, the *Triple Entente* was formed between Great Britain, France, and Russia, in opposition to the *Triple Alliance* that had been formed between Germany, Austria-Hungary, and Italy. These two alliances divided Europe into two opposing military camps.

In case of war, Germany was depending on the use of the Schlieffen Plan, sending 90 percent of the German forces immediately against France. According to the plan, French troops would be crushed within four or five days. Then full German forces could be sent against Russia in the east. Russia's long mobilization time meant it would be unable to help defend France, and Russian forces would be only partly ready by the time Germany attacked Russia.

On June 28, 1914, Archduke Ferdinand, heir to the Austro-Hungarian throne, was assassinated

▲ *Ghostly stumps of shell-blasted trees show the terrible destruction of World War I. Millions lost their lives on mud-soaked battlefields like this.*

▼ *The last survivors of a British artillery battery keep firing their gun during the battle at Mons, Belgium, early in World War I.*

▼ *Before the United States entered the war in 1917, there were already some American pilots flying French planes, such as this Spad. Here, an American pilot destroys a German observation balloon. The leading American "ace" (a pilot who shot down five or more enemy planes) was Eddie Rickenbacker.*

CHRONOLOGY OF WORLD WAR I

1914 June 15: Assassination of Archduke Franz Ferdinand at Sarajevo
Aug. 1: Germany declares war on Russia
Aug. 4: Britain declares war on Germany
Aug. 30: Germans defeat Russians at Tannenberg
Sept. 12: French and British halt German advance at Battle of the Marne

1915 Dec.: British withdraw from Gallipoli

1916 Feb.–July: German attack on Verdun
May 31–June 1: Naval battle of Jutland; indecisive
June–Sept.: Brusilov offensive
July 1–Nov. 18: Battle of the Somme

1917 Mar. 3: Russia makes peace with Germany at Brest-Litovsk
Mar. 11: British occupy Baghdad
Apr. 6: U.S. enters war against Germany

1918 Mar.: Great German offensive begins
Oct. 28: Mutiny in German navy at Kiel
Nov. 9: German Kaiser (Emperor) Wilhelm II abdicates
Nov. 11: Ceasefire on western front

THE FIRST MODERN WAR

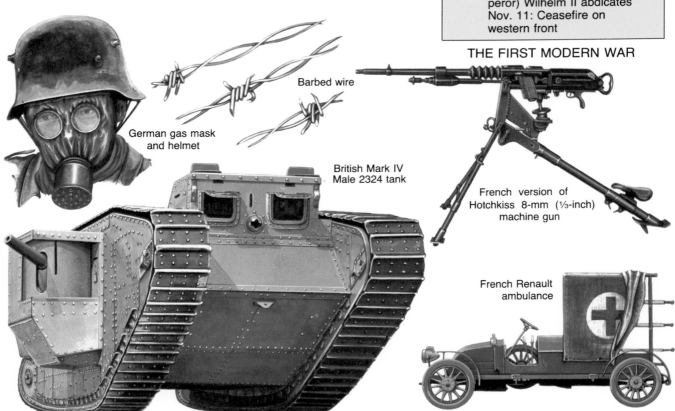

German gas mask and helmet

Barbed wire

British Mark IV Male 2324 tank

French version of Hotchkiss 8-mm (⅓-inch) machine gun

French Renault ambulance

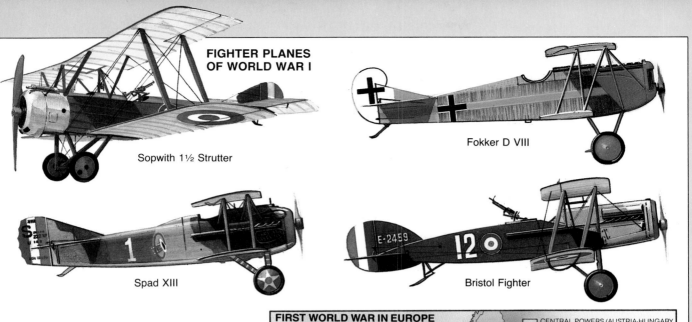

FIGHTER PLANES OF WORLD WAR I

Sopwith 1½ Strutter

Fokker D VIII

Spad XIII

Bristol Fighter

British soldier

U.S. soldier

German soldier

FIRST WORLD WAR IN EUROPE

- CENTRAL POWERS (AUSTRIA-HUNGARY, GERMANY, OTTOMAN EMPIRE)
- ALLIED POWERS (ENGLAND, FRANCE, RUSSIA)
- NEUTRAL COUNTRIES
- JOINED ALLIES AFTER 1914
- TERRITORY OCCUPIED BY CENTRAL POWERS AT END OF WAR
- UNITED STATES ENTERED WAR IN 1917
- JOINED CENTRAL POWERS IN 1915

ATLANTIC OCEAN · Shetland Is. · NORWAY · SWEDEN · NORTH SEA · BALTIC SEA · DENMARK · GREAT BRITAIN · NETHER-LANDS · GERMAN EMPIRE · BELGIUM · LUXEM-BOURG · FRANCE · SWITZER-LAND · AUSTRIA — HUNGARY · RUSSIA · CASPIAN SEA · MONTENEGRO · RUMANIA · SERBIA · BLACK SEA · BULGARIA · ALBANIA · PORTUGAL · SPAIN · Corsica · ITALY · Sardinia · GREECE · TURKEY · PERSIA · Gibraltar · MEDITERRANEAN SEA · Sicily · Crete · Cyprus · ARABIA · MOROCCO · ALGERIA · TUNISIA

EUROPE AT THE END OF THE FIRST WORLD WAR

- FORMER CENTRAL POWERS
- FORMER ALLIED POWERS
- FORMER NEUTRAL COUNTRIES
- NEW COUNTRIES
- TERRITORIES LOST BY CENTRAL POWERS

ATLANTIC OCEAN · Shetland Is. · NORWAY · SWEDEN · FINLAND · NORTH SEA · BALTIC SEA · DENMARK · ESTONIA · GREAT BRITAIN · NETHER-LANDS · LATVIA · LITHUANIA · GERMANY · BELGIUM · POLAND · SOVIET UNION · FRANCE · SWITZER-LAND · CZECHOSLOVAKIA · AUSTRIA · HUNGARY · RUMANIA · CASPIAN SEA · YUGOSLAVIA · BLACK SEA · PORTUGAL · SPAIN · Corsica · ITALY · BULGARIA · ALBANIA · GREECE · TURKEY · PERSIA · Gibraltar · MEDITERRANEAN SEA · Sardinia · Sicily · Crete · Cyprus · ARABIA · MOROCCO · ALGERIA · TUNISIA

▲ *Britain's empire came to its aid in World War I. Here, Indian troops ride through a French village.*

▲ *U.S. artillery soldiers fire a heavy shell at a German army headquarters almost 20 miles (32 km) away. The huge gun is mounted on a flatcar.*

by a Serbian member of a terrorist group that wanted to free Serbia from Austro-Hungarian rule. On July 28, 1914, Austria-Hungary declared war on Serbia. Russia began mobilizing troops to defend Serbia. Germany had promised unlimited military support for Austria-Hungary. German forces began mobilizing, and the Schlieffen Plan went into action.

The Fighting   The course of World War I can be divided into three parts, or phases.

PHASE ONE.   Once the Schlieffen Plan was begun, German forces immediately tore through Belgium to attack northern France. Seeing the danger, France mobilized her troops. The weak Belgian army gave way in the face of German artillery guns. The French army met the German forces at the northern border of France, but the well-trained Germans pushed them back almost to Paris. Britain came into the war, and the combined armies of Great Britain and France stopped the Germans at the Marne River.

The Germans tried another maneuver. They struck northward toward the English Channel to cut off the flow of supplies coming from England. The Belgians had other ideas. They opened the dikes (walls along waterways, built to prevent floods), flooded the battlefield, drowned many Germans, and stopped the attack.

By the winter of 1914–1915, the Schlieffen Plan had obviously failed. The Germans had failed in their attempt to crush France quickly. Germany had misjudged the strength of the French and British forces. The war was deadlocked. Two lines of opposing trenches were dug that stretched across about 600 miles (965 km) of France from Belgium to Switzerland. Between the trench lines was an area called "No Man's Land."

On the eastern front, Russian forces attacked Prussia and were beaten back. But a Russian force in the south soundly defeated Austro-Hungarian forces. These Russian attacks forced Germany to defend its eastern borders, which relieved some of the pressure on France in the west.

British and German battle fleets confronted each other in the North Sea. German ships retreated, and Britain tightened a sea blockade on Germany that lasted throughout the war. Germany's only superior vessels were its submarines.

PHASE TWO.   From 1915 through 1917, the Central and Allied Powers tried various maneuvers to break the trench deadlock and gain a decisive battle success. But both sides on the western front had equal forces. Thousands of lives were lost in unsuccessful attempts to break through enemy positions. The more lives that were lost, the more the leaders felt they must gain a victory.

In 1915, the Germans brought out a "secret weapon"—poison gas—that was then used by both sides throughout the war. Gas masks became standard military equipment. In 1916, the British introduced their own "secret weapon"—the tank. Tanks were a new military invention. They were called "land battleships." Although tanks were the weapons that eventually ended the trench deadlock, the ones used in 1916 bogged down in the mud and stopped because of mechanical defects. In spite of this, they were frightening to see, and German soldiers fled in panic.

In 1916, the German high command decided to try wearing down French forces at the town of Verdun. The Germans planned to break the French line by applying a slow, long-term, steady pressure on Verdun. This would eat away French military strength as more and more French troops, sent to defend Verdun, were killed by German artillery fire. The first German attack on Verdun came on February 21, 1916. The Verdun garrison was under siege for almost six months. Aircraft played an important part in keeping the Germans from taking Verdun. The Germans had superior air power at the start. But by April, the French had gained control of the skies over Verdun.

On June 4, Russia made an overwhelming surprise attack against Austria-Hungary, taking around 12,000 square miles (32,000 sq. km) of territory. The siege of Verdun was suspended, and German troops were sent to the eastern front to fight the Russians. Attacks on Verdun were resumed on June 22, but the Germans made no progress. Two powerful French attacks pushed the Germans back, and the deadlock continued.

In January 1917, Germany announced a policy of unlimited submarine warfare. All ships, even those of neutral nations, were now targets for German attack. U.S. merchant ships were torpedoed and sunk, and U.S. losses rose steeply. In 1915, German submarines had sunk the British passenger ship *Lusitania* with U.S. citizens aboard. This catastrophe had aroused U.S. opinion against Germany. President Woodrow Wilson had sent sharp messages to Kaiser Wilhelm telling him to suspend German attacks on U.S. ships. Finally, on April 6, 1917, the United States declared war on Germany.

On March 12, 1917, a major revolution of civilians and military officers broke out in St. Petersburg (now Leningrad), Russia. The Russian people had been suffering the effects of a corrupt government, an oppressive social system, and a poor economy for many years. Supplies had become scarce, and Russian troops at the front were starving. They had few weapons, not enough ammunition, and their clothes were in rags. On March 15, Czar Nicholas II abdicated and a provisional government was set up. But the new government was equally unable to support Russian participation in the war. Russian troops mutinied and began streaming

homeward by the thousands.

In November 1917, the revolutionary Bolshevik (Communist) party, led by V. I. Lenin and Leon Trotsky, overthrew the provisional government. Lenin soon announced his intentions to make peace with Germany, and negotiations began in December. Russia was out of the war.

In June 1917, the first troops of the American Expeditionary Force (AEF), under General John J. Pershing, arrived in France. German submarine warfare increased against ships going to and from Britain. Britain was in danger of having all its supplies cut off. U.S. destroyers arrived in British waters to aid British convoys. Merchant ships were made to sail together in convoys, protected by escorts of warships. More German submarines were destroyed as Allied antisubmarine warfare improved. By 1918, the Germans were losing submarines faster than they could build them.

PHASE THREE. In the early months of 1918, the Germans decided on a new plan for victory. German troops on the eastern front would be sent quickly to the west. There they would overwhelm the Allied forces before many more U.S. troops arrived.

On March 21, the Germans launched their great attack. They broke through Allied lines at one point. Instead of sending more troops through that gap, German officers ordered attacks at other places along the Allied line. Those attacks did not work. The Allies began coordinating their armies under the command of the French leader Marshal Ferdinand Foch. The Germans tried several more attacks, the last of which resulted in a shattering German defeat.

On August 8, the Allies launched a huge artillery attack using a forward line of tanks with thousands of foot soldiers behind. The German army collapsed. With air and ground attacks, Allied armies kept pushing the

▲ *German troops in the trenches during World War I. Conditions were appalling. Soldiers lived—or did not live—in seas of mud among the corpses of their comrades or enemies.*

The largest mutiny in history took place during World War I. About 650,000 French soldiers under General Robert G. Nivelle refused to obey orders during the Aisne offensive in April and May, 1917.

▲ *The armistice ending World War I was signed in a railroad car near Compiègne, France, on November 11, 1918. Marshal Foch, the French leader, is holding a briefcase containing the armistice papers.*

▼ *The leaders of the Allied powers met at Versailles, France, to prepare the peace treaty that officially ended World War I. Seated from left to right are: Premier Vittorio Orlando of Italy; Prime Minister David Lloyd George of Great Britain; Premier Georges Clemenceau of France; and President Woodrow Wilson of the United States.*

German forces back. German supplies ran short. German sailors mutinied, and riots broke out in several German cities. The German people demanded the abdication of Kaiser Wilhelm II, and he was sent into exile on November 10. A provisional German government surrendered to the Allied Powers on November 11, 1918. All fighting on the western front ended.

The Outcome In 1918, the world's political leaders had the job of trying to build a lasting peace out of the ruins of war. Representatives from nations involved in the war met at the Paris Peace Conference to decide the conditions of peace with Germany. The principal negotiators were President Woodrow Wilson of the United States, Prime Minister David Lloyd George of Great Britain, Premier Georges Clemenceau of France, and Premier Vittorio Orlando of Italy. Germany, however, was barred from the conference and had no voice in forming the peace plans. The result of the negotiations was the Treaty of Versailles, which was signed on June 28, 1919, at the Palace of Versailles, located just outside the city of Paris, France.

The first part of the treaty established the League of Nations, an international organization that would try to insure world peace. The treaty temporarily barred Germany from membership in the League. The treaty made Germany primarily responsible for the war, and the terms that Germany was forced to agree to were designed to make sure that Germany would never again be able to become a military threat against the rest of Europe. Germany was required to pay about 33 billion dollars to the Allied Powers. Germany was to be completely disarmed and was not allowed to produce or import any military equipment. The German Army was limited to 100,000 men. Parts of Germany were to be occupied by Allied forces, while other parts were to be ceded to Allied countries or to the League of Nations. All of Germany's overseas territories were to be given over to the Allied Powers.

The Treaty of Versailles was ratified by all the nations that signed it, except the United States. The Senate would not approve U.S. membership in the League of Nations, so the United States concluded a separate treaty with Germany in 1921.

The German people did not expect such harsh treatment, and their anger against the Allies grew over the years. The severe terms of the Versailles treaty were partly responsible for the terrible economic and political conditions in Germany during the 1920's and 1930's. Money and goods were scarce, and the German people were unable to get jobs. These circumstances and the smoldering anger against the Allies created the conditions in which Adolf Hitler rose to power and which led to World War II.

ALSO READ: AIRPLANE; ARMY; BISMARCK, OTTO VON; HITLER, ADOLF; INTERNATIONAL LAW; INTERNATIONAL RELATIONS; LEAGUE OF NATIONS; LENIN, VLADIMIR ILYICH; NAVY; SUBMARINE; TANK; TREATY; TROTSKY, LEON; VERSAILLES; VETERANS DAY; WAR; WILSON, WOODROW; WORLD WAR II.
See article at name of each country involved.